SPATIAL JUSTICE AND DIASPORA

Spatial Justice and Diaspora

Edited by

Emma Patchett and Sarah Keenan

COUNTERPRESS
OXFORD

First published (revised) 2017
Counterpress, Oxford
http://counterpress.org.uk

ISBN: 978-1-910761-05-2 (paperback)

Typeset in 10.5 on 12 pt Sabon

Cover image: 'Hypoxic Highway' © Jerome Flinders

Global print and distribution by Ingram

FOREWORD

Parvathi Raman

When Emma Patchett and Sarah Keenan asked if I would write a foreword for their new edited volume, Spatial Justice and Diaspora, I was delighted to be able to make a small contribution to this important, and timely, new book.

In our current political moment, we urgently require engaged scholarship on questions of space-making, the politics of diaspora, and the racialization of inequality.

Global disparity has reached unprecedented levels. Mass displacement, fuelled by wars, environmental change and the gross disparity of wealth and opportunity, along with the increasing racialization of 'differential inclusion', now shape the contours of a world primarily defined by injustice. The concept of spatial justice, an approach that recognizes that always-already spatial nature of political, economic, and social struggles, can serve to highlight the conflictual and often violent nature of co-existence in an inequitable world. It has the potential to provide a powerful lens for empirical analysis, and can act as an instrument for political change.

In turn, as struggles for meaningful political and social inclusion proliferate, a radical politics of diaspora opens up the possibility of undermining hegemonic borders of political (un)belonging, and can challenge the exclusionary, and power laden, practices of the neoliberal state. When the concepts of spatial justice and diaspora are brought into conversation with each other, and interrogated through a focus on the empirical, they can offer new insights into the micro-politics of everyday existence. Such engagement requires the type of politically committed, innovative academic scholarship to be found in this edited volume.

The book brings together thought provoking approaches to spatial justice (as the conception of, the struggle over, and the use of space) and diaspora (as a progressive potential to disrupt hegemonic and exclusionary political orders) with empirical studies of communities who are contesting space in contexts as varied as Chile, Germany, South Africa, Guantanamo Bay, and Britain.

Neoliberal democracy, the dominant political framework of our times, is in crisis. One of its core characteristics, the relationship between the state and the market, is not functional for the vast majority of people. We are witnessing intensified inequalities and social polarization, which starkly illustrate the limits of capital accumulation coupled with state-market relations. What is required of academics at this time is both evidence making research, and political critique, which holds power to account, but also illuminates the multiple ways that people are fighting for justice and democratic inclusion. Both are abundantly apparent in this impressive volume.

Another reason I was pleased to contribute this foreword is the nature of the scholarship which is evident throughout the book. Traversing the disciplinary boundaries of law, politics, anthropology, and the broader social sciences, the authors engage with an open ended, contextual enquiry which evokes Susan Buck-Morss' idea of 'undisciplinarity.'[1] For me, the call to be 'undisciplined' is both a way of exceeding the limits of disciplinary borders, and a refusal to conform to the requirements of neoliberal academia. It can open up new possibilities for radical research. Undisciplinarity means challenging the demands of an increasingly policy oriented and 'problem solving' academic landscape; confronting the idea of 'impartial' research; and upsetting notions of pragmatic, seemingly non-ideological results-measured solutions to complex problems. It requires a recognition of the conflictual nature of academic labour, which can generate a productive politics of discomfort, and act as a call to action.

In this volume, such an approach is skilfully interlinked with the perceptive use of radical theoretical paradigms. Academic approaches to issues of space and diaspora have generated some of the most exciting innovations in thinking in recent years, as well as many indulgent and abstract exercises which serve to reinforce academic privilege. This volume transcends the multicultural/hybridity limitations of much writing on space and diaspora. Here, the contributions pioneered by authors such as Massey, Harvey, and Soja on space, as well as Hall, Clifford, and Brah on diaspora, are utilized both incisively and creatively. It is scholarship that seeks to collapsing the false distinction between academia and activism; as is evident in the following pages, knowledge production is always a form of political action.

Without doubt, ethnography has now moved beyond its anthropological 'home.' The ethnographic studies in this volume provide both a sensitivity to context, and act as political critique. They illuminate the everyday arts of space making and diasporic resistance, at a time when our institutions are increasingly dysfunctional, and the state's norms of control are, at once, less powerful, and more pernicious. The

---

[1] Susan Buck-Morss, *Hegel, Haiti, and Universal History* (University of Pittsburgh Press, 2009).

studies deftly illustrate the ways in which people attempt to escape the everyday governance of the state, and the 'normalizing force' of state power.

The micro-politics of our everyday lives can often be hidden from view, giving the impression of monolithic institutions which render us powerless. But by giving centre stage to the creative art of people's everyday socio-political space-making and diasporic practices, we can highlight not only how contemporary governance can be challenged, but can also be escaped, and on occasion, overturned.

The vocabularies we use can render things visible. And visibility has the potential to open up the agency present in all of us. It confronts the notion that we are powerless to bring change to an unequal world. As Lefebvre has highlighted, we make space, and construct our own geographies. It is therefore also our responsibility to make an intervention in space making and diasporic practices, and help render them more just. This volume is a valuable contribution to that wider struggle. It reflects genuine conceptual innovation in the fields of spatial justice and diaspora, and contributes to an understanding which is both transformative and productive. It is the work of a group young scholars who are making their intervention for change.

CONTENTS

CONTRIBUTORS

Tekalign Ayalew is a PhD candidate at the department of Social Anthropology, Stockholm University, Sweden. His research interests are young peoples' life, mobility, borders and diaspora. His PhD project deals with High-Risk migration process from Horn of Africa (Ethiopia and Eritrea) until Scandinavia (Sweden). Taking up migrants' stories and experiences of borders as point of departure; he explores how individual identities (such as gender, age, religion, class), social networks and political forces shape conditions of departures from homelands, vulnerabilities and (im) mobility en route and struggles of settlement and homing practices in destination location. His PhD project is part of the EU Marie Curie Initial Training Network 'Diasporic Constructions of Home and Belonging-CoHaB.' His recent publications include *Risks, Resilience and Adaptations in Child and Young Life*; and, together with Ayalew Gebre and Helmut Kloos, *Gender inequalities, power relations and HIV/Aids: exploring the interface.*

Jaco Barnard-Naudé is Professor of Jurisprudence in the Department of Private Law in the Law Faculty at the University of Cape Town. He is a past recipient of the UCT Fellows Award and the Faculty Research Prize. He also holds a National Research Foundation rating and is a past Honorary Research Fellow at the Birkbeck Institute for the Humanities and Visiting Professor in the School of Law at Westminster University. His research interests include critical jurisprudence, spatial justice, psychoanalysis, queer legal theory and law & literature. Recent publications include work on Derrida's reading of Nelson Mandela and a consideration of the relevance of Rancière's notion of presupposed equality for contemporary debates on queer freedom in Africa.

Nadine El-Enany joined Birkbeck as Lecturer in Law in 2013. Between 2010 and 2013 she lectured at Brunel University, London where she also co-directed the Brunel Human Rights Centre. After graduating with an LLB in 2006 from the London School of Economics, she completed her doctoral thesis in the field of EU and UK refugee law at the European University Institute, Florence. She has taught EU law at the London School of Economics, where she is presently a research fellow in the Migration Studies Unit. She was Guest Lecturer in European and Public Law on the London School of Economics Executive Education programme in May 2010. Nadine is currently Recent Developments

Editor for the International Human Rights Law Review. Nadine was selected to join the Runnymede Trust Race Equality Forum in 2012 and is a member of the European Association of Lawyers for Democracy and Human Rights. She is on the organising committee of the Defend the Right to Protest campaign and has published several comment pieces in The Guardian.

Sarah Keenan is a Lecturer in Law at Birkbeck College. Her research draws on legal geography, feminist and critical race theory to rethink the relationship between membership and ownership, offering new perspectives on a range of social, legal and political issues. Her book *Subversive Property: Law and the Production of Spaces of Belonging* (Routledge 2014) develops a theory of property as a spatially contingent relation of belonging - a relation that can be understood as a blurring of ownership and membership, but that will only form property when it is 'held up' by the space in and through which it exists, that is, when the wider social processes, structures and networks that constitute space give force to that relation. She is currently researching the relationship between land title registration, time and race.

Le Anh Nguyen Long is a post-doctoral fellow at the Center for Environmental Policy and Behaviour working on a project which seeks to elucidate how social networks influence the diffusion and innovation of local-level hydraulic fracturing policy. Her research interests center on three trans-border governance research areas: immigration, sustainable development, and local-level hydraulic fracturing policy. She has been a Research Associate at the I.U. Institute for Development Strategies and has taught at the Institute for Political Science at the University of Muenster.

Dafina Paca completed her PhD in September 2015 at the Cardiff School of Journalism Media and Cultural Studies. She currently teaches on numerous undergraduate and postgraduate courses. Her research interests are interdisciplinary, ranging from diaspora, migration and the media, to conflict and international interventions. Her current research focuses on the discursive construction of identity, by migrants and diaspora in the UK as well as how homeland discourses construct diaspora. Her PhD research examines the discursive construction of UK Kosovo Albanian Diaspora identity by Kosovo Albanians in both the UK and Kosovo. Dafina has published on the 'Schatzi' phenomenon, which is a discourse that developed in Kosovo to describe the diaspora especially the diaspora in Germany and Switzerland. She is continuing work on numerous publications, one of which is a monograph based on her

PhD thesis. Dafina also regularly publishes in journalistic publications around the world, most recently in the International Political Forum, Fabrikzeitung in Switzerland and Kosovo 2.0.

Emma Patchett is currently a Research Fellow at the Käte Hamburger Kolleg 'Recht als Kultur' in Bonn, where she is working on postdoctoral research focusing on European spatial imaginaries and minority legal cultures in law. Prior to this, she was Visiting Research Fellow at the Menzies Centre for Australian Studies, King's College London, where her research centred on the convergence between spatiality, literature, and contemporary immigration legislation in Australia. She received her PhD from the University of Muenster in 2015, as a Marie Curie Research Fellow in the CoHaB (diasporic Constructions of Home and Belonging) ITN. Her doctoral research explored migration and legal spatiality in the context of the contemporary literature of the Roma diaspora. Her work has been published in Polemos, the Australian Feminist Law Journal, and Law and Literature.

Parvathi Raman is a senior lecturer in social anthropology. She is the current chair of the SOAS Centre for Migration and Diaspora Studies. Her research interests include the politics of migrant subjectivity, diaspora and identity and questions of (un)belonging.

Julia Rushchenko (PhD) is a Lecturer in Policing and Criminal Investigations at the University of West London. Previously, she held a Doctoral position of Erasmus Mundus Fellow in Cultural and Global Criminology at the University of Kent, Utrecht University, and the University of Hamburg. In the framework of this inter-university project funded by the European Commission Julia conducted her PhD research in Germany. She was a teaching fellow at the Willem Pompe Institute for Criminal Law and Criminology at Utrecht University in 2014-2015 and a visiting scholar at the University of California, San Diego. Her research focuses on transnational migration, security and organized crime.

Siri Schwabe is a PhD Candidate at the Department of Social Anthropology at Stockholm University. She joined the department in 2012 as part of the Marie Curie Initial Training Network 'Diasporic Constructions of Home and Belonging' (CoHaB) after receiving her MSc in Anthropology at the University of Copenhagen. She lived in Santiago from 2013 to 2014 and conducted fieldwork there as part of her doctoral research on Palestinianness, memory, and politics in post-dictatorship Chile. In Santiago, she found herself as fascinated with the (development of the) city itself as with its people, and since then her research has continued to focus on the politics in and of memory, place, and protest.

Melanie R. Wattenbarger graduated from Ohio Wesleyan University with a BA in Religion, Pre-Theology, and Humanities-Classics. She earned her MA in Liberal Studies from Ohio Dominican University. Ms. Wattenbarger is currently ABD in the PhD program at the University of Mumbai and served as an Early Stage Researcher for the European Union's Marie Curie Initial Training Network Diasporic Constructions of Home and Belonging (CoHaB) project. She specializes in contemporary South Asian and Canadian literatures, Diaspora Studies, and Gender and Sexuality Studies. Her publications include articles for the *South Asian Review, Symbolism: An International Annual of Critical Aesthetics* and the edited collection *New Perspectives in Diasporic Experience*. She serves as the Co-Editor of *Salaam*, the newsletter for the South Asian Literary Association.

INTRODUCTION

Spatialities of Diaspora: Race, Justice, and Contentious Topographies

Emma Patchett and Sarah Keenan

This volume seeks to bring ideas of spatial justice into conversation with empirical studies of displacement and racism, and to thereby challenge and extend existing discussions of both spatial justice and diaspora. The groundwork for today's discussions of spatial justice was laid by geographers illustrating that space is not simply and defiantly 'there': space is never neutral.[1] David Harvey wrote in 1973 that

> space is neither absolute, relative or relational in itself, but it can become one or all simultaneously depending on the circumstances … The question 'What is space?' is therefore replaced by the question 'how is it that different human practices create and make use of different conceptualisations of space?'[2]

Reflecting on this understanding of space 30 years later, Harvey saw no reason to shift his position of focussing not on what space 'is', but rather on how different conceptualisations of it are utilised for particular purposes.[3] Doreen Massey's conceptualisation of space as 'dynamic, heterogenous simultaneity' also highlights the malleability of 'space' as a concept with broad political potential.[4] These insights from critical geographers have allowed interdisciplinary scholars to find both hope and complicity in the various networks that constitute space, and to make demands for spatial justice. Recent discussions of spatial justice

---

[1] See, for example, Andreas Philippopoulos-Mihalopoulos, 'Spatial Justice in the Lawscape' in *Urban Interstices: The Aesthetics and the Politics of the In-between,* ed. Andrea Mubi Brightenti (London: Routledge, 2016) 87–103; J. J. A. Shaw and H. J. Shaw, 'Mapping the technologies of spatial (in)justice in the Anthropocene,' *Information and Communications Technology Law* 25/1 (2016), 32–49.

[2] David Harvey, Social Justice and the City (Oxford: Blackwell, 1973) 13-14.

[3] David Harvey, 'Space As a Keyword,' in *David Harvey: A Critical Reader*, eds. Noel Castree and Derek Gregory (Oxford: Blackwell, 2006), 275.

[4] Doreen Massey, *For Space* (London: Sage, 2005), 9.

have built upon both poststructuralist and materialist understandings of space, and have addressed a range of grounded political issues.[5] Yet there has so far been a paucity of work bringing ideas of spatial justice to bear on grounded issues faced by communities labelled 'diasporic.'

The politics of diaspora make the normative coding of space clear by revealing hegemonic attempts to obscure the construction of the spaces we all inhabit. The concept of diaspora offers a useful tool for analyzing the ongoing relationality that is space, as it represents an encounter between 'the global' and 'the local.'[6] Derived from the Greek *dia* ('across') and *speirein* ('scatter'), diaspora is a spatial concept. As diasporic communities are often scattered because geopolitical forces have rendered their homeland a difficult or impossible place to live, diaspora is also a concept that tends to be close to questions of justice. The idea of people scattered far from their homeland and forced to produce new homes elsewhere without losing their cultural identity has been of great interest to sociologists examining the hybridization of culture, the preservation of collective (if disenfranchised) memory and the negotiation of Return.[7] We argue that there is a need to extend the critical potential of diaspora to reach beyond questions of culture and return, and to look toward Avtar Brah's productively fertile concept of 'diaspora space' as a means of implicating both 'natives' and 'migrants' in the production of space, whereby 'entanglements and genealogies of dispersion [are foregrounded] with those of staying put.'[8] Brah's 'diaspora space' is 'the intersectionality of diaspora, border and dis/location as a point of confluence of economic, political, cultural and psychic processes,'[9] and we hope that by bringing grounded work inspired by this concept into the realm of 'spatial justice,' new conversations might begin. In diaspora space, the subject positions of the native and the migrant are both contested. Consistent with Stuart Hall's work de-essentializing identity by showing how diaspora identities produce

---

[5] See, for example, Stephanie Jones et al., 'Childhood Geographies and Spatial Justice: Making Sense of Place and Space-Making as Political Acts in Education,' 53 *American Education Research Journal* (2016), 1126–58; Komali Yenneti, Rosie Day, and Oleg Golubchikov, 'Spatial Justice and the Land Politics of Renewables: Dispossessing Vulnerable Communities through Solar Energy Mega-Projects,' *Geoforum* 76 (2016), 90–9.

[6] James Clifford, 'Diasporas,' *Cultural Anthropology* 9/3 (1994), 302–38.

[7] Homi K. Bhabha, *The Location of Culture* (New York and Abingdon: Routledge, 2004), 163–211; Robin Cohen, *Global Diasporas: An introduction* (New York and Abingdon: Routledge 2008), 166.

[8] Avtar Brah, *Cartographies of Diaspora* (London and New York: Routledge, 1996), 181.

[9] Brah, *Cartographies*, 181.

and reproduce themselves, Brah's work on diaspora space challenges the very distinction between those who are 'settled' and those who are not, shifting the focus onto space and subject position.[10] Sarah Keenan has argued that diasporas appear to 'take space with them' across great distances, performing and producing distinct practices and structures from their homeland despite being physically remote from it.[11] The very existence of diasporas undermines closed and essentialist understandings of space and home, throwing into doubt any version of justice that relies on such understandings.

As a result of this shift in focus onto space and subject position, new ways of thinking about a range of issues have emerged. It has been possible, for example, for writers to observe an indigenous burial ritual as a process of 'entanglement,' a local election as transfused with practices of the global, and poetic identities as coming to exist in a legislative site of extra-territorial emergence.[12] The social, legal, cultural, and political narratives in this collection seek to reflect upon the multiple complicities involved in the shaping of diaspora space, and to thereby bring into question what spatial justice would look like for communities labelled diasporic. This collection does not intend to provide a smooth journey but rather to find potentially uncomfortable juxtapositions in a range of lived contexts in which diasporic identities are involved. We hope to open up new articulations of diaspora as a critical tool, and in so doing to provoke a vigorous discourse on spatial justice, racism, and socio-political paradigms of order. Our aim is to explore refractions of diasporic spatiality, and in doing so to critique the readings of space implied by the very term 'diaspora.' Here we draw on Merleau-Ponty's concept of refractions as a recognition of the multisensory textures of the spatial: refractions of light are not only seen but 'inhabited,'[13] leading to a questioning of what it means to 'live in it from the inside,' to be 'immersed in it.'[14] In other words, a focus

[10] Stuart Hall, 'What Is This "Black" in Black Popular Culture?' *Social Justice* 20/1–2 (1993), 104–14; David Morley and Kuan-Hsing Chen, eds., *Stuart Hall: Critical dialogues in cultural studies* (London and New York: Routledge, 1996).

[11] Sarah Keenan, *Subversive Property—Law and the Production of Spaces of Belonging* (New York and Abingdon: Routledge, 2015), 153.

[12] Wendy Walters, *At Home in Diaspora: Black International Writing* (Minneapolis: University ofMinnesota Press, 2005), ix.

[13] Chris Horrocks, 'You Want to See? Well, Take a Look at This! Ethical Vision, Disembodiment and Light in Marcel Duchamp's Etant DonnéS,' in *Secret Spaces, Forbidden Places: Rethinking Culture*, eds. Fran Lloyd and Catherine O'Brien (New York: Berghahn Books, 2000), 210.

[14] Maurice Merleau-Ponty, *The Primacy of Perception*, ed. James M. Edie (Evanston: Northwestern University Press, 1964), 178.

on refractions of diasporic spatiality turns away from a logocentric geometry to an immersive and yet contentious topography of the local and the global.[15]

As Avtar Brah notes, the notion of border is inscribed within the narrative of diaspora, suggesting a bounded and static concept of space which acts as a platform for peoples' lives rather than an understanding closer to Massey's reading of space as the constantly shifting hetero-geneity that constitutes the world.[16] Borders are an attempt to flatten and enclose space, a task which requires great violence and which will be forever incomplete, hence the constant crossing and redrawing of borders. Striving for articulations of spatial justice in diasporic contexts might be a means by which to wrest the notion of 'scattering' from its essentialist focus on origins and cartography, and instead introduce (or at least evoke) a notion of chaos, an implosion of space at the point of ontology. Striving for spatial justice in the context of diaspora is an attempt to 'embrace the uncertainty of space.'[17]

This volume is not simply a collection of essays which seeks to immerse the reader in a spectacle of fragmentation. Rather, it encour-ages new readings of spatial justice. In this reading, diaspora must be taken seriously as an analytical framework through which to navigate transdisciplinary routes through issues as varied as decolonization, property and planning legislation, counter-terrorism policy, local government, genealogy, and lived experiences of resistance. This book began with a stream of conversations at the Critical Legal Conference 2014, and has grown into a collection comprising in most part the work of junior scholars doing innovative empirical work on local contemporary issues of diaspora and spatial justice around the world. Each of the chapters addresses, in different ways, the construction of spaces textured through socio-legal practices of experience and figura-tive manifestations of particular and peculiar acts of spacing. We have put together this intentionally dischordant, multidisciplinary collection which critiques essentialist readings of space and home, grounds issues of justice in lived experiences, and insists that we ask difficult questions about justice and its spatiality.

Through this collection we want to insist that work on spatial justice be attentive to lived experiences of the local, and that work on diaspora not only be read as a series of displacements. In insisting that we ask difficult questions about justice and its spatiality, this

---

[15] See for example David Delaney, *Nomospheric Investigations: The Spatial, The Legal and the Pragmatics of World-Making* (Glasshouse 2010).

[16] Brah, *Cartographies*, 16; Massey, *For Space*, 139.

[17] Keenan, *Subversive Property*, 13; Massey, *For Space*, 153.

volume necessarily looks beyond concepts such as multiculturalism, cosmopolitanism and hybridity.[18] Instead this collection takes its cue from post-colonial scholarship which encourages academic engagement as a way of 'reading otherwise, against the grain.'[19]

Whose Spatial Justice?

Scholars from a range of disciplines are embracing the concept of 'spatial justice.'[20] Edward Soja wrote extensively on spatial justice and the possibility of constructing political strategies through the amalgamation of these terms.[21] For Soja, justice has a geography, and spatial justice involves the equitable distribution of resources, services, and access as basic human rights. Soja's spatial justice is a way of looking at justice, namely with an intentional and focused emphasis on its spatial or geographical aspects.[22] As a starting point, Soja suggests, spatial justice 'involves the fair and equitable distribution in space of socially valued resources and the opportunities to use them.'[23] Similarly, Peter Marcuse identifies two forms of spatial *injustice*, first as physical confinement, and secondly as the unjust allocation of resources (inequality), arguing that 'these broader injustices cannot be dealt with without attention to their spatial aspect.'[24] Attending to the refractions of diasporic spatialities proposes a framework for reading these injustices not as external to the rhetoric of the spatial but as a necessary rupture within the spatio-temporal topographies mapped out in this collection. Andreas Philippopoulos-Mihalopoulos puts forward a different form of spatial justice which focuses specifically on the subjects's locationality in space, and the way in which the 'dispute between my and your claim to "here" rises above the law while relying on it.'[25] Philippopoulos -Mihalopoulos' spatial justice arises out of 'the conflict between bodies that are moved

---

[18] Paul Gilroy, *Against Race: Imagining Political Culture Beyond the Color Line* (Massachusetts: Harvard University Press, 2000). Ulrich Beck, *Cosmopolitan Vision* (Oxford: Polity Press, 2006).

[19] Stuart Hall, 'Avtar Brah's Cartographies: Moment, Method, Meaning,' *Feminist Review* 100 (2012), 35.

[20] See fn. 5.

[21] Edward Soja, 'The City and Spatial Justice,' *Spatial Justice* 1 (2009), 2, accessed 14 October 2014, http://www.jssj.org.

[22] Soja, 'The City and Spatial Justice,' 2.

[23] Soja, 'The City and Spatial Justice,' 2.

[24] Peter Marcuse, 'Spatial Justice: Derivative but Causal of Social Injustice,' *Spatial Justice* 1 (2009), 3, 5, accessed 12 October 2014, http://www.jssj.org.

[25] Andreas Philippopoulos-Mihalopoulos, 'Spatial Justice: Law and the Geography of Withdrawal,' *International Journal of Law in Context* 6/3 (2010), 202.

by a desire to occupy the same space at the same time.'[26] In his work, the key question is of 'a spatiotemporally positioned question: not what can happen, but what happens when bodies claim the same space at the same time.'[27] This notion of dialectical corporeality operating in a lawscape is a productive way to interrogate the multi-layered condition of emplacement. However it does not explicitly take account of race in the conflict between bodies out of which spatial justice arises, which we argue is useful to address.[28]

Soja's and Philippopoulos-Mihalopoulos's work on spatial justice is part of a broader 'spatial turn' in the humanities, social sciences, and law, which has powerfully demonstrated the political meaning and potential of space as both an analytic framework and everyday reality.[29] In line with this spatial turn, this collection seeks to explore spatial justice in the context of diaspora, asking what possibilities exist for justice against the realities of severely imbalanced post-colonial geographies, state borders, and systemic racism. As Sherene Razack and others have demonstrated, space is racialized—place can *become* race through law.[30] While Razack is writing in the context of settler colonialism, her approach of interrogating bodies travelling in spaces as a way of tracking how multiple systems of domination come into existence in and through each other is clearly relevant to diasporic contexts.[31] Examining diaspora space not only shows how cultural identities and spaces of belonging can be retained despite movement from one side of the globe to another, it also shows how colonial histories continue to shape the life chances of communities of both the North and the South, how nation-state borders can operate well outside the limited zones of inhabitation insinuated by a map, and how racism operates through histories and increasingly pervasive borders.

---

[26] Andreas Philippopoulos-Mihalopoulos, *Spatial Justice: Body, Lawscape, Atmosphere* (Abingdon and New York: Routledge, 2014), 3.

[27] Philippopoulos-Mihalopoulos, *Spatial Justice*, 5.

[28] Arventina Washington Cherry, 'Spaces of Possibilities: Using Diaspora as a Tool to Unravel Complex Ideological Frameworks that Impact Diasporic Encounters among African Americans, Afro Latinas/os, and Latinas/os of African Descent in a Prince George's County, Maryland Public Middle School,' *Transforming Anthropology* 23/1 (2015), 28–42.

[29] Nicholas Blomley, *Law, Space and the Geographies of Power* (London: The Guildford Press, 1994); Davina Cooper, *Governing out of Order: Space, Law and the Politics of Belonging* (London and New York: Rivers Oram and New York University Press, 1998); Graham, Nicole. *Lawscape: Property, Environment, Law* (Abingdon and New York: Routledge, 2011).

[30] Sherene Razack, *Race, Space, and the Law: Unmapping a White Settler Society* (Toronto: Between the Lines, 2002), 1.

[31] Razack, *Race, Space, and the Law*, 15.

This collection does not advocate any one definition of spatial justice, but rather gathers together work that exposes the relation between juridical and spatial orders in ways which resonate with and, we hope, take further the engagements with spatial justice that have preceded it. Rather than focus on defining spatial justice, the pieces in this collection discuss specific diasporic contexts in which the relation between juridical and spatial orders is both exposed and refracted in ways that are often unexpected. In chapter one, Jaco Barnard-Naudé presents a reading of nomos as counter-memorial responsiveness. Drawing on Giorgio Agemben, Carl Schmitt, and Hannah Arendt, he focuses on a spatio-legal reading of slave burial sites in Cape Town. The longest piece in the collection, this chapter engages in depth with the theoretical debates around spatial justice. Barnard-Naudé explores the process of encountering a memorial space through the spatial legacy of apartheid, provoking an inevitable confrontation with the exteriority of the nomos, and locating justice as that which always lies 'beyond.' In chapter two, Siri Schwabe draws on her fieldwork research conducted in Santiago with the Palestinian-Chilean community to explore the politics of presence in a mobilized ethics of resistance in exile. Schwabe identifies mobilization as a process of securing presence despite being 'out of place,' forging a diasporic politics of resistance which critiques static conceptions of place, space, and locality. In the third chapter Julia Rushchenko discusses crimmigration discourse in the context of the German state, and explores the uneasy narrative of 'sham' cross-border marriages, family reunification and border controls in the context of the state's policing of citizenship. In chapter four, Dafina Paca analyzes interviews undertaken at the Kosovo Ministry of Diaspora to consider how the homeland constructs the diaspora. Paca critiques the use of biopolitics at a distance, or what she terms 'tele-biopolitics,' to control and discipline the Kosovan diasporic body and construct a homogenized diaspora. In chapter five, Melanie Wattenbarger reads the spaces of Guantanomo Bay through a literary analysis of poetry written by those detained inside the infamous prison. Her work reflects upon a form of corporeal resistance to ongoing detention, asking how home spaces can come to be evoked in the condition of controlled place and embodied presence. In chapter six, Le Anh Nguyen-Long considers socio-political representations of diasporic groups and the ideology of the 'European space' in the context of Italy. Looking at case studies of different attitudes to the Bangladeshi and Filipino diasporic communities in Italy, she argues that diasporic use of space represents a particular political engagement with space which plays on previously disenfranchising discourses of visibility. In chapter seven, Nadine El-Enany discusses the removal from office of Lutfur Rahman,

Britain's first Muslim mayor, in the London borough of Tower Hamlets. Providing a contextualized critique of the judgment which removed Rahman, El-Enany demonstrates law's reassertion of racist colonial exclusion in an area with a significant Muslim population and progressive socio-economic leadership. El-Enany argues that any concern with spatial justice demands an engagement with the way in which spaces of injustice are often racialized. In chapter eight, Tekalign Ayalew discusses research conducted with Ethiopian diasporic communities in Sweden. Engaging with the complex and dynamic processes of making 'home' in the 'host' land, Ayalew focuses on the importance of community activities in forging economic and political connections to place as a means of shaping space. In chapter nine Emma Patchett conducts an interdisiciplinary analysis of the evictions of the Dale Farm Traveller site in 2011, exploring this case in the context of legal access to space in domestic and international law and the history of anti-nomadic exclusion, framed through a reading of the novel *Tribe* by John F. McDonald.

The volume seeks to pose a series of questions which move beyond the fixation on the static categorizations of authenticity, legitimacy, and 'non-belonging' that tend to dominate the field of diaspora studies.[32] The authors seek to broaden out the notion of spatiality in diaspora from issues of remittances and the homesick gaze of return (where the diasporic is situated as forever caught in a metaphorical no-man's land), and to simultaneously inform and empirically ground current debates on 'spatial justice.'[33] There is much scope for further research in this area, taking inspiration from scholarship which is unpicking the potentially vast new readings of space available in the context of diaspora;[34] the

---

[32] Mette Louise Berg, '"La Lenin Is My Passport": Schooling, Mobility and Belonging in Socialist Cuba and Its Diaspora,' *Identities* 22/3 (2015), 303–17; Alison Booth, 'Whose Diwali is it? Diaspora, Identity, and Festivalization,' *Tourism Culture & Communication* 15/3 (2016), 215–26; Edmund Gomez and Gregor Benton, *Belonging to the Nation: Generational Change, Identity and the Chinese Diaspora.* (New York and London: Routledge, 2016).

[33] Stefano Breschi et al., 'Foreign Inventors in the US: Testing for Diaspora and Brain Gain Effects,' *Cahiers du GREThA* 2015/25 (2015); Anastasia Christou and Russell King, *Counter-Diaspora: The Greek Second Generation Returns ' Home'* (Cambridge, MA, and London: Harvard University Press, 2015); Mariana Guzzardo et al., '"Half Here, Half There": Dialogical Selves Among Older Puerto Ricans of the Diaspora,' *Journal of Constructivist Psychology* (2015), 1–15; Elaine Lynn-Ee Ho and Mark Boyle, 'Migration as Development Repackaged? The Globalizing Imperative of the Singaporean State's Diaspora Strategies,' *Singapore Journal of Tropical Geography* 36/2 (2015), 164–182; Anca Turcu and Robert Urbatsch, 'Diffusion of Diaspora Enfranchisement Norms A Multinational Study,' *Comparative Political Studies* 48/4 (2015), 407–37.

[34] Rizwangul NurMuhammad et al., 'Uyghur Transnational Identity on Facebook:

ambiguous complexity of new and unfolding networks of participation taking place;[35] and in the dexterity with which evolving legal orders defy any dichotomous understanding of the public/private divide.[36] The questions, therefore, that we hope this volume will provoke in the reader are diverse: is it possible to be 'out of place,' if you can take space with you? Does lexicography induce new potentialities which will no longer rely on metaphor for an approximation of spatial justice? Are all diasporic practices inherently spatial, and can this spatiality be used to instigate a new paradigm of justice? Can the concept of spatial justice adequately grapple with historical and contemporary discourses of race, ethnicity, and migration? While this volume cannot provide answers to these questions, we hope that asking them will be a productive process for those attempting to find spatial justice.

On the Development of a Young Diaspora,' *Identities* (2015), 1–15.

[35] Cherry, 'Spaces of Possibilities.'

[36] Reza Banakar, 'Introduction: Emerging Legal Uncertainty,' *Normativity in Legal Sociology*, ed. Reza Banakar (New York: Springer International Publishing, 2015); Harry Blagg, 'From Terra Nullius to Terra Liquidus?' *Punishing the Other: The Social Production of Immorality Revisited*, ed. Anna Eriksson, (New York and London: Routledge, 2016); Irus Braverman et al., *The Expanding Spaces of Law: A Timely Legal Geography* (Stanford, CA: Stanford University Press, 2014); Peer Zumbansen, 'Where the Wild Things are: Journeys to Transnational Legal Orders, and Back.' *TLI Think! Paper* 07/2016, 28 January 2016. King's College London Law School Research Paper No. 16-11, accessed 10 November 2016, http://dx.doi.org/10.2139/ssrn.2723990.

1

Law, Memory and Post-Apartheid Spatiality: 'Reading Nomos Otherwise,' 'Mapping the Heterotopic'

Jaco Barnard-Naudé

Introduction: Phocion's Widow

In this chapter, I reflect on what a spatial consideration of law—law as nomos—might contribute to its confrontation with a past of injustice; an injustice that is hauntingly re-presented spatially when the remains of the unknown, unnamed, and unconsecrated dead make their appearance in the very heart of the postcolonial city.[1] Throughout, I ask the question of how to hold the law responsible, or rather, *responsive* in and with regards to this uncanny place. Commentators in the field of post-apartheid jurisprudence have noted the intricate connection between memory and justice with reference to the distinction between two spatial metaphors: the monumental and the memorial.[2] The founding of the post-apartheid Constitution is, in such commentary, characterized as a monumental achievement which *celebrates* the South African transition as *the* historical moment that 'recognizes the injustices of the past' and, through the constitutional provisions, continues to inaugurate justice for the victims of the past. Indeed, the South African Constitutional Court has often emphasized the importance of memory in the interpretation of the meaning of the Constitution. On the other hand, critical commentators that are more skeptical of the extent to which positivized constitutional law can do justice, have insisted on

---

[1] Julian Jonker makes the point that even without this appearance of the remains the structural legacy of apartheid is visible in the post-apartheid city in the planning of the urban built environment and is experienced through the popular racial imaginary; see Julian Jonker, 'Excavating the Legal Subject: The Unnamed Dead of Prestwich Place, Cape Town,' *Griffith Law Review* 14/2 (2005), 203.

[2] Lourens Du Plessis, 'The South African Constitution As Memory and Promise,' *Stellenbosch Law Review* 11 (2000), 385–6.

justice as radical incompletion,[3] have emphasized the memorial dimension of constitutionalism and have insisted on the *commemoration* of those for who, and that in relation to which, justice can never be done. This contribution represents an association with memory that is closer to the latter form of commentary than it is to the former. As such, it asks how to commemorate and thus memorialize the slave burial site as a space and a place, how to hold open the possibility of beginning to do justice not only to the remains as a representation of past injustice but also to the remains in the widest, metaphorical sense of that word, in other words, the remains that are always other to the law's claim to be doing justice. Like Jonker, to whose work I will be referring extensively, I am interested in discerning the 'ethical and political spirit' which animates the relationship between law and those whose remains serve as a poignant reminder of the injustice of a past, here particularly the unjust past of apartheid.[4] We shall encounter these remains by revisiting the discovery in recent years of two slave burial sites in Cape Town.

I justify my enquiry as one that attends to a consideration of specifically the involvement of *law* in this context, with reference to Giorgio Agamben's claim that responsibility is 'irremediably contaminated by law.'[5] For Agamben, ethics is the 'doctrine of the happy life.'[6] The assumption of responsibility, on the other hand, means that one takes leave of ethics and enters the domain of law. Jonker draws out the implication of this point for the relationship between law and memory: 'ethics aims at the good life, and no duty to remember can produce "good" memory. Instead demands upon memory are juridical, and imply a juridical technology, a *tekhnē* of memory, a way to imprison memory and to sponsor mnemonic debts.'[7] For Agamben then, these questions of remembrance are juridical as much as they are questions of responsibility, or rather, they are juridical *because* they are questions of responsibility. 'It must be recalled,' Agamben writes, 'that the assumption of moral responsibility has value only if one is ready to assume the relevant legal consequences.'[8] Accordingly, an enquiry into the kind of

---

[3] The Derridean deconstruction of the relationship between law and justice is, of course, in play here; see Jacques Derrida, 'Force of Law: The "Mystical Foundation of Authority",' *Cardozo Law Review* 11 (1990), 921.

[4] Julian Jonker, 'The Silence of the Dead: Ethical and Juridical Significances of the Exhumations at Prestwich Place, Cape Town, 2003–2005' (MPhil dissertation, University of Cape Town, 2005), 132.

[5] Giorgio Agamben, *Remnants of Auschwitz: The Witness and the Archive* (New York: Zone Books, 1999), 20.

[6] Agamben, *Remnants of Auschwitz*, 24.

[7] Jonker, 'The Silence of the Dead,' 70.

[8] Agamben, *Remnants of Auschwitz*, 23.

law or approach to law that will assume this responsibility, is indicated.

A consideration of the spatial dimension of law is necessitated by this kind of enquiry, not least because the remains are invariably topographically located or emplaced. As these remains pertaining to the slave burial site both instantiate and reflect layers of spatiality or spatial orientations, they consequently highlight multiple ways in which the relationship between law and space can be understood. In this contribution, I am ultimately interested in how space can inform or shape a modality of law as transformative. But our encounter with the slave burial site as remains will, first of all, make apparent another, older, conservative and historically oppressive relationship between law and space. For the slave burial site as a memorial space invariably evokes or remembers the spatial legacy of apartheid as a nomos in Carl Schmitt's sense of the term, that is to say the law as a concrete unity of order and orientation that here originates in a land-appropriation as the foundational act of a colonization.[9] The relationship between law and space that comes to the fore here is one of containment as exclusivity coupled with jurisdiction as domination. I will illustrate this by arguing that the resurfacing—via the slave burial site—of the colonial nomos on the post-apartheid landscape confronts us with the exteriority of the nomos of apartheid's political community. Such a confrontation with exteriority becomes appreciable when one admits to a reflexive understanding of nomos and of the designation of the slave burial site as what Hans Lindahl calls a 'strange place'—a place that serves as a spatial marker of and as such represents those who are *dis*placed.[10] Here displacement must be understood as a primary effect of the nomos of apartheid: 'these unnamed and unmarked dead became the tangible signs of the city's displacement of so many others, both living and dead.'[11]

Yet, the encounter with the remains as a confrontation with the exteriority of nomos as the 'place' of the displaced invites a postcolonial re-consideration of the nomos—a consideration of nomos 'otherwise.'[12] Relying on Chryssostalis, I locate the rudiments of a consideration of nomos 'otherwise' in the work of Hannah Arendt. This involves

[9] Carl Schmitt, *The Nomos of the Earth in the International Law of the Jus Publicum Europaeum* (New York: Telos Press Publishing, 2006), 48.

[10] Hans Lindahl, 'Give and Take: Arendt and the *Nomos* of Political Community,' *Philosophy & Social Criticism* 32/7 (2006), 888.

[11] Louise Green & Noëleen Murray, 'Notes for a Guide to the Ossuary,' *African Studies* 68/3 (2009), 372.

[12] Julia Chryssostalis, 'Reading Arendt, 'Reading' Schmitt: Reading Nomos Otherwise?' in *Feminist Encounters with Legal Philosophy*, ed. Maria Drakopoulou (London: Routledge, 2013), 158.

a reading of nomos that retains its character as a spatial concept but causes this spatial instantiation of law to turn not on the primacy of a land-appropriation, but rather on the primacy of the relationship between space, memory and political action. My claim here is that 'place' or 'site' represents the nodal point of the interconnection between space, memory, and political action and that law as nomos is that which secures and as such renders a degree of permanence to, or preserves, the site.[13] In Lindahl's words, this understanding of nomos 'provides a durable structure for "spaces of appearances" in which men, in the plural, can disclose and distinguish themselves through word and deed.'[14] As we shall see, reading nomos *otherwise* hints at law's memorial responsiveness and places it in relation to the justice that forever exceeds it—a futural justice to which it is nevertheless required to accede in each and every of its instantiations in a spatio-temporal present as law.[15]

As for the law's past, reading nomos otherwise allows for an appreciation of how this responsive potentiality of law is, in turn, activated by its capacity for memory. Reading nomos otherwise is thus always already a memorial reading, not simply of law, but of space as the concrete instantiation of relations of counter-memory or what I call memory-as-difference.[16] With its focus on alterity, reading nomos *otherwise* necessitates, to put it in Andreas Philippopoulos-Mihalopoulos's words, that one privileges the point of view that '*spatiality is an ethical position.*'[17] Such a reconsideration of nomos as a (counter-)memorial responsiveness prompts, in this context, a consideration of the slave burial site as heterotopic and heterotopic specifically as a counter-site and of the involvement of transformative law at the burial site as constituting what Jonker has called 'mapping the heterotopic.'[18] This mapping of the burial site as heterotopic re-orientates nomos in that it places it in a responsive memorial relation with its spatial and temporal exteriority, with what lies beyond it. In elaborating such a responsive and transformative nomos, I rely on Golder and Fitzpatrick's reading

---

[13] Hannah Arendt, *The Human Condition* (Chicago: University of Chicago Press, 1998), 175–247.

[14] Lindahl, 'Give and Take,' 885.

[15] Jacques Derrida, 'Force of Law,' 921.

[16] In following Foucault, Rosi Braidotti defines 'countermemory' as 'a space of resistance,' the memory of the 'nomadic subject ... who has forgotten to forget injustice'; see Rosi Braidotti, *Nomadic Subjects: Embodiment and Sexual Difference in Contemporary Feminist Theory* (New York: Columbia University Press, 1994), 25.

[17] Andreas Philippopoulos-Mihalopoulos, 'Law's Spatial Turn: Geography, Justice and a Certain Fear of Space,' *Law, Culture and the Humanities* 7/2 (2011), 9.

[18] Jonker, 'The Silence of the Dead,' 132.

of Foucault on law.[19] Indeed, mapping the heterotopic necessitates acts of law-as-counter-memory that crucially entails a breach of nomos in its definition as a 'wall of law.'[20] Such a breach radically destabilizes the very distinction between inside and outside, 'us' and 'them,' by understanding, first of all, that space is 'constantly in transit and open to the infinite.'[21] I suggest, following Gillian Rose, that this breach allows us to contemplate what she calls the 'just city.'[22]

As a way of visually highlighting the concerns of this contribution, I want to begin with the story that forms the subject of Alexander Poussin's painting, *Gathering the Ashes of Phocion*.[23] This is the story, as it is told by Rose in her book *Mourning Becomes the Law*, of the widow of the Athenian statesman, Phocion who was sentenced to his death by a corrupted government on a false charge of treason.[24] As an additional disgrace, Phocion's proper burial inside the city was forbidden. No Athenian was allowed to provide fire for his funeral. Consequently, his body was burnt outside the city by a paid alien who left the ashes untended on the pyre.[25]

Poussin's painting represents the moment when Phocion's widow and a woman servant—defiant of the decree that his remains be left unconsecrated—venture outside the city to collect his ashes. The viewer is presented with a landscape that contains the two women hidden in shadows in the central foreground. The positioning of the two women in the shadowy foreground stands in stark contrast with the brightly lit Athens in the background. Phocion's wife is presented with her back to the city, bending downwards to scoop up the ashes, while the servant is positioned between her and the city, almost as if she is guarding or shielding her mistress against the danger she is putting herself in by transgressively collecting the ashes. This positioning adds a sense of suspense to the painting.[26]

[19] Ben Golder and Peter Fitzpatrick, *Foucault's Law* (Abingdon: Routledge, 2009).
[20] Hannah Arendt, 'The Great Tradition I: Law and Power,' *Social Research* 74/3 (2007), 717.
[21] Jonker, 'The Silence of the Dead,' 138.
[22] Gillian Rose, *Mourning Becomes the Law: Philosophy and Representation* (Cambridge: CUP, 1996), 26.
[23] The painting can be viewed via Wikipedia, accessed 29 October 2016, http://upload. wikimedia.org/wikipedia/commons/9/90/Nicolas_Poussin_-_Landscape_with_the_ Gathering_of_the_Ashes_of_Phocion_by_his_Widow_%28detail%29_-_WGA18326. jpg.
[24] Rose, *Mourning Becomes the Law*, 23.
[25] Rose, *Mourning Becomes the Law*, 23.
[26] Rose, *Mourning Becomes the Law*, 25 and 35. It is noteworthy to relate this sense of suspense to the suspension of the law at stake in this decision to collect the ashes illegally. This suspension of the law, is, as Derrida taught, the condition of all decision

There are at least two versions of what happens next. Plutarch's original version has it that Phocion's wife returns to the city where she dedicates the remains to the household gods by burying the ashes by the hearth.[27] Another version claims that Phocion's wife consumes his ashes giving her husband's unhappy soul a final tomb within her.[28] Important for current purposes, both versions insist that Phocion's wife returns (with) the remains to the city. Rose contends that in this return, Phocion's wife re-engages the ethical and political processes of the city and so comes to challenge—in mourning—the tyranny that culminated in her husband's dishonorable death.[29]

As is clear from the story, law is intricately involved in these events, most prominently in its manifestation as a decree that the remains be left unconsecrated outside the city walls. Indeed, law determines the very notion of what constitutes 'outside the city walls.' Phocion's wife, much like Antigone, transgresses this law and, in her protest, comes to politically contest and confront the law of the city with itself and with another law—a law that would respond to the remains, a law that attempts to do justice to the remains, a law that Phocion's widow comes to embody and emplace. The representations in the painting also clearly juxtapose the emplacements of these different registers of law. Although Rose is critical of such a reading, there is nevertheless a juxtaposition in the painting between the brightly-lit architectural order of the law of the city and the dark, obscure emplacement of the burial site outside the city. While one can agree with Rose that the 'magnificent, gleaming, classical buildings' may not in themselves represent tyranny and injustice, it is nevertheless the case that Poussin provided a *spatial contrast* between the illegal ethico-political act of gathering the ashes, on the one hand, and the no less political but positivized law of the order of the city, on the other.[30]

(See Derrida, 'Force of Law,' 961–2). Rose contends that it is the servant who in the picture bears the political risk in her contorted posture. In other words, she is suspension, the suspension of the law. She is in-between spaces—the ethical space of her mistress, on the one hand, the juridical space of the city, on the other. As such she represents undecidability. This presence of the slave who, at the burial site, is made to bear the political risk for the master, is, as we shall see later on, not insignificant when it comes to reflecting on the responsibility of the postcolonial living for the dead who remain as the victims of colonization and slavery. On the relationship between suspension and responsibility, Elisabeth Weber argues that the responsible decision passes through 'the space or lapse of undecidability'; see Elisabeth Weber, 'Suspended from the Other's Heartbeat,' *South Atlantic Quarterly* 106/2 (2007), 325.

27 Rose, *Mourning Becomes the Law*, 25.
28 Rose, *Mourning Becomes the Law*, 25.
29 Rose, *Mourning Becomes the Law*, 25–6 and 36.
30 Rose, *Mourning Becomes the Law*, 25. In my description of the act as

Rose warns that a reading of the painting which opposes 'the act of redeeming love' on the part of Phocion's widow, to 'the implacable domination of architectural and political order ... is completely to efface the politics of this painting.'[31] Rather, Rose sees political defiance in the action of these women—the act of infinite love is also a transgressive, 'finite act of political justice.'[32] Further, if the buildings are taken to represent the city as the space of rational order then it throws into relief the 'specific act of injustice' that takes place outside of the city as the bounded political entity. And further still, while 'the city' implies the bounded political entity, it also implies 'the breaches in its wall.'[33] The 'missing resources,' says Rose, 'may be found ... in the politics which has been disowned.'[34]

A transformative encounter of nomos with the remains would take Rose's warning seriously. It would thus not be motivated by a compulsion to oppose 'power and law as such' by emphasizing that tending to the remains constitute pure ethical acts of infinite love that do not and cannot have legal ramifications.[35] Rather, it would be interested in the breaches in the wall, in the politics and the law that have been disowned and as such concerned with the ways in which tending to the remains through finite acts of political justice can breach the wall, making available a transformative relation of the nomos to itself. Haverkamp remarks that 'justice, in other words, has to deal with the other—but the law "deal[s] pain and death." In dealing death and pain, the law deals with the other, mercilessly. The law creates within the nomos the other of the nomos.'[36]

I contend that what is at issue in the postcolony and in post-apartheid law today is this merciless dealing and along with it, this creation of 'the other of the nomos' within the nomos. When the remains of the dead surface in the very heart of the city, it confronts the nomos not only with its other, but also with the ways in which it mercilessly deals

---

'ethico-political,' I follow Slavoj Žižek's contention that 'politics is the very space in which, without any external guarantee, ethical decisions are made and negotiated.' Slavoj Žižek, *Less Than Nothing: Hegel and the Shadow of Dialectical Materialism* (London: Verso, 2012), 963. Yet, as I have already indicated through my reliance on Agamben, there is an irreducibly juridical dimension to this act, which takes as its point of departure the 'facticity' of the act as illegal.

[31] Rose, *Mourning Becomes the Law*, 25.
[32] Rose, *Mourning Becomes the Law*, 25.
[33] Rose, *Mourning Becomes the Law*, 10.
[34] Rose, *Mourning Becomes the Law*, 10.
[35] Rose, *Mourning Becomes the Law*, 26.
[36] Anselm Haverkamp, 'Rhetoric, Law and the Poetics of Memory,' *Cardozo Law Review* 13 (1991), 1649.

and mercilessly has dealt with this other. In doing so, the confrontation invites the law to *reflect* upon itself. In other words, it invites a *reflexive* reflection. Philippopoulos-Mihalopoulos explicitly identifies this type of reflection as a characteristic of an authentic encounter of space with law: 'space forces law to turn toward itself and judge its own judgements: space is the terrain of law's questioning *par excellence*.'[37] What is ultimately at issue then is a constitution or re-constitution of the nomos by way of which the city wall is breached; through which the inside does not only become responsive to the outside, but through which the very demarcation of inside and outside is constitutively politicized and the idea of a *transformative* nomos—a nomos that disconfirms itself—appreciable.[38]

Encountering the Remains: The Truth and Reconciliation Commission, Prestwich Place, and the Rustenburg Burial Ground

Ever since the ethical, political, and legal processes that surrounded the life of the South African Truth and Reconciliation Commission (TRC), post-apartheid South Africa has been haunted by the question of the remains. One can even go as far as saying that a significant part of post-apartheid law and politics—at least in the TRC period—could be seen to have consisted in the overt attempt not only to encounter the physical remains of the previously condemned, but also in an attempt to return these remains to the *polis;* to welcome the specter of the condemned at the walls, inviting it to pass through it, as ghosts do and perhaps more importantly, will. Indeed, it would be justified to refer to this period as the institution of a hauntology of apartheid.[39] This pre-occupation with the remains is not surprising from the point of view that, as Mark Sanders writes, apartheid significantly

---

[37] Andreas Philippopoulos-Mihalopoulos, 'Law's Spatial Turn: Geography, Justice and a Certain Fear of Space,' *Law, Culture and the Humanities* 7/2 (2011), 195.

[38] In this regard Drucilla Cornell's description of transformation, which she rigorously distinguishes from evolution, is highly relevant. Cornell writes that 'a system can so alter itself that it not only no longer confirms its identity, but disconfirms it and, indeed, through its very iterability, generates new meanings which can be further pursued and enhanced by the sociosymbolic practice of the political contestant within its milieu.' Drucilla Cornell, *Transformations: Recollective Imagination and Sexual Difference* (New York: Routledge, 1993), 2.

[39] On the history of hauntology, see Colin Davis, 'État Present: Hauntology, Spectres and Phantoms,' *French Studies* 59/3 (2005), 373: 'Hauntology supplants its near-homonym ontology, replacing the priority of being and presence with the figure of the ghost as that which is neither present nor absent, neither dead nor alive.'

constituted a proscription on the work of mourning, 'specifically of the other' and, as such, amounted to a devastating obstruction of the ethico-politico-juridico encounter with the remains:[40]

> The petitions for funeral rites heard at the Truth Commission's hearings, especially those calling for their proper completion, tell us that apartheid brought with it not only an attempt to disrupt the work of mourning through restrictions on political funerals and attacks on mourners, but, in so doing, effectively also entailed a refusal to join with survivors in the work of mourning. Going one better than the vengeful decrees of Creon that Antigone defied, apartheid was, in other words, a systematic prohibition on mourning and a withholding of condolence.[41]

The (still) overwhelming need to encounter the remains in post-apartheid South Africa is not restricted only to efforts through which physical encounters with the remains of the dead become possible. Indeed, the mandate of the TRC, namely that it had to provide as complete a picture as possible of the causes, nature and extent of the gross human rights violations of apartheid can be stated otherwise as the task to encounter the remains. In addition, it is a widely held (and judicially endorsed) view that the very task of the law of post-apartheid South Africa, in its form as the project of transformative constitutionalism, consists in dealing with or addressing the legacy/ghost of the apartheid past and in this sense it is the task of encountering the remains. As Pierre de Vos writes, the very interpretation of the South African Constitution has been made to hinge upon the construction of a grand narrative of the 'dark, apartheid' past in the sense that the meaning of the constitutional text is said to be discoverable by reading it in the context of the country's recent past:

> Put bluntly, according to this approach one can get to grips with the meaning of the constitutional text if one refers to the specific apartheid past to identify all the wicked attitudes and practices that existed before commencement of the interim Constitution. It is thus only with reference to this shameful history that we can really understand what the text of the Constitution is trying to achieve.[42]

We will leave suspended, for the moment, the successes and failures that have been attendant upon this general or wide sense in which the

[40] Mark Sanders, *Ambiguities of Witnessing: Law and Literature in the Time of a Truth Commission* (Johannesburg: Wits University Press, 2007), 35.

[41] Sanders, *Ambiguities of Witnessing*, 48–9.

[42] Pierre de Vos, 'A Bridge Too Far? History as Context in the Interpretation of the South African Constitution,' *South African Journal on Human Rights* 17/1 (2001), 11.

law is mandated with the task of encountering the remains, although our encounter with specific physical remains in what follows ultimately leads back to and causes the stress to fall on this generality and on what Douzinas and Geary have referred to as a 'general jurisprudence.'[43] If we restrict the focus to the TRC—as a creature of post-apartheid statute—one can, despite the pervasive emphasis on encountering the remains, discern a more or less dismal failure in its role of facilitating physical encounters with, and the return of, the remains to the city. In the first place, as Sanders has indicated, the TRC's mandate did not, strictly speaking, allow for the investigation of violations of custom such as the insistence on burial rites.[44] Yet, this custom—and its denial—was of utmost importance for many apartheid victims' families. Sanders argues that the positing of the law of apartheid but also (although less so) of the TRC against custom, in fact served to thwart the encounter with the remains of those previously condemned by apartheid.

Nevertheless, the witness testimonies before the TRC forced it to reach beyond its legal mandate. Witnesses repeatedly spoke of 'undiscovered bodies, of bodies denied a proper burial' and sought the help of the commission in 'rectifying this state of affairs.'[45] Sanders remarks that this constituted a request from the witness to the TRC to participate 'materially and affectively' in the work of mourning.[46] This caused the commission to alter its actual practices by responding to these appeals in the form of, for instance, carrying the cost of several exhumations. But despite also having set up a Missing Persons Task Team, the TRC failed satisfactorily to facilitate the location of the remains of struggle activists believed to have been killed by apartheid security forces. According to a report issued by the victim support group, Khulumani, 'the number of reports "officially recognized" by the TRC as "the disappeared" are only about a third of those who are believed to have disappeared while engaged in political activities under apartheid.'[47]

Moving beyond the physical encounter with the remains, the TRC has also been accused of thwarting the encounter with the remains on a more symbolic, if no less important, level. Terry Bell and Dumisa Ntsebeza have described it as a 'widely propagated myth' that the TRC

---

[43] Costas Douzinas & Adam Geary, *Critical Jurisprudence: The Political Philosophy of Justice* (Oxford: Hart Publishing, 2005), 4–5.

[44] Sanders, *Ambiguities of Witnessing*, 65.

[45] Sanders, *Ambiguities of Witnessing*, 35.

[46] Sanders, *Ambiguities of Witnessing*, 40.

[47] Marjorie Jobson, 'Respect the Bereaved as well as the Bones,' 2008, accessed 29 October 2016, http://www.khulumani.net/khulumani/statements/item/139-respect-the-bereaved-as-well-as-the-bones.html.

uncovered the 'hidden history' of apartheid.[48] Grunebaum and Henri argue that the TRC created a speaking subject

> whose selfhood was defined by a disempowering and passive interiority: the 'victim.' The 'victim' of human rights abuse and atrocity was represented as a damaged survivor coming to voice in order to be publicly heard and to heal, not as a self-defining author and agent of history, of social action and meaningful change.[49]

The authors believe that the TRC did not intend to collect three hundred and fifty years worth of evidence of the theft and destruction that was colonialism and apartheid. Rather,

> the TRC also diminished the possibility for people who lived and suffered to explore and understand these histories in ways that make real the chance to transform present reality into a time of mourning, of refinding a language of humanity and of recovery. As part of broader political, historical and human processes in which conflict and post-conflict are not so easily separated the TRC process nurtured rather the possibility for those who benefited and continue to benefit from colonial and apartheid rule to consolidate socio-economic relations of power informed by direct socio-economic structuring based on previously legally defined 'race' categories.[50]

As Jonker and Till have pointed out, relying on the work of Mahmood Mamdani, the restriction of the TRC's mandate to investigate only narrowly defined 'gross' human rights violations that occurred after the 1960 Sharpeville massacre, meant that it narrated apartheid 'as a history of the few': what has been left out is "unfinished business," ... the violence of the everyday and the continuities of the colonial past.'[51] One of the legacies of South Africa's colonial and imperialist past that was most glaringly overlooked by the official discourse of transition and nation building is that of slavery. It is against this general background of a post-apartheid insistence that the law transformatively encounters the remains, as well as the repeated failure to do just that, that I want to revisit this history by looking at two recent discoveries of slave

---

[48] Terry Bell and Dumisa Buhle Ntsebeza, *Unfinished Business: South Africa, Apartheid and Truth* (London: Verso, 2003), 2.

[49] Yazir Henri and Heidi Grunebaum, 'Re-Historicising Trauma: Reflections on Violence and Memory in Current-Day Cape Town,' Direct Action Centre for Peace and Memory, 2005, accessed 20 November 2011 http://www.medico.de/download/report26/ps_henrigrunebaum_en.pdf, 2.

[50] Henri and Grunebaum, 'Re-Historicising Trauma,' 2.

[51] Julian Jonker and Karen E Till, 'Mapping and Excavating Spectral Traces in Post-apartheid Cape Town,' *Memory Studies* 2/3 (2009), 316.

burial sites in Cape Town, reading them as what Jonker and Till call 'landmarks of a cartography of incomplete political transformation.'[52]

I shall begin with the latest discovery as it is the one closest to home. In 2006, the University of Cape Town (UCT) proposed a site on its Middle Campus, where a new building—opposite the existing Law Faculty building and adjacent to a residence called All Africa House—was to be constructed to house the University's School of Economics.[53] The Law Faculty building was erected during the apartheid-era and All Africa House in 1996,[54] the year in which the democratic South Africa's Final Constitution came into effect. UCT occupies an area of land that used to be the location of a colonial farm called Rustenburg.[55] It is undeniable that the labour on this farm, as well as on all the other farms in the area along the Liesbeeck River, would have been carried out by slaves in the 17th and 18th centuries.

Documentary evidence and archival research commissioned by UCT suggested the presence of an old cemetery on the site proposed for the new development.[56] All available evidence point to the conclusion that this cemetery originated as a Dutch East India Company (VOC) slave cemetery in which the remains of the slaves who worked the farms in the area were buried.[57] The archival study notes that 'the burial ground is repeatedly referred to as a slave cemetery, and not by any other association. It was overgrown and neglected by the late 19th Century, and was no longer in use by 1895.'[58] A wall was built around the cemetery between 1894 and 1902 and the Surveyor General established the boundaries of this wall in 1917.[59] A great deal of the burial ground was destroyed by developments during the apartheid era. The study noted that it had 'not been visible above ground level since approximately 1930 (between 1927 and 1934), when the university built tennis courts on the site.'[60] Anecdotal evidence, however, suggested that human remains were uncovered during the building of these tennis

[52] Jonker and Till, 'Mapping and Excavating,' 316.
[53] Lita Webley and Tim Hart, *Archeological Impact Assessment: Exploratory Excavation of the Area outside the Rustenburg Walled Cemetery at the University of Cape Town, City of Cape Town, Western Cape* (2008), 4.
[54] Gerda Kruger, 'Media Release: UCT Consults Public about Commemoration of Historic Slave Burial Ground,' *UCT*, 2008.
[55] Anonymous, 'Student Design Competition for Rustenburg Slave Memorial,' *UCT*, accessed 29 October 2016, http://www.uct.ac.za/dailynews/?id=8809.
[56] Webley and Hart, *Archeological Impact Assessment*, 2.
[57] Anonymous, 'Student Design Competition for Rustenburg Slave Memorial.'
[58] Kruger, 'Media Release.'
[59] Webley and Hart, *Archeological Impact Assessment*, 5 and 11.
[60] Bongani Kona, 'UCT Speaks to Communities about Heritage Sites,' *UCT*, 2008, accessed 29 Octobter 2016, https://www.uct.ac.za/dailynews/archives/?id=6602.

courts.[61]

In 2007, UCT launched a public participation process with respect to the burial ground (known, after the name of the farm, as 'Rustenburg'). This was done pursuant to its legal obligations in terms of the regulations published under the National Heritage Resources Act, which stipulates that 'local communities' and 'interested parties' must be consulted with a view to 'reaching agreement' about the future of burial grounds that stand to be affected by new developments.[62] This process raised the question of how best to memorialize those who were buried at Rustenburg. Then Deputy Vice-Chancellor, Prof Martin Hall, said at the time that 'the line of connection between UCT's middle campus in Rondebosch and Mowbray and the slave plantations of the 17th and 18th centuries remains largely unacknowledged.'[63] Yet, 'the landscape of slavery is literally beneath the ground we walk on at the university.'[64]

In 2008, excavation work took place as the culmination of the year-long public participation process. No human remains or relics—other than pieces of the old graveyard wall—were uncovered during the extensive excavation undertaken by the University's Department of Archaeology.[65] Yet, a human skull, which had been housed for years in the department of human anthropology, was found to have originated at the site.[66] It is believed that the skull was moved from the burial site in the 1930s when the now demolished tennis courts next to All Africa House were built. Today, a portion of the wall that was uncovered during excavations is visible under a transparent glass pane in a memorial garden still under construction in the space between the New Economics Building, the Kramer Law School Building and All Africa House. This is the sole physical reminder and remainder of the 'landscape of slavery' that once existed there. That the physical location of the memorial site is concretely a liminal space between the economic, the juridical, and the universal is more than just somewhat uncanny. Recently, the University announced a student design competition for

[61] Webley and Hart, *Archeological Impact Assessment*, 8.

[62] See section 36 (5) National Heritage Resources Act 25 of 1999 as well as regulations 38–42 published in terms of section 25 (2) (h) of the Act on 2 June 2000 in Government Gazette no. 21239, Pretoria: Government Printer.

[63] Anonymous, 'UCT to Commemorate Slave Burial Grounds,' *UCT*, 2007, accessed 29 October 2016, http://www.uct.ac.za/mondaypaper/archives/?id=6369.

[64] Anonymous, 'Memory of Slavery Resurrected through Powerful Work of Fiction,' UCT, 2007, accessed 29 October 2019, http://www.uct.ac.za/mondaypaper/archives/?id=6628.

[65] Webley and Hart, *Archeological Impact Assessment*, 11.

[66] Jessica Bel, 'UCT slave excavation to start soon,' *IOL*, 2008, http://www.iol.co.za/news/south-africa/uct-slave-excavation-to-start-soon-1.423068#.VEal6b4a_TQ.

the continued memorialization of the site and the winning design was revealed in December 2014.[67] At the time of writing, it remains to be seen what the final memorial will look like. UCT has, however, also committed to an ongoing memorialization of the site beyond the construction of a memorial. In this regard, it launched, in December 2013, a public seminar series entitled the Rustenburg Memorial Conversations.

The discovery of the Rustenburg cemetery reactivated the memory of an earlier discovery of a slave burial site known as Prestwich Place on the other side of the city in Green Point in 2003.[68] During the apartheid era, Green Point was known as District One and in the 1960s and early 1970s it became one of the areas from which black and Coloured residents were forcibly removed to 'one of the scores of ghettoes that were being set up across the Cape Flats.'[69] The discovery at Prestwich Place (and the processes that ensued as a result) proved to be far more controversial than the events surrounding the Rustenburg site. What sets Prestwich Place apart is that a large number of human skeletal remains were unearthed when—as a direct result of rapid gentrification in the area—construction was undertaken at the site.[70] A profound conflict of interests arose as regards the question of what was to be done with/about these remains.[71] On the one hand, there were those who demanded a permanent cessation of all construction activities on the site. This group also resisted archeological exhumation of the remains, insisting that it be left interred in the ground in which it was originally buried so that the site could be preserved as 'an open space for memory.'[72] This sentiment was forcefully expressed when, during the public consultations about the site and in the face of exhumations that were at that point already taking place—arguably, illegally—one person shouted from the floor: 'Stop robbing graves! Stop robbing graves!'[73]

[67] Abigail Calata, 'Slave Memorial to Recover Histories of the Dispossessed,' *UCT*, 2014, accessed 29 October 2016, http://www.uct.ac.za/dailynews/?id=8921.

[68] Nick Shepherd, 'Archeology Dreaming: Post-apartheid Urban Imaginaries and the Bones of the Prestwich Street dead,' *Journal of Social Archeology* 7/3 (2007), 7. The discovery at Prestwich Place, in turn, activated the memory of other controversies (both in the recent and more distant past) surrounding burial sites in and around Cape Town. See Jonker and Till, 'Mapping and excavating,' 310.

[69] Grunebaum & Henri, 'Re-Historicising Trauma,' 3.

[70] Shepherd, 'Archeology Dreaming,' 7. Jonker and Till, 'Mapping and Excavating,' 304: 'Yet, capital's vision of a future built on gentrification was interrupted by the dead, aided by their living mourners.'

[71] Shepherd, 'Archeology Dreaming,' 7–13.

[72] Xolelwa Kashe-Katiya, 'Prestwich Place Memorial: Human Remains, Development and Truth,' *The Archival Platform*, 2010, accessed 29 October 2016, http://www.archivalplatform.org/blog/entry/prestwich_place/.

[73] Shepherd, 'Archeology Dreaming,' 8.

On the other hand, there was the group consisting mainly of UCT archeologists who wanted to study the remains before a reburial at an alternative, formally established burial site.[74] This group expressed the sentiment that a significant part of Cape Town's social history would be lost if archeological study of the bones was to be prohibited.[75] And then there was the South African Heritage Resources Agency (SAHRA), which had legal 'authority' over the remains and finally decided that no scientific studies would be conducted on the bones and that they were to be moved to a newly established ossuary in the immediate vicinity of the original burial site.[76]

The concern of the living with the memorialization of slave burial sites in the post-apartheid city underscore that these sites confront us over and over again with the ongoing presence of the past in the present. In this regard, Shepherd remarks that sites like Prestwich Place describe what the historian Premesh Lalu has called a 'history of the present': 'By this he means that the condition of post-coloniality requires a form of history that constantly interrupts and unsettles the present.'[77] In the same vein, Jonker writes that the unearthing of remains at Prestwich Place came to mark a 'metaphorical unearthing' of the city's unfinished business:

> These sites, and the broader emerging cultural landscape that they represent, are claimed as the 'unfinished business' of transitional justice, markers on a cartography of incomplete political transformation. Occupying central and prominent spaces in the city, as well as places of desire in the plans of development capital, these places speak to the continuity of racial stratification and the haunting presence of the past.[78]

Because the urban landscape in which these sites are located is also always already a lawscape,[79] these sites irreducibly confront us with

[74] Shepherd, 'Archeology Dreaming,' 9.

[75] Shepherd, 'Archeology Dreaming,' 9. Environment & Science Writer, 'Some of City's Social History Lost Forever,' *IOL News*, 2008, accessed 29 October 2016, http://www.iol.co.za/news/south-africa/some-of-city-s-social-history-lost-forever-1.421175#.VGMrf4esa-I.

[76] Shepherd, 'Archeology Dreaming,' 13. Green and Murray, 'Notes for a Guide to the Ossuary,' 371–2.

[77] Shepherd, 'Archeology Dreaming,' 24.

[78] Jonker, 'Excavating the Legal Subject,' 204.

[79] Andreas Philippopoulos-Mihalopoulos describes the lawscape as the 'interrelation between law and the city' where the 'and' between 'law' and 'the city' is always already indicative of the co-extensivity of the two: 'lawscape is the ever-receding horizon of prior invitation by the one (the law/the city) to be conditioned by the other (the city/the law). It is the topos where logos and polis are fused in an embrace of escaping distance. In lawscape, the city and the law are found to operate in a double state

the presence of the law in this past, how it has shaped and continues to shape this present and it is this confrontation of the present with its spectral (neither absent nor present) past that I want to foreground in what follows. I claim that if 'the condition of post-coloniality' requires a form of history that constantly challenges the certitudes of the present, this condition no less importantly requires a form of law that both constantly disrupts a spatial logic of closure, exclusion, and fixity as well as a law that is *disrupted by* a space or spatiality that posits itself against such an oppressive spatial logic and in this sense is aimed at a transformation of the lawscape.

As regards the latter, Jonker describes the disruptive spatiality of the remains at Prestwich Place by alluding to its 'uncanny' interruption of the post-apartheid 'development' of the city,[80] development that testifies as it does to the economic terms of the South African transition as the country's 'admission' to and inscription into global neoliberal capitalism. To come back momentarily to the TRC, it is a common criticism of the South African transition in general and of the TRC in particular that it failed to provide a progressive critique of the political economy of apartheid and consequently failed to provide the parameters of an economic transformation that could operate as an alternative to apartheid style capitalism.[81]

From this point of view, it could indeed be argued that the discovery of remains such as these not only heightens the continued material inscription in the city of this legacy, but also that these remains obstruct, even if only temporarily and in a radically incomplete way, the development of the new neoliberal order and, as a return of the repressed, confronts the economic with a non- or uneconomic moment in which the stakes of responsibility to a past of injustice are raised anew. Green and Murray note in this regard that the discovery of and interventions around the bones at Prestwich Place constituted a 'minor

---

of co-presence and absence, as expressed by the conjunction "and"'; see Andreas Philippopoulos-Mihalopoulos, 'Introduction: In the Lawscape' in *Law and the* City, ed. Andreas Philippopoulos-Mihalopoulos (Abingdon: Routledge, 2007), 1 and 10.

[80] Jonker, 'Excavating the Legal Subject,' 190.

[81] As Sampie Terreblanche has argued, this failure is attributable to the fact that two sets of negotiations took place during the transitions. One, the formal negotiations, centred around the political terms of the transition and favoured the democratic movement. These negotiations defeated the political establishment of the apartheid regime. The second, informal, set of negotiations were concerned with the economic terms of the transition and did not remotely defeat the white corporate sector, nor the system of racialized capitalism that was produced by apartheid; see Sampie Terreblanche, *A History of Inequality in South Africa: 1652–2002* (Pietermaritzburg: University of Natal Press, 2002), 125.

irritation' for the extension of global capitalism in South Africa.[82] And as Jonker and Till remark more forcefully: 'The (re)discovered burial ground defamiliarized and made inhospitable an area that had been regarded as a safe home for white and foreign capital, well known for its upmarket restaurants, trendy design boutiques and luxury living.'[83] Put bluntly, the slave burial site violently disrupts/stops in its tracks the logic of accelerated capitalist accumulation. In the case of Rustenburg, it is more than somewhat ironic that the slave burial site resurfaced as part of the construction of what is now known as the New Economics Building.

As Jonker puts it: 'the postcolonial phantom appears at the frontier of inner city gentrification and development,' and, in so doing, provides an opportunity for enquiry into how the law is implicated in this responsibility.[84] Indeed, it pertinently resurrects the age old question of the validity of the Marxist critique of law as superstructure.[85] Jonker quotes South African archeologist Antonia Malan in reflecting on Prestwich Place. She remarks that if you stand there '"the urban landscape can be read like a political history book".'[86] What Malan is referring to is how the post-apartheid urban landscape continues spatially to reflect the history of segregation and forced removal in the city.

But it is perhaps more accurate to say that in Cape Town the urban landscape can be read like a *legal* history book, a history book of how the law's *enforcement* came to represent spatially its colonial and segregationist origin. It is in this sense that the urban landscape of Cape Town and of the post-apartheid city in general can be described as constituting veritable lawscapes, that is to say, landscapes that are both shaped by law and that at the same time shapes law and legal practices.[87] And the question of how to encounter the remains, what to do with the remains, how to return the remains to the city, attends all the more urgently at the very place where the law encounters the

[82] Louise Green and Noëleen Murray, 'Housing Cape Town's Forgotten Dead: Conflict in the Post-apartheid Public Sphere,' *Africa Development* 35/4 (2010), 91.

[83] Jonker and Till, 'Mapping and Excavating,' 316.

[84] Jonker, 'Excavating the Legal Subject,' 190.

[85] In South African legal academia, Drucilla Cornell has been at the forefront of the positing of this question in her work on Ubuntu; see Drucilla Cornell, *Law and Revolution in South Africa* (New York: Fordham University Press, 2014), 34–44. The 'foundational' text here, however, is of course Jacques Derrida's *Specters of Marx* (New York: Routledge, 1994).

[86] Jonker, 'Excavating the Legal Subject,' 188.

[87] As Philippopoulos-Mihalopoulos remarks, the description of the lawscape initiates a discussion 'on the itinerant manner in which the city appropriates the law and the law the city'; see Philippopoulos-Mihalopoulos, 'Introduction,' 2 and 7–10; see also Nicole Graham, *Lawscape: Property, Environment, Law* (Abingdon: Routledge, 2011), 5.

remains of its own (monumental) enforcement, indeed of its origin as nomos, a land-appropriation.

Van Riebeeck's Hedge of Bitter Almonds:
The Nomos of Apartheid

Malan's comment on Prestwich Place puts me in mind of what Alistair Sparks writes in his reflections on the 'oldest living monument of European settlement'[88] at the Cape: Jan van Riebeeck's hedge of bitter almonds, the remains of which can still be found in Kirstenbosch Botanical Gardens, located on the slopes of Table Mountain, a short distance away from Rustenburg. Planted shortly after the arrival of the Dutch at the Cape, the hedge was meant to, in Sparks's words, 'keep out the KhoiKhoi cattle herders who inhabited this southernmost tip of the African continent, with the mountain barrier behind.'[89] The hedge 'cut off Van Riebeeck's little white community from the great African continent stretching away to the north, creating their own little enclave of Europe—six thousand miles from home.'[90] As such, the hedge spatially represented the first attempt at marking off, through a land-appropriation, the boundaries of colonial territory at the Cape. It was arguably the first spatial instantiation of modern colonial law on the Southern African landscape.[91] Viewed in this way, the hedge constituted the boundaries of the first colonial polity in South Africa as the self-closure of a community as 'an inside over against an outside.'[92] From this point of view, Van Riebeeck's hedge designated the first

[88] HB Rycroft, 'The Van Riebeeck Hedge at Kirstenbosch: Past, Present and Future,' *Journal of the South African Forestry Association* 31/1 (1958), 23. Rycroft records that in 1936 the remains of Van Riebeeck's hedge in Kirstenbosch was declared a 'monument' in terms of the applicable legislation. Rycroft goes on to describe the efforts to re-establish the hedge in anticipation of the 1960 tercentenary of its planting. He informs the reader that young wild almond plants are being raised at Kirstenbosch and that these will be planted where blanks occur in the Kirstenbosch hedge. In addition, he suggests, with all the requisite seriousness of the imperial intellectual, that 'if the precise position of the old boundary can be determined, property owners will be given young plants and requested to establish them at suitable sites.'

[89] Allister Sparks, *The Mind of South Africa* (Cape Town: Jonathan Ball Publishers, 1990), xiii.

[90] Sparks, *The mind of South Africa*, xiv. Also see Rycroft, 'The Van Riebeeck Dedge,' 21.

[91] From Arendt and Schmitt we have it that the wall or hedge spatially represents the law (nomos) of the polis. See Arendt, *The Human Condition*, 63–4; Schmitt, *The Nomos of the Earth*, 70.

[92] Lindahl, 'Give and Take,' 882.

geographical jurisdiction of colonial law in South Africa. In planting his hedge, Van Riebeeck became the first to draw 'the line that would come to divide the highly stratified white and native communities of South Africa for so many centuries.'[93]

In his 1990 book, *The Mind of South Africa*, Sparks elaborates on this point when he illustrates how apartheid's 'geography of exclusion' can physically and concretely be traced from Van Riebeeck's hedge:[94]

> Stand there beside the strip of hedge in the Kirstenbosch Garden and look north—in the middle distance are the twin cooling towers of Athlone Power station ... to the left and west of that line lie the white suburbs of Claremont, Kenilworth, Rondebosch, Newlands, Mowbray, Wynberg and Pinelands. On the sandy flats to the right and east of it lie the 'coloured' townships—Athlone, Hazendal, Bonteheuvel, Heideveld, Bellville, Elsies River, Lavender Hill and Mitchells Plain—and beyond them, in a descending order of social status, the black townships and squatter camps of Langa, Nyanga, Gugulethu, Crossroads and Khayelitsha. There before you lies apartheid in all its obscenity.[95]

This is apartheid, then, as apart-ness, the 'spectacle of empire as separation,' 'a spatial ordering of society through segregation and suburbanization: dividing and distancing being central to the politics and culture of apartheid';[96] and law as a rigid spatial ordering that originates in a land-appropriation. In the terms of the German jurist, Carl Schmitt, this is law as nomos, a concrete unity of order and orientation—the nomos of apartheid in its full spatial immediacy.[97] In his widely discussed *The nomos of the Earth in the International Law of the Jus Publicum Europaeum*, Schmitt undertook a thorough excavation of the original Western name of law which in the Greek was 'nomos.' In it, Schmitt set out to restore to nomos 'its energy and majesty' and pointed out that 'originally the word did not signify a

---

[93] Sarah Hogan, 'Of Islands and Bridges: Figures of Uneven Development in Bacon's "New Atlantis",' *Journal for Early Modern Cultural Studies* 12/3 (2012), 29.

[94] Hogan, 'Of Islands and Bridges,' 29.

[95] Sparks, *The Mind of South Africa*, xiii–xiv.

[96] Hogan, 'Of Islands and Bridges,' 29. Suzanne M Hall, 'Book reviews' *Antipode* 1 (2012).

[97] Note the spatial metaphors to which Derrida resorts when describing apartheid: 'APARTHEID: by itself the word occupies the terrain like a concentration camp. System of partition, barbed wire, crowds of mapped out solitudes. ... The word concentrates separation, raises it to another power and sets separation itself apart ... By isolating being apart in some sort of essence ... the word corrupts it into a quasi-ontological segregation.' Jacques Derrida, 'Racism's Last Word,' *Critical Inquiry* 12/1 (1985), 292.

mere act whereby is and ought could be separated.'[98] Rather, nomos was the word for the 'first measure of subsequent measures, for the first land-appropriation understood as the first partition and classification of space.'[99] For his argument, Schmitt traced the origin of nomos to the pre-Socratic works of Heraclitus and Pindar, arguing that originally the word signified, specifically, fundamental law as the spatial structure of a concrete order and orientation. Emphasizing that nomos comes from the verb *nemein* which means 'to divide' and 'to pasture,' Schmitt argued that 'nomos is the immediate form in which the political and social order of a people becomes spatially visible.'[100] In other words, nomos is the word for the first land-appropriation as the 'constitutive act of spatial ordering,' where such appropriation or ordering 'marks the first partition and classification of space,' the 'original distribution of land.'[101] Thus, nomos is 'the initial measure and division of pasture-land, i.e. the land-appropriation as well as the concrete order contained in it and following from it. In Kant's words, it is the "distributive law of mine and thine," or, to use an English term that expresses it so well, it is the "radical title."'[102]

For Schmitt, then, nomos originally complicates the simplistic understanding of law as the legality of 'the functional mode of a state bureaucracy' which concerns itself with 'enactments of acts emanating from the central command-post responsible for this bureaucracy.'[103] Nomos is the *'full immediacy* of a legal power' unmediated by laws.[104] It is 'a constitutive historical event,' an 'act of *legitimacy*' 'whereby the legality of a mere law first is made meaningful.'[105] The nomos of the earth, as Richard Ek points out, was the spatial ordering 'conceptualized on the basis of an "us inside—them outside" divide,'[106] a spatial ordering that both excluded and included the sovereign himself. This spatial orientation of the sovereign was a result of the fact that it was precisely only ever the sovereign's decision as regards who (and what) could be included and who (and what) could be excluded. This is why Schmitt writes that 'nomos is precisely the full *immediacy* of a legal power *not mediated* by laws; whereby the legality of a mere law is first

[98] Schmitt, *The Nomos of the Earth*, 67, 69.
[99] Schmitt, *The Nomos of the Earth*, 67.
[100] Schmitt, *The Nomos of the Earth*, 70.
[101] Schmitt, *The Nomos of the Earth*, 71, 67–8.
[102] Schmitt, *The Nomos of the Earth*, 70.
[103] Schmitt, *The Nomos of the Earth*, 71.
[104] Schmitt, *The Nomos of the Earth*, 73 (emphasis supplied).
[105] Schmitt, *The Nomos of the Earth*, 73.
[106] Richard Ek, 'Giorgio Agamben and the Spatialities of the Camp: An Introduction,' *Geografiska Annaler: Series B, Human Geography* 88/4 (2006), 365.

made meaningful.'

Both Schmitt and Arendt refer to nomos as quite literally the walls of the *polis*, that is, the spatial demarcation of the normative political community, the concrete manifestation of the boundary by way of which the inside and the outside is constituted. Quoting Trier, Schmitt notes that nomos is a fence-word: '"In the beginning was the fence. Fence, enclosure, and border are deeply interwoven in the world formed by men, determining its concepts."'[107] Schmitt went on to consider this meaning of nomos as the coincidence of space and law in the context of the imperialist and colonialist projects. On this he wrote the following: 'The history of colonialism in its entirety is as well a history of spatially determined processes of settlement in which order and orientation are combined. At this origin of land-appropriation, law and order are one; where order and orientation coincide, they cannot be separated.'[108]

The appearance of the slave burial ground in the postcolonial city takes us back by unearthing or excavating the origin of the positive law in its colonial moment of land-appropriation—a land-appropriation from which all subsequent divisions and partitions ensued. This is the case because the slave, as a labourer in his relation with a master owner, is, in the colonial setting at least, an embodiment of that appropriation, a cipher of an excluded inclusion in that nomos. Sparks's words above vividly illustrate how one can trace apartheid's later segregationist demarcations from the original colonial nomos. Indeed, the appearance of slave burial ground like Prestwich Place and Rustenburg comes to re-visit upon the postcolonial landscape the legacy of this rigid spatial logic of Schmitt's nomos, this 'history of spatially determined processes of settlement.'

For the above reasons, Jonker is at pains to draw our attention to the fact that the slave burial ground represents the *exteriority* of the colonial nomos. Prestwich Place is located outside the borders of the original colonial city:

> The frontier along Buitengracht Street and Bree Street, marking the western end of the city and beyond which lay the 'menace of wild animals [and] the depredations of marauding Hottentots,' would come to prescribe the (dis)location of the informal burials of the city's slaves, freed slaves and poor, who were excluded from burial grounds within city walls.[109]

In the case of the Rustenburg slave cemetery, the archival research

---

[107] Schmitt, *The Nomos of the Earth*, 74.
[108] Schmitt, *The Nomos of the Earth*, 81.
[109] Jonker, 'Excavating the Legal Subject,' 204–5.

commissioned by UCT notes that the immediate geographical area in which the cemetery is located was, during colonial times, known as a place of exile or imprisonment, since people were kept there 'who were considered by the VOC to be in some way threatening or insurrectionary.'[110] Today, the site, located as it (tellingly and suggestively) is between the Law Faculty building, All Africa House and the New Economics building, occupies a space that confronts us differently with exteriority, but with exteriority nevertheless.

Thus, the surfacing of this place of the buried dead not only calls forth the spatiality of the 'full immediacy' of the colonial power as nomos, it also confronts that nomos with the question of its outside or its exteriority—its remainder.[111] On this point, Lindahl's consideration of the nomos, with reference to Arendt, is instructive. Lindahl argues for a *reflexive* account of nomos, an account that understands that 'no political community is possible ... that does not close itself off as an inside over against an outside.'[112] This understanding of nomos in turn illustrates 'a strong form of exteriority called forth by the self-closure of a polity.'[113] Lindahl argues that taking seriously Arendt's claim that nomos is constitutive for political community requires that one makes sense of this exteriority 'and of how a polity deals with it.'[114] He continues to argue that this strong form of exteriority can be designated as the contrast between an 'own place' and a 'strange place.'[115] In a strange place, individuals are not 'in-legal-place.'[116] Rather, they are *displaced*—'that is to say, they claim a legal place of their own for which there is no place within the distribution of places made available by a region.'[117] This means that we have to understand exteriority incisively, namely as the space of an included exclusion: the 'exterior' is a space occupied by or representing those who have been excluded from political community, while at the same time they have been included by politics, that is, 'affected by the more or less violent consequences

---

[110] Sally Titlestad, *Historical Analysis of Primary Research regarding the University of Cape Town Middle Campus Burial Ground* (2007), 17.

[111] What I call the remainder accords with what Philippopoulos-Mihalopoulos, 'Law's Spatial Turn,' 8 calls the 'truly "irritating," disturbing, upsetting facets of space.'

[112] Lindahl, 'Give and Take,' 882.

[113] Lindahl, 'Give and Take,' 882.

[114] Lindahl, 'Give and Take,' 882.

[115] Lindahl, 'Give and Take,' 888.

[116] Lindahl, 'Give and Take,' 889.

[117] Lindahl, 'Give and Take,' 889.

of politics.'[118] As Lindahl remarks, the original land-appropriation from which nomos arises in fact 'inscribes strangeness in ownness in the very process of differentiating them,'[119] or as Augsberg puts it 'the logic of exclusion implies that the expelled person has been part of the expelling community.'[120] Such a reading reveals that the logic of Schmitt's nomos proceeds from the premise that 'the exclusion of otherness' is a precondition of political community.[121] This is how the nomos creates from within itself the other of the nomos with which it, as Haverkamp suggests, deals mercilessly.

Slave burial sites, then, are strange places in Lindahl's sense, because they spatially represent those who were displaced by the colonial as well as the apartheid nomos. At the slave burial site, nomos encounters the remains in a way that constitutes a confrontation with the displaced as its outside / exteriority and, indeed, alterity. As regards the way in which the living, in the post-apartheid time-space, take up this confrontational encounter of nomos with the dead as exteriority, we can return to the cry at the Prestwich Place public consultation which Jonker transcribes not simply as 'Stop robbing graves!,' but as 'Stop robbing *our* graves!'[122] Such a cry is expressive of the claim to a legal place for which there is no place. Greene and Murray remark that the discovery of the remains as signs of earlier historical occupation of this part of the city, confirm that people who do not occupy this part of the city, nevertheless have an association with it. As such, the burial site comes to foreground 'the residual trauma of colonial and apartheid dispossession.'[123] Grunebaum and Henri provocatively radicalize this insight by arguing that the association can in fact be translated as a claim to occupation (which can and in this context does sound as a claim to reparation). The uncovering of these remains provided the 'haunting evidence that could no longer be denied by the majority of those who live, work and "own" property in the city and in all of the

---

[118] Ek, 'Giorgio Agamben and the spatialities of the camp,' 366. As Ek continues to point out, Foucault defined as racism, this 'political' categorization and separation of groups that exist within a population. Needless to say, since this racism was the very principle of apartheid state power, the whole experience was a spectacular illustration of what happens when 'racism goes biopolitical.' A consideration of how the slave burial site reflects the camp as the biopolitical nomos of the modern will require a separate paper.

[119] Lindahl, 'Give and Take,' 895.

[120] Ino Augsberg, 'Carl Schmitt's Fear: Nomos-Norm-Network,' *Leiden Journal of International Law* 23 (2010), 745.

[121] Augsberg, 'Carl Schmitt's Fear,' 745.

[122] Jonker, 'Excavating the Legal Subject,' 191.

[123] Greene and Murray, 'Notes for a Guide to the Ossuary,' 372.

forced removal areas of the peninsula: that people who now live on the Cape Flats have a claim to this part of the city.'[124]

Here, then, the present of postcolonial law is confronted with the legacy of its colonial and apartheid instantiations which serves as the basis for a claim to legal place. As a concretized space of injustice, the slave burial ground throws into relief the chiasmus between a justice that remains to be done and a present law that is already attempting to cover over or 'finalize' its responsibility to the remains. Heritage legislation in post-apartheid South Africa, with its emphasis on the 'management' of heritage resources, is aimed at and is doing precisely this.[125] Grunebaum and Henri remark that in the case of Prestwich Place, the legislation was engaged from within old epistemological paradigms and instrumentalized in such a way that the dominant theme of the public participation process became the question of finding, as expediently as possible, an appropriate alternative site for the remains.[126] Similarly, Shepherd documents the anxiety on the part of SAHRA about the 'disastrous consequences' that the conservation of the burial site as a heritage site would have for the developer and about the commercial urgency of the matter given that apartments in the development had been pre-sold.[127]

All of this meant that questions relating to how the remains came to be located where they were found and about a consecration of the site where they were discovered, were conveniently set aside. As Shepherd remarks:

> SAHRA's heritage managers showed little political will to take on entrenched interests in the city or creativity in acknowledging the trauma of both the deep and more recent pasts. Instead, they opted for a narrow, and at times questionable, interpretation of the heritage legislation.[128]

At the opening of the student design exhibition for Rustenburg, Professor Iain Low of UCT's School of Architecture, Planning and Geomatics remarked that the heritage domain in South Africa is generally governed by 'notions of whiteness, where legal and economic concerns surface, rather than hidden histories.'[129] From this point of

---

[124] Henri and Grunebaum, 'Re-Historicising Trauma,' 4.

[125] As Achmat Dangor's character, Mikey, wryly remarks: 'Managers dull the process. They cannot make miracles, because they refuse to believe in them.' Achmat Dangor, *Bitter Fruit* (Cape Town: Kwela Books, 1998), 196.

[126] Henri and Grunebaum, 'Re-Historicising Trauma,' 5.

[127] Shepherd, 'Archeology Dreaming,' 11.

[128] Shepherd, 'Archeology Dreaming,' 4.

[129] Yusuf Omar, 'Rustenburg Slave Memorial: Remembering the Past, Planning for the Future,' *UCT Monday Paper*, 2014, accessed 29 October 2016, http://www.uct.

view, it can certainly be argued that a certain 'fear of space' as the 'fear of alterity' and, hence a fear of 'what the law can become,'[130] marks the dominant approach to heritage legislation in South Africa.

Yet, the blunt instrumentalism of heritage authorities to 'regularize' the site by re-inscribing it into the spatial logic of a neo-liberal post-modernity does not succeed in tempering its irreducibility: 'what these sites represent to us are archeological potentialities, places where excavation might unearth the relationship between the memory of the past and the juridical self.'[131] To resort to a spatial metaphor: what happens in the moment of the unearthing of the slave burial ground in a postcolonial present is precisely that the wall of the law is breached and as Rose argues, this breach of the wall invites us to locate what she calls 'the missing resources' in the politics that has been disowned, it invites us to reinvent political life or political community through mourning or what Jonker calls 'practices of memory as resistance' or what I referred to earlier as counter-memory.[132] Jonker argues in this context that critique needs to shift away from the immediate question of law's responsibility, 'the question of to whom does the law respond,' towards a questioning of law's myths and the 'source of law' that is responsible for the founding of law in the first place. For Jonker it is this questioning that founds (as opposed to finds) legal activism. Its potential exists precisely in this visitation of the past through memory and 'the presence of the past in the very constitution of law.'[133]

As an example of such a founding of legal activism, Jonker discusses the work of the District Six Museum which was founded to commemorate the apartheid forced removals of residents from the area called District Six, located on the eastern side of Cape Town's inner city boundary. He argues that the work of the museum concerns itself not only with the commemoration of the discrete community of the district but 'with questions about race and citizenship in the city generally, about the re-imagination of the built environment generally, and about what indigeneity and creolization might mean in the city generally.'[134] With reference to a public sculpture project that was held on the site of the removals, he describes an 'archeology of the site's hauntologies' through which emerge 'the traces with which the contemporary city's

ac.za/dailynews/?id=8837.

[130] Philippopoulos-Mihalopoulos, 'Law's Spatial Turn,' 2.

[131] Jonker, 'The Silence of the Dead,' 56.

[132] Jonker, 'Excavating the Legal Subject,' 196.

[133] Jonker, 'The Silence of the Dead,' 41. These remarks returns us of course to and, by so doing emphasizes, the historical self-consciousness of the ultimate 'source of law' in South Africa—the Constitution.

[134] Jonker, 'The Silence of the Dead,' 47.

memorial and constitutional topographies are formed and inscribed.'[135] Jonker goes on to argue that the 'creative struggle for memory' made of District Six a constitutional monument, in the sense that it is 'the remembrance of such sites and events that inform a new constitutional regime's monumental vision of justice and legality.'[136] I want to contend that Jonker's description of the memory-work of the District Six Museum as informing the new constitution's 'monumental' vision of justice and legality necessarily points to a memorial activist practice that underlies this monumental vision, indeed without which the monument will not endure. Lourens du Plessis reminds us that the post-apartheid Constitution is both a monument *and a memorial*, that the monument is quick to celebrate (with all the finalities and forgetfulness—even oblivion—that that entails), while the memorial commemorates.[137] Du Plessis argues that the 'reading' of the Constitution as memorial recognizes that it is not '*an overarching, all-encompassing super law.*'[138] Instead, it serves as a reminder of our 'human obligation' to achieve (social) justice. This obligation is necessarily excessive—it overflows and thus cannot be (wholly) assigned to any particular 'law-text'—it breaches the wall.[139]

The memorial approach to constitutionalism emphasizes an enlarged understanding of constitutional interpretation as being assigned to an open (or public) community of interpreters that includes individuals and groups in civil society who are affected by the exercise of public power. Du Plessis goes on to plead for a creative or productive tension between the monumental and the memorial approach:

> The Constitution's promise of a democratic constitutional state can only be kept if the Constitution as monument does not overpower the Constitution as memorial, but also when the Constitution as memorial does not enervate the Constitution as monument.[140]

If it is, as Jonker argues, 'recognition' that 'links the commemorative past with the juridical subject,'[141] I want to argue below that it is the memorial approach that should at this time be foregrounded in our imagination of the law that attends in the moment of haunting. As we shall see below, this memorial approach is inscribed in nomos, provided that we are prepared to read it 'otherwise.'

---

[135] Jonker, 'The Silence of the Dead,' 48.
[136] Jonker, 'The Silence of the Dead,' 50.
[137] Du Plessis, 'The South African Constitution as Memory and Promise,' 385–6.
[138] Du Plessis, 'The South African Constitution as Memory and Promise,' 388.
[139] Du Plessis, 'The South African Constitution as Memory and Promise,' 388.
[140] Du Plessis, 'The South African Constitution as Memory and Promise,' 390.
[141] Jonker, 'The Silence of the Dead,' 57.

Reading Nomos Otherwise?

From the point of view that the resurfacing of the burial site metaphorically constitutes a breach in the wall of a certain and indeed overwhelming 'business as usual' approach to law and legality, I want to consider in this section whether another reading of nomos can indicate a direction in which to think a version of law that retains the spatial dimension of its instantiation as nomos, but that places emphasis on the transformative potential of space and, to that extent, triggers a certain disruption of the rigidity of the spatial logic of nomos in Schmitt. Whilst it is true, as we have seen, that the post-apartheid Constitution and post-apartheid constitutional discourse places an explicit emphasis on the importance of the role of history and memory in the interpretation (and perhaps, enforcement) of the law, it also has to be said that the 'business as usual' approach or the approach that would have it that we can 'close the book' on the past, tends to overshadow law's responsiveness to questions of its responsibility to the past and the dead in that past.[142]

In short, the monumental approach to justice and legality indicates a monumental approach to space and this approach seems to be pervasive in post-apartheid South Africa. It is not surprising that monumentalism enjoys hegemony, given the self-congratulatory, celebratory geopolitical context that resulted from the 1989 collapse of the Berlin Wall, accompanied as it was (and still seems to be) by the pervasive belief that we now live in the time and space of the end of history as the 'global triumph of free market economies.'[143] Yet, a specter, indeed more than one specters, continues to haunt this space. The slave burial site, as I have indicated, raises this specter in the postcolonial city, dislocating the time(s).[144] The dislocation of time for which the specter is responsible, opens up possibilities and, first of all for us, possibilities for a different understanding of space, which may lead to a different understanding of law and hence, a different understanding of the relationship between law and space.[145]

My starting point here is Hannah Arendt's consideration of the

---

[142] Terry Bell and Dumisa Ntsebeza remark that 'there is now a strong move to close the door on the past, to pretend that all is not just forgiven, but forgotten; to bury many aspects of our recent history'; see Bell and Ntsebeza, *Unfinished Business*, 3

[143] Jacques Derrida, *Specters of Marx: The State of the Debt, the Work of Mourning and the New International*, trans. Peggy Kamuf (New York: Routledge, 1994), vii.

[144] Derrida, *Specters of Marx*, 24–5.

[145] Derrida notes that when Hamlet remarks that 'the time is out of joint' he is 'speaking in the space' opened up by the question of justice as the (Levinassian) 'relation to others'; see Derrida, *Specters of Marx*, 23.

nomos as discussed by Julia Chryssostalis. In her reading of Schmitt and Arendt, Chryssostalis is interested in 're-imagining the spatiality of nomos in non-territorial terms and emplacement without the priority of appropriation.'[146] Chryssostalis begins by pointing to the similarities in the reading of nomos between Arendt and Schmitt—both turn to nomos in order to emphasize law's 'original spatial significance'[147] and both authors rely on the same etymology according to which nomos derives from '*nemein*' which means to distribute, to possess that which has been distributed and to dwell.[148] Yet, for Arendt nomos does not involve an act of appropriation and subsequent distribution as it does in Schmitt. In Arendt, nomos is primarily thought of as 'a boundary, both wall-like and constitutive of the *polis*, since without this wall-like law there cannot be a *polis*.'[149]

Chryssostalis, however, argues that in Arendt, while nomos names a boundary it is not constitutive of political community in the same sense as it is for Schmitt. This is the case because what nomos encloses is not a territorial entity—the *polis* is the organization of the people wherever they may be, it does not have 'a set physical location' and exists wherever the people create between them a space of disclosure in action and speech.[150] At Prestwich Place, for instance, the creation of such a disclosive space of action and speech was constituted when what Till calls the activist 'memory-work' of citizen groups shifted the 'taken-for-grantedness of urban space in the city' through a claim that the space belongs to them as a place in the larger urban landscape of post-apartheid society—an urban landscape that does not (yet) reflect the becoming of a post-apartheid being-in-common.[151]

Chryssostalis's discussion of the *polis* as a particular set of relations between people implies, in turn, that the existence of the *polis* predates and precedes 'any formal constitution and organization of its space.'[152] At the same time, it implies that the *polis* is inherently fragile and fleeting: it comes into existence wherever and whenever the people are disclosively orientated to one another in action and in speech, but it disappears whenever such speech and action cease.[153] Nomos is intended to counteract this fragility of the *polis* by providing the

---

[146] Chryssostalis, 'Reading Arendt "Reading" Schmitt,' 158.
[147] Chryssostalis, 'Reading Arendt "Reading" Schmitt,' 167.
[148] Chryssostalis, 'Reading Arendt "Reading" Schmitt,' 167.
[149] Chryssostalis, 'Reading Arendt "Reading" Schmitt,' 167.
[150] Chryssostalis, 'Reading Arendt "Reading" Schmitt,' 167.
[151] Karen E Till, 'Wounded Cities: Memory-work and a Place-based Ethics of Care,' *Political Geography* 31/3 (2012), 11.
[152] Chryssostalis, 'Reading Arendt "Reading" Schmitt,' 168.
[153] Chryssostalis, 'Reading Arendt "Reading" Schmitt,' 168.

political realm with a measure of continuity, permanence, stability and durability: 'nomos, by delimiting the political realm and assigning to it a place it can inhabit, keeps it from dissipating and floating away.'[154] The function of nomos, then, is not to create the political realm but rather 'to secure its space, to shelter and guarantee the political life of the community.'[155]

Nomos provides the political as *polis* with its defining features:

> It gives the *polis* a form, configures its space, and ensures its unique identity, ie those features that make Athens, for example, different from Thebes, from Megara, Corinth or Sparta. Just as the walls of the city render 'a city identifiable by virtue of its shape and boundary marks,' Arendt notes, 'the law determines the identity of its inhabitants, the features that distinguish and set them apart from all other cities and their inhabitants.'[156]

Nomos is constitutive of the *polis* in the sense that it, as a 'stabilizing force,' provides the fragile *polis* with durability—its constitutive character lies in the continuity that it provides to an otherwise fleeting organization.[157] In this aspect, Chryssostalis notes that nomos is conservative in the sense that it is what conserves the political realm, what guards it against the boundlessness of action by lodging action within it.[158] In its spatial character it reminds us that 'all legislation creates first of all a space within which it is valid, and this space is the world in which we can move in freedom'[159] and that freedom 'wherever it existed as a tangible reality, has always been spatially limited.'[160] In the end, the function of nomos for Arendt is 'to lodge political action within it and guarantee the durability of the "common world" of the *polis*.'[161] Volks argues that all of this points to an understanding in Arendt that law is a 'relational concept'—it describes, reveals and arranges the 'relations among people within a political community.'[162] Volks contends that 'the relation-establishing dimension' of law is present in Arendt's idea of nomos.[163] We can see how this is so when we bear in mind that

---

[154] Chryssostalis, 'Reading Arendt "Reading" Schmitt,' 168.
[155] Chryssostalis, 'Reading Arendt "Reading" Schmitt,' 168.
[156] Chryssostalis, 'Reading Arendt "Reading" Schmitt,' 168–9.
[157] Chryssostalis, 'Reading Arendt "Reading" Schmitt,' 168.
[158] Chryssostalis, 'Reading Arendt "Reading" Schmitt,' 169.
[159] Chryssostalis, 'Reading Arendt "Reading" Schmitt,' 172.
[160] Chryssostalis, 'Reading Arendt "Reading" Schmitt,' 172.
[161] Chryssostalis, 'Reading Arendt "Reading" Schmitt,' 173.
[162] Christian Volks, 'From *Nomos* to Lex: Hannah Arendt on Law, Politics, and Order,' *Leiden Journal of International Law* 23/4 (2010), 775.
[163] Volks, 'From *Nomos* to Lex,' 776.

nomos in Arendt secures the *polis* as a space in which a set of (political) relations amongst people prevails—to abbreviate: these are the relations of action and speech as external freedom. As Volks contends, Arendt's nomos shifts the consideration of legal space from a container theory with a strong emphasis on boundaries to a relational theory that in my reading places an emphasis on memory or, better, the memorial aspect of relationality: 'because it surrounded itself with a permanent wall of law, the *polis* as a unity could claim to ensure that whatever happened or was done within it would not perish with the life of the doer or endurer, but live on in the memory of future generations.'[164]

But it is also crucial to note for my purposes that while, on Arendt's reading, nomos hedges in the new beginnings resulting from action, it is also the case that nomos is never entirely successful in terms of containing action; because of 'action's dynamically excessive character' it has the tendency to 'force open all limitations and cut across all boundaries.'[165] This is why nomos is never entirely coincidental with the formation of the political—action will always exceed the space of nomos or as Arendt puts it: 'the limitations of the law are never entirely reliable safeguards against action from within the body politic, just as the boundaries of the territory are never entirely reliable safeguards against action from without.'[166] In this regard, Volks argues that a durable and stable political order, from the Arendtian point of view, 'is not meant to be static; rather, it could be characterized as a dialectic of acting and preserving.'[167] To this Keith Breen adds the crucial point that nomos as 'the spatial and normative constitution of a polity does not occur simply at its beginning but is an ongoing process, the polity's wall of law, like a physical wall, requiring maintenance, revision, and addition over time.'[168]

Having made this point about Arendt's reading of nomos, Chryssostalis explores how feminism in recent years has focused on Arendt's stress that the political is 'freedom-centred,' 'disruptive,' 'space-generating,' 'performative and relational' as well as 'inter-active' and 'local.'[169] Chryssostalis argues, however, that these feminisms have underestimated how law and other normative frameworks can conserve

---

[164] Hannah Arendt, 'The Great Tradition I: Law and Power,' *Social research* 74 (2007), 716.

[165] Chryssostalis, 'Reading Arendt "reading" Schmitt,' 169.

[166] Arendt, *The Human Condition*, 191.

[167] Volks, 'From *Nomos* to Lex,' 774.

[168] Keith Breen, 'Law Beyond Command? An Evaluation of Arendt's Understanding of Law' in *Hannah Arendt and the Law: Law and Practical Reason*, eds. Marco Goldoni and Christopher McCorkindale (Oxford: Hart Publishing, 2012), 28.

[169] Chryssostalis, 'Reading Arendt "Reading" Schmitt,' 173–74.

political space.[170] Arendt's theorization of the political does not only involve its constitution through speech and action; it also considers its preservation (through nomos).[171] Here Chryssostalis reminds us that the *polis* is the 'organized remembrance' of a political experience and that nomos is for the political what memory is for man's historical existence—'it guarantees the pre-existence of a common world, the reality of some continuity.'[172]

In Chryssostalis's account, we need nomos as law to secure the space of freedom as action which constitutes itself as a set of relations amongst people. Moreover, Chryssostalis shows us that nomos exists for the sake of memory, for the sake of the 'organized remembrance' that is the political. As Volks puts it: 'due to its "stabilizing force" and "permanent wall", the Greek nomos guaranteed that political agents would stay "in the memory of future generations".'[173] At the same time (and perhaps more controversially) Chryssostalis's discussion of Arendt's nomos reveals that nomos remains responsive to or orientated towards the political that is logically prior to it and that can, at times, exceed it. While Arendt is at pains to point out that, for the Greeks, nomos was not itself a political activity,[174] it cannot be gainsaid that nomos, in order to fulfill its function of securing the political by hedging in the new beginnings, could not remain static but had to be responsive to the vicissitudes of action, precisely because action could exceed the established nomos.

This is a nomos, then, that, if pushed in a radical direction, is unlike Schmitt's, is not married to a rigid spatial logic of containment 'conceptualized on the basis of an "us inside—them outside" divide.' In terms of the metaphor that I have used throughout, this version of nomos is responsive to the breach in the wall, to the politics that has been disowned, to the ghost that haunts the archive understood as a beginning and a commandment.[175] It is simultaneously also a nomos that understands that freedom and action requires a durable space for its performance—a space that stabilizes action while remaining faithful to its initiatory and unpredictable character. As Volks remarks, the rationality of this conception of law 'derives from its ability to establish a public space in which an active and vivid citizenry could act.'[176]

It is this memorial, 'shifting' version of nomos in(to) which the

[170] Chryssostalis, 'Reading Arendt "Reading" Schmitt,' 175.
[171] Chryssostalis, 'Reading Arendt "Reading" Schmitt,' 175.
[172] Chryssostalis, 'Reading Arendt "Reading" Schmitt,' 175.
[173] Volks, 'From *Nomos* to lex,' 777.
[174] Arendt, *The Human Condition*, 194–195.
[175] Jonker, 'Excavating the Legal Subject,' 205.
[176] Volks, 'From *Nomos* to Lex,' 779.

containment theory of space unravels to a significant extent, that Carrol Clarkson expounds in her invocation of the colonial story of Oom Schalk Lourens as told by the celebrated South African writer, Herman Charles Bosman.[177] Clarkson argues that literary texts like the story of Oom Schalk expose, in the context of the colonial and postcolonial setting, the fraught relationship 'between territorial boundaries and the limit of what is just.'[178] Oom Schalk tells a story of a high fever he had suffered as a result of malaria. In the fever he thought that he was likely to die and had a vision of the whole world as one enormous burial ground: 'I thought that it was the earth itself that was a graveyard, and not just those little fenced-in bits of land dotted with tombstones in the shade of a Western Province oak-tree or by the side of a Transvaal koppie.'[179] When Oom Schalk recovers, he is grateful for the fact that 'we Boers had properly marked-out places on our farms for white people to be laid to rest in, in a civilized Christian way, instead of having to be buried just anyhow.'[180]

Oom Schalk discusses his vision with a friend who tries to offer him some consoling words against the abominable vision of death as the great equaliser. The friend (called Stoffel Oosthuizen) tells a story of one Hans Welman's death in a bush skirmish in the same place where Oosthuizen had killed a black man. Six months later, Stoffel and friends have the task of bringing back Welman's remains to his widow for burial. The only problem is that it has become impossible to distinguish between the remains of the black man and that of Welman. Long after the funeral, the black man's dog can still be seen at the grave where Welman was supposedly buried. Oom Schalk remarks that by the time Oosthuizen's story was finished, all his uncertainties had come back to him.[181]

Clarkson observes that the matter of the failure of the boundary to properly enclose what is proper to it, is a general theme in Bosman's work: 'images of fences and graveyards are striking in that they invite thoughts of the mutability and contingency of the human boundaries they are meant to set and stabilize' and 'fences and tombstones are poignant reminders of the very phenomena they are meant to keep at bay, to the extent that "those fenced-in bits of land" seem hardly up to the task of isolating and defining the perimeters of "Boer," "white

---

[177] Carrol Clarkson, *Drawing the Line: Toward an Aesthetics of Transitional Justice* (New York: Fordham University Press, 2013), 30.

[178] Clarkson, *Drawing the Line,* 30.

[179] Clarkson, *Drawing the Line,* 30.

[180] Clarkson, *Drawing the Line,* 30.

[181] Clarkson, *Drawing the Line,* 31.

people," "Christian," "civilized".'[182] The irony of Stoffel Oosthuizen's story is that, instead of providing comforting words with which to counter Oom Schalk's vision, it insists on 'the uncertainties it is meant to fence out.'[183]

Clarkson argues that when considering the logic of the limit, one is led to think of that which is excluded or fenced out.[184] With reference to Drucilla Cornell's work on the philosophy of the limit, she draws attention to the question of the limit as assuming an 'ethical resonance' in contemporary legal and political philosophy.[185] In this regard, Clarkson quotes Peter Fitzpatrick's remark on the 'irresolution of law's spatial determinations': to the extent that such a determination can never be spatially fixed, 'responsiveness cannot be ever completely unformed.'[186] This insight is remarkably resonant with Chryssostalis's description of the nomos as never entirely able to contain the vicissitudes of action, of nomos as always in one or the other way responsive to and thus the product of action even as it attempts to lend the space of action some continuity or permanence. Lindahl similarly contends that the corollary of the reflexive understanding of nomos is that 'no collective ever entirely succeeds in stabilizing the claim to a territory as its own place.'[187] For Lindahl this means that 'from the very beginning community is also, albeit latently, *outside* the enclosure.'[188] This, in turn, means that the question as to '*who* is an interested party to a territory and its boundaries is never exhausted by any legal institutionalizations of spatial unity.'[189] Clarkson comments that it is precisely the *irresolution* of what is inside the boundary that causes a positive ethicity of the limit in that it is in and as this irresolution that the boundary takes on a 'responsive relation' to what supposedly lies beyond it.[190]

'Mapping the Heterotopic'

Jonker concludes his analysis of Prestwich Place with an argument, relying on Foucault, that these burial sites tend toward the

---

[182] Clarkson, *Drawing the Line*, 31.
[183] Clarkson, *Drawing the Line*, 31.
[184] Clarkson, *Drawing the Line*, 32.
[185] Clarkson, *Drawing the Line*, 32.
[186] Clarkson, *Drawing the Line*, 32.
[187] Lindahl, 'Give and Take,' 892.
[188] Lindahl, 'Give and Take,' 895.
[189] Lindahl, 'Give and Take,' 896.
[190] Clarkson, *Drawing the Line*, 32.

'heterotopic.'[191] He begins his brief argument here by stating that these sites are spatial markers of an 'anomaly.' He, however, does not draw out the consequences for nomos that this lexical choice entails. Yet, in his discussion of a series of South African cases involving burial and graves, Jonker comes close to these consequences when he shows how the treatment of burial sites as *res religiosa* has proceeded from a compulsion to 'manage the unmanageable thing, as if *nomos* could not abide an anomaly.'[192] In this context he goes on to refer to Foucault's 'Of other spaces' in which Foucault proposed the notion of the heterotopia.[193] Jonker does not, however, engage in a fuller analysis of the slave burial site as heterotopic. A consideration of what Foucault writes about the heterotopia will aid in an understanding of Jonker's resort to the heterotopic in his description of the slave burial site.

Foucault begins this text with the statement that the present epoch will perhaps, above all, be the 'epoch of space' and that this is an epoch in which space takes the form of 'relations among sites.'[194] The external space in which we live testifies to this relation of sites because it is 'in itself' a 'heterogenous space' in the sense that 'we live inside a set of relations that delineates sites which are irreducible to one another.'[195] Moreover, sites themselves are defined by the sets of relations that they represent. In short, Foucault is proposing here a thoroughly relational theory of space—space understood as 'a product of interrelations and embedded practices, a sphere of multiple possibilities, a ground of chance and undecidability, and as such always becoming, always open to the future.'[196] He goes on to proclaim his interest in those sites that are in relation with all the other sites but in such a way that they 'contradict' all the other sites with which they stand in relation.[197] Because of this, these spaces are referred to as 'counter-sites.' These spaces constitute a relation of absolute difference from the sites that they reflect and speak about and so Foucault calls them 'heterotopias.'[198] Hook and Vrdoljak characterize the heterotopia as follows:

> Heterotopia are the potentially transformative spaces of society from which meaningful forms of resistance can be mounted. These are the places capable of a certain kind of social commentary, those sites where social commentary may, in a sense, be written into the arrangements and

[191] Jonker, 'The Silence of the Dead,' 132.
[192] Jonker, 'The Silence of the Dead,' 137.
[193] Michel Foucault, 'Of Other Spaces,' *Diacritics* 16/1 (1986), 22.
[194] Foucault, 'Of Other Spaces,' 23.
[195] Foucault, 'Of Other Spaces,' 23.
[196] Philippopoulos-Mihalopoulos, 'Law's Spatial Turn,' 8.
[197] Foucault, 'Of Other Spaces,' 24.
[198] Foucault, 'Of Other Spaces,' 24.

relations of space.[199]

Foucault takes as his primary example of a heterotopia as counter-site, the cemetery.[200] It is a place unlike ordinary cultural spaces whilst being at the same time connected with all the sites of the city, since all of us have 'relatives' in the cemetery. He undertakes a brief historical sketch of the location of the cemetery in the city over the ages and points out that it is only at the beginning of the nineteenth century, at that moment when we are no longer certain that we have a soul or that our bodies will come to life again, that cemeteries began to be located at the outside border of cities: 'the cemeteries then came to constitute, no longer the sacred and immortal heart of the city, but "the other city," where each family possesses its dark resting place.'[201] The cemetery, then, from this moment on, confronts the living with the absolute difference/alterity of death. As heterotopia, the cemetery is also heterochronic in that it represents a sort of absolute break with traditional time. In the cemetery, the individual is presented with the loss of life/death as heterochrony, 'this quasi-eternity in which her permanent lot is dissolution and disappearance.'[202] We can see here how Foucault separates 'eternity' from the notion of 'eternal life.' In its heterochrony, the cemetery contradicts the sites of life to which it is related. This description of the heterotopia as heterochronic resonates well with the earlier description of the slave burial site as dislocating the monumental time of the post-apartheid.

Jonker builds upon these features of the heterotopia in claiming that it embodies an 'anomalous energy, a tendency towards a limit, that limit being the site of an impossibly different and discontinuous space.'[203] The 'hallowed thing' / the remains can then be thought as tending towards this limit because it is located at the 'haunted place' where the city is out of joint with itself and out of joint with linear time and smooth, continuous space. The idea of the heterotopic, then, captures in spatial terms the anomaly that these sites represent. In Lindahl's terms, slave burial sites as strange places, as heterotopia, are anomalous in the strong sense of being anomos—lawless.[204] Even if positive legislation attempts to appropriate and regulate the earth

---

[199] Derek Hook and Michele Vrdoljak, 'Gated Communities, Heterotopia and A "Rights" of Privilege: A "Heterotopology" of the South African Security-Park,' *Geoforum* 33/2 (2002), 209.

[200] Foucault, 'Of Other Spaces,' 25.

[201] Foucault, 'Of Other Spaces,' 25.

[202] Foucault, 'Of Other Spaces,' at 25.

[203] Jonker, 'The Silence of the Dead,' 139.

[204] Lindahl, 'Give and Take,' 882.

on which they are located, even if such legislation moves quickly to regularize the irregularity of the space as place, something irregular—a lawlessness—remains that escapes this regularization and thus escapes the nomos understood as land appropriation and the fixing of boundaries. Lindahl argues that strange places are 'protoplaces' in that they represent spaces where, as Hook and Vrdoljak suggest, transformative processes of resistance become possible. In this respect Lindahl again quotes Arendt who remarks that 'the law can ... stabilize and legalize change once it has occurred, but the change itself is always the result of extralegal action [that] takes place outside of *nomos*' but for this very reason can redraw or transform nomos.[205] Jonker concludes that the juridical significance of burial sites like Prestwich Place and Rustenburg should finally be located here: 'between nomos and anomaly.'[206]

The location of the juridical significance of the slave burial site as 'between' nomos and anomaly means that it is here where nomos is pushed to its limit, which is to say that if we were to follow Clarkson's 'logic of the limit' it is here where nomos is called upon in its response-ability. Golder and Fitzpatrick's reading of law in Foucault's work is highly relevant here. They argue that there are in Foucault 'two crucial dimensions of law' at work. The first is a 'determinate law which expresses a definite content.'[207] This is the law that is 'to be resisted and transgressed' because it is law on the side of the instantiation of the disciplinary norm.[208] The second dimension of law is that in which it is constitutively engaged with resistance and transgression in such a way that it 'extends itself illimitably in its attempt to encompass and respond to what lies outside its definite content.'[209] Thus, in Foucault 'law is not simply rendered in terms of determinacy and closure. Rather, law can be seen to engage responsively with exteriority, with an outside made up of resistances and transgressions that assume a constituent role in law's very formation.'[210]

Golder and Fitzpatrick show that this 'responsive dimension' of law originates in Foucault's alternative understanding of modernity not as an epoch but as 'an *attitude* that one adopts towards the present.'[211] This attitude entails a critical imagining of the present as otherwise than it is. As a critical enterprise, such an imagining requires a '*limit-attitude*' that moves beyond 'the outside-inside alternative' towards a 'crossing-over

---

[205] Lindahl, 'Give and Take,' 896.
[206] Jonker, 'The Silence of the Dead,' 139.
[207] Golder and Fitzpatrick at 71.
[208] Golder and Fitzpatrick at 71.
[209] Golder and Fitzpatrick, *Foucault's Law*, 71.
[210] Golder and Fitzpatrick, *Foucault's Law*, 56.
[211] Golder and Fitzpatrick, *Foucault's Law*, 71, 107.

of limits.' As Foucault writes: 'we have to be at the frontiers.'[212] This, then, is modernity at the frontier, modernity 'as constituent lability and contestation, and modernity as *rupture*.'[213] From such an attitude of modernity, Golder and Fitzpatrick derive a 'sociality of law' that is dedicated to the 'unworking of the space of the social': 'the law of the law of modernity thus resides in law's responsive dimension, in its being able to open society to alterity, to an ethic of constantly being otherwise.'[214]

Such an approach to law proceeds from the insight that resistance is constitutive of power.[215] If, as Foucault argues, power is relational and 'everywhere,' indeed if it defines the social, then power formations exist in a constituent relationship with counter-formations of resistance.[216] Power relations, argue Golder and Fitzpatrick, derive their very existence from 'the impelling movement of resistance.'[217] This means that resistance is never in a relationship of simple or demarcated exteriority to power, resistances 'invest and inhabit power': 'Foucault thus does not posit a stable and determinate instantiation of power, but rather a mobile and constantly shifting relation between power and that which contests it from outside.'[218] Transgression thus plays a central role in the very constitution of the limit: 'a limit could not exist if it were absolutely uncrossable and, reciprocally, transgression would be pointless if it merely crossed a limit composed of illusions and shadows.'[219] From this characterization of the constitutive relationship between power and resistance, Golder and Fitzpatrick show that Foucault derived a modality of a law 'of mutability, a law which practices an "infinitely accommodating welcome" to what lies beyond it.'[220] It is 'the darkness beyond its borders,' 'obsessed with exteriority.'[221]

Here then we have law or at least a 'mode of becoming' of law as trans-formative, as attuned to alterity, as extending itself, 'constantly opening itself to new possibilities, new instantiations, fresh determinations.'[222] If there is to be a 'mapping' (and as such the imposition of a 'law') of the heterotopia it must be as this illimitable law 'which comes

[212] Golder and Fitzpatrick, *Foucault's Law*, 108.
[213] Golder and Fitzpatrick, *Foucault's Law*, 109.
[214] Golder and Fitzpatrick, *Foucault's Law*, 109.
[215] Golder and Fitzpatrick, *Foucault's Law*, 75.
[216] Golder and Fitzpatrick, *Foucault's Law*, 74–5.
[217] Golder and Fitzpatrick, *Foucault's Law*, 75.
[218] Golder and Fitzpatrick, *Foucault's Law*, 75–6.
[219] Golder and Fitzpatrick, *Foucault's Law*, 77.
[220] Golder and Fitzpatrick, *Foucault's Law*, 77.
[221] Golder and Fitzpatrick, *Foucault's Law*, 78.
[222] Golder and Fitzpatrick, *Foucault's Law*, 79.

from beyond law's present positioning.'[223] This would not be a law that is geared towards the regulation and normalization of the heterotopia. Rather, it would be a modality of law that emanates from claiming the burial site as a heterotopia, as a site that generates a resistance (through memory-work as the work of difference) to closure and enclosure, to geographies of exclusion and the spectacles of empire. It would, as such, be interested in the constitution of (legal) relations of resistance and irreducible difference—relations that are themselves constituted through acts of memory by way of which an unjust past is re-inscribed in the present as an aspiration to the post-apartheid.

Van Marle, De Villiers and Beukes, relying on the work of Shane Graham, have suggested that 're-imagining the law by re-membering' could be stated in spatial terms and in the context of post-apartheid South Africa as the 'mapping of loss': 'The notion of mapping loss entails the literal and figurative re-mapping of place, space and memory. It is a process of taking ownership of conceptual landscapes, of excavating and reclaiming the memory of social spaces.'[224] This, they argue would entail a resistance to and a refusal of the 'hegemonic forces that drew the maps and legislated the spaces.'[225] Here, then, is a shift in the constitution of nomos by way of its encounter with the remains as alterity. We have here nomos no longer as the act by way of which an inside is separated and fenced off from an outside, but rather a thoroughly relational and memorial nomos—a nomos that shifts and displaces boundaries, a nomos that not only re-relates the past to the present and the future, but does so by making the inside responsive to the outside and, in so doing, insists on a dynamic legal relationality and a legal spatiality characterized by the processes of radical change that are immanent to transformation.

It cannot admit of any doubt that this nomos can only be constituted in and through a certain approach and claim to space. In this regard, Philippopoulos-Mihalopoulos pleads for an understanding that 'spatiality is an ethical position' in that it is an approach to space that conceives of the interrelations that constitute a space also as a force—a force that forces law to 'question its ethics':[226] 'the lack of certainty, direction, orientation, predictability, causality that space brings, shakes law's judgement, the certainty of legal decisions, the irreversibility of

---

[223] Golder and Fitzpatrick, *Foucault's Law*, 79.

[224] Shane Graham, *South African Literature after the Truth Commission: Mapping Loss* (New York: Palgrave MacMillan, 2009); Karin van Marle, Isolde de Villiers and Eunette Beukes, 'Memory, Space and Gender: Re-imagining the Law,' *SAPL* 27 (2012), 568.

[225] Van Marle, De Villiers and Beukes, 'Memory, Space and Gender,' 569.

[226] Philippopoulos-Mihalopoulos, 'Law's Spatial Turn,' 9.

judgement, the causal link on which a judge relies.'[227] Philippopoulos-Mihalopoulos asks the pertinent question of how to prevent the law from imploding, if we are to admit that space (as infinite and 'infinitely open') 'destabilizes, shakes up and resemiologizes the law.'[228] Here, he makes the reflexive move that I advocated in the beginning as crucial to the understanding of law as *transformative*: 'it can only be the law that turns *itself* spatial.'[229] It is space that brings the law to reflection and to reflection upon itself, a reflexive reflection then that is a pre-condition of law's transformation as a moment in which 'the host becomes hostage and the law, a willing victim of its own transcendence, ultimately fails to resist its own inviting twists and turns.'[230]

Conclusion

We have come a long way from Van Riebeeck's hedge of bitter almonds and Schmitt's nomos as a land-appropriation that establishes a definitive legal separation between inside and outside, with a preference for the inside as the claim to political community. Yet, as Graham observes, while many of the 'policies of spatial regimentation' have collapsed in post-apartheid South Africa, 'the racial legacy of apartheid is perpetuated by the remains of its built environment and by conservative elements in the society that struggle to limit wealth and privilege to those (white and black, now) who already possess it.'[231] This observation echoes Jennifer Robinson's earlier warning that

> the complex relations between urban spatial arrangements and state power which we can observe in the past should alert us to the possibility that current restructurings of the state and the emergence of a post-apartheid urban form may also be closely related to one another. In addition, we might expect to find some continuities in planning practices and racialized urban management strategies.[232]

In short, the specter of the old nomos of separation and exclusion, of the close relationship between space and law as domination, continues to haunt our contemporary condition. Moreover, as Graham continues

---

[227] Philippopoulos-Mihalopoulos, 'Law's Spatial Turn,' 9.

[228] Foucault, 'Of other spaces,' 23; Philippopoulos-Mihalopoulos, 'Law's Spatial Turn,' 9.

[229] Philippopoulos-Mihalopoulos, 'Law's Spatial Turn,' 9.

[230] Philippopoulos-Mihalopoulos, 'Law's Spatial Turn,' 10.

[231] Graham, *South African Literature after the Truth Commission*, 2.

[232] Jennifer Robinson, 'The Geopolitics of South African Cities: States, Citizens and Territory,' *Political Geography* 16/5 (1997), 366.

to point out, South Africa's post-apartheid subjection to the global flows of late capitalism has thwarted the inscription of memory onto urban spaces and has produced an 'amnesiac effect.'[233]

The slave burial site represents a rupture in the urban post-apartheid landscape, a rupture that both intensifies the haunting of the ghost of this old nomos whilst also powerfully raising the specter of apartheid's displaced. In so doing, it opens up a space for reading nomos otherwise. Because the specter is always already a memory. To this extent, the remains reminds. And first of all, it reminds the law. Indeed, it serves as a powerful demand upon law's conscience.[234] The slave burial site is not only a space where social memory can be inscribed onto the urban landscape—it is also a space in which memory can be re-inscribed into law in the name of a call upon the law to respond to the idea of justice. It is of this relationship between memory and justice that Paul Ricoeur has written as follows: 'it is justice that turns memory into a project; and it is this same project of justice that gives the form of the future and of the imperative to the duty of memory.'[235] As such it is a transformative space, a space that challenges and disturbs the law, that calls it to account, that demands a response.

Far too often, this response comes exclusively in the form of the building of a monument or even a memorial, a structure in space, aimed at conserving the memory, but that does precious little, if anything, in terms of securing or stabilizing the transformative relations that constitute the space. One only needs to read Greene and Murray's bleak account of the Prestwich Place memorial ossuary (where well-heeled, post-modern, post-apartheid city dwellers can have designer coffee at 'Truth Coffee Shop') to surmise that whatever this response may be it is certainly not transformative. Rather, the response testifies to law's resistance to transformation, to its preference for closure, its penchant for looking the other way—indeed, its fear of space. In this moment, 'we hand the responsibility of memory to the sign, to the object,' writes South African artist William Kentridge. 'It becomes a canned memory, like canned laughter on a TV show, which laughs on our behalf, it remembers on our behalf, it does the work for us. We are let off the hook.'[236] And so is the law.

---

[233] Graham, *South African Literature after the Truth Commission*, 2.

[234] As Costas Douzinas and Adam Geary observe, there can be no talk of jurisprudence if it does not take the prudence of ius—law's conscience—seriously; see Costas Douzinas and Adam Geary, *Critical Jurisprudence: The Political Philosophy of Justice* (Oxford: Hart Publishing, 2005).

[235] Paul Ricoeur, *Memory, History, Forgetting* (Chicago: University of Chicago Press, 2004), 88.

[236] William Kentridge, *Six Drawing Lessons* (Cambridge: Harvard University Press,

I have argued here that the slave burial site, as remains, as a remainder, nevertheless invites a refusal, on law's part, of the 'business as usual' approach. A reading of nomos 'otherwise' will place memory at the centre of the law's encounter with space. Through such an encounter with the remains as memory the law may become both responsive to and conducive of relations of memory-as-difference, that is to say of memory as a disconfirmation and contradiction of the given present. Unfortunately, it is true that the law (as nomos) has seldom lived up to this task in post-apartheid South Africa. Memorialization, for all its symbolic import, has done little in terms of a material transformation of post-apartheid space. Where such transformations have taken place, be they in the form of an attempt to 'read' nomos otherwise or in the form of a mapping of loss, they have been like a *polis* without a nomos—fragile, transient, and ultimately elusive. Put succinctly, the law has failed to secure a lasting space for the transformation of space. All over the country, the spatial demarcations and degradations of apartheid remain firmly in (legal) place.

Yet, the slave burial site, like injustice, remains and remains as dislocation. And as Derrida remarks, for those who are still interested in justice 'it is necessary to appeal unconditionally to the future of another law and another force lying beyond the totality of this present.'[237] The juridical significance of the slave burial site is finally that it facilitates this appeal by itself appealing in silence, from a past, in a present, to a future. The slave burial site watches, it bears testimony and it waits: 'it keeps watch on that which is not, on that which is not yet, and on the chance of still remembering some faithful day.'[238]

2014), 80.

[237] Jacques Derrida, 'Racism's Last Word,' trans. Peggy Kamuf, *Critical inquiry* 12/1 (1985), 298.

[238] Derrida, 'Racism's Last Word,' 299.

2

A Struggle for Space (Elsewhere): Marching for Gaza in Santiago de Chile

Siri Schwabe

M arching down La Alameda in protest was almost like marching down La Alameda in victory. It was early August 2014 when I joined thousands of Santiaguinos in a manifestation of discontent with Israel's Operation Protective Edge in Gaza and the relative passivity of the Chilean government on the matter. Walking in procession from the Plaza Italia in central Santiago toward the presidential palace La Moneda, we took over the grand avenue of La Alameda like a wave of bodies, banners, and noise which seemed to overflow the usual barriers of the city as we moved through it. Perhaps that is why it felt like victory; no matter the outcome, everyone who came together in protest that day made for a Palestinian presence in the centre of Santiago, notably occupying public space and disrupting the usual flow of the city. To understand this as cause for celebration, however, a number of circumstances must be scrutinized.

This chapter will explore the dynamics of protest among Palestinian-Chileans and supporters of the Palestinian cause in Santiago. By examining these dynamics as they play out within a space that is, in geographical terms, far removed from Palestine, it will seek to approach an understanding of the various ways in which a politics of Palestinianness is constituted in the Chilean context through a peculiar interplay between the absent and the present.[1] It will do so through an investigation of the various instances of protest that came

---

[1] In this article, I use the term Palestinianness as an umbrella category for the various practices and narratives that go into 'being Palestinian' in the context of Santiago. The purpose of this article is not to discuss identity as such; however, my understanding of the term Palestinianness is much in line with Rosemary Sayegh, who takes Palestinianness to indicate a 'strategic fusion of objective and subjective identity'; see Rosemary Sayegh, 'Palestinian Refugee Identity/ies: Generation, Region, Class,' in *Palestinian Refugees: Different Generations, but One Identity*, ed. Sunaina Miari (Birzeit: Birzeit University, 2012), 13.

about in Santiago in connection with Israel's Operation Protective Edge in mid 2014. These instances took place toward the end of my doctoral fieldwork in the Chilean capital (between September 2013 and August 2014). While they only made up a fraction of Palestinian life in Santiago, they made explicit and expressive a politics of Palestinianness that had until then only taken more subtle forms.

Chile is popularly known to be home to the most numerous—and most notable—Palestinian population outside the Arab world. With immigration going back as far as the late 1800s and intensifying in the years leading up to World War I, the first Palestinians arrived in Chile holding Ottoman passports and were held to their status as *turcos* for decades.[2] As more Palestinians came to Chile from the old villages around Bethlehem while tensions mounted all around the old land, Palestinians in the capital of Chile and beyond gradually experienced a heightened awareness and commitment to their Palestinianness, and Palestinian organizations and institutions began springing up in earnest. Indeed, the commitment to Palestinianness continues to be a commitment to engage with the ongoing Palestinian-Israeli conflict and, with that, a commitment to the Palestinian cause. As such, politics—and in particular a politics of resistance—have since permeated much of Palestinian social life in Santiago as well as the rest of Chile.

It was not surprising then, that when Israel launched another wave of attacks on the Gaza Strip in the middle of the Chilean winter of 2014, a corresponding wave of protests in support of the Palestinian struggle surged the streets of Santiago. Growing in size with each round of mobilization, the protests included Santiaguinos of a wide range of backgrounds. At the same time, however, efforts at mobilization were centred around Palestinian-Chilean organizations, and Palestinians and their descendants showed up in large numbers to call for an end to the violent and bloody conflict. Through an exploration of these protests, I want to argue that *presence* is not only at the very core of the Palestinian struggle, but also pivotal to the social dynamics surrounding diasporic Palestinianness and popular politics in Santiago. First, presence is a central issue to the Palestinian struggle for land and the right to a sustainable presence on that land. Secondly, remaining part of that struggle in the capital of Chile is about creating a place for Palestinianness and keeping Palestine present in the wider sense of the term, not least through an expressive mode of contestation which draws heavily on the broader Chilean context. Rather than theorizing 'spatial

---

[2] Patricia Arancibia Clavel, Roberto Arancibia Clavel, and Isabel Jara Hinojosa, *Tras la huella de los árabes en Chile. Una historia de esfuerzo e integración*, (Santiago: Instituto Democracia y Mercado, 2010).

justice', this chapter offers a lived example of a diasporic community struggling to obtain it.

The Place of Protest

The march which took over La Alameda on that day at the height of Israel's onslaught in Gaza was but one in a series of similar actions. Besides running campaigns on social media and spreading the word on Palestine through various events and happenings, a small core of Palestinian-Chilean organizations had been the leading force behind several mass demonstrations which called for the Chilean government to break ties with Israel in support of Palestine. As they drew together masses of people to fill up various public spaces in the city, they created a spectacle of colour, noise, and movement. Homemade banners, flags, and balloons filled the air above our heads as we marched slowly through Santiago, and several groups which had brought instruments from home filled our ears with the sound of music pouring out from large drums, cymbals, and trumpets. At the march going down La Alameda, supporters of the popular Chilean football team Colo-Colo walked behind a huge banner which marked the front of their huddle as they raised their voices in song. Further along the procession large groups of people were joining together in chants easily learned and repeated: *¡Gaza resiste, Palestina existe!* and the unfaltering *¡Palestina vencerá, el sionismo caerá!* ('Palestine will overcome, Zionism will fall!'). Several little groups were performing choreographed dance routines to their own music, and scattered along the snakelike formation a few people were passing around megaphones into which fellow protesters were encouraged to lead the chants or otherwise hype the crowd. Just like the other *marchas por Gaza* which took place during the course of Operation Protective Edge, this manifestation clearly took its cue from a well-traversed repertoire of protest, formed over decades of political unrest in Chile, and featured a wide array of protesters who all seemed to be drawing on the same collective expressions of discontent.

Perhaps especially since the first so-called 'march of the empty pots and pans' in 1971—during which large numbers of mostly conservative women banged on their kitchenware in an effort to express their rejection of the socialist policies of then-president Salvador Allende—marches have been a popular means of protest in the Chilean capital.[3] *Marchas*, as these manifestations are known, are perhaps still

[3] Margaret Power, *Right-Wing Women in Chile: Feminine Power and the Struggle Against Allende 1964–1973*, (University Park: The Pennsylvania State University Press,

to a great extent associated with what might be thought of as leftist politics, but the reality is that they have been employed over the years by a wide spectrum of political movements whose objectives have by no means been limited to one side of any ideological divide. What characterizes these outbursts of politics into the cityscape, then, is not some overarching political theme, but rather the form through which politics is expressed and acted out by the masses. Central to the means of popular political action—from marches to the so-called *funas* and other expressive political performances—is that they disrupt the space which they come to occupy, if only for a limited period of time.[4] None of these actions could take place outside of the spaces within the city that are available to their participants. No matter the format, popular manifestations rely on, and indeed exploit, the cityscape. At the same time, they transform spaces with their presence and make for a popular politics which is at the same time grounded and in movement.

Particular to the prevalence of spectacular public protest in the Chilean capital is a history of greatly divisive and violent political conflict. Especially since the years leading up to the military coup in 1973, Chile has in many ways been a country divided along the lines of economic inequality as much as political ideology.[5] After decades of military rule imposed by Augusto Pinochet followed by a de facto continuation of the neoliberal politics implemented during his time as head of state, Chile has witnessed a widespread decline in political involvement among its citizens. With a population left with little faith in the political system after seeing very little change, popular politics is marked by what has been described as a 'widely held belief in Chilean politics' that 'politics, if discussed at all, is best left to technocrats and party bosses.'[6] At the same time, however, Santiago lends turf to public political manifestations, and especially marches, on a monthly if not weekly basis. The massive student movement has been breathing new

---

2002), 88–9.

   [4] The funa emerged as a form of protest in the late 1990s. As something of a 'shaming technique' (Temma Kaplan, *Taking Back the Streets: Women, Youth, and Direct Democracy* [Berkeley and Los Angeles: University of California Press, 2004], 6), the funa outed former contributors to torture and disappearances during dictatorship by very publicly and quite spectacularly calling attention to the complicity of specific persons—shaming them, as it were; see also Steve Stern, *Reckoning with Pinochet: The Memory Question in Democratic Chile, 1989–2006*, (Durham & London: Duke University Press, 2010).

   [5] Clara Han, *Life in Debt. Times of Care and Violence in Neoliberal Chile*. Berkeley: University of California Press, 2012).

   [6] Joshua Frens-String, 'A New Politics for a New Chile,' *NACLA Report on the Americas* 46/3 (2013), 29.

life to the political playing field in the Chilean capital and beyond since it was reawakened in 2011, and squares, parks, and roads are regularly appropriated into arenas for promoting a variety of causes. Rather than general disengagement with politics then, what seems to be at stake in Santiago and in Chile, is a move away from party politics and toward mobilization around specific causes.[7]

The marches for Gaza which took place in the Chilean winter of 2014 are part of this tendency toward mobilization around specific causes. While a few prominent Palestinian surnames appear on ballots in Santiago as the persons behind them run for office—representing political parties all along the ideological spectrum—party politics do not figure prominently within the realm of collective Palestinian politics. Quite the contrary: Palestinian-Chilean organizations most often make it their explicit aim to avoid divisive ideology and rather aim to serve as a neutral meeting ground for political mobilization and engagement with Palestine. During a conversation with Ana, a young Palestinian-Chilean woman, she explained to me that even the Palestinian-Chilean organizations considered the most popular continue to refuse to 'pick sides' when it comes to ideology and party politics.[8] Ana had been very active in the mobilization based around these organizations and had been very open with me about her conservative stance on politics from Chile to Palestine and beyond. At the same time, she made it clear that the Palestinian cause should always come front and centre, and no ideological discordances should ever get in the way of promoting a free Palestine. As she explained:

I never understood why there's a problem with the communists when the right-wingers never lend their support. It's like we're waiting for our knight in shining armor to arrive, so we won't do anything with the frog because when our knight comes he'll get mad. But the frog is always there and the knight never is. It's the same, it's like we're waiting for the day when the right-wing will see and support us, but they haven't showed up yet.

To Ana, getting caught up in party politics only takes away from the message and causes frustration and conflict. In her words, 'it's just

[7] Simón Escoffier, 'The Dictatorship Has Not Ended: Chile's September Riots,' Open Democracy, 2014, accessed 1 November 2016, https://www.opendemocracy.net/sim%C3%B3n-escoffier/dictatorship-has-not-ended-chile%E2%80%99s-september-riots; Kirsten Sehbruch and Sofia Donoso, 'Chilean winter of discontent: are protests here to stay?,' Open Democracy, 2011, accessed 1 November 2016, https://www.opendemocracy.net/kirsten-sehnbruch-sofia-donoso/chilean-winter-of-discontent-are-protests-here-to-stay.

[8] For the sake of anonymity, I have not used Ana's real name.

stupid, crazy to mix and confuse the issues for no good reason, and I don't like that.' While the reality of popular politics in Santiago is complicated and cannot easily be slotted into a simple formula of pushing party politics to the side in order to keep the focus on particular issues, the resurgence of mobilization across ideological convictions is reconfiguring the place of politics in Santiago. Indeed, the marches for Gaza which took place during Operation Protective Edge, albeit occupying but a fraction of public space, saw an impressive diversity. Marching along with hundreds of Palestinian-Chileans were a wide array of Santiaguinos representing organizations and groups of various persuasions while many were simply there as individuals who had come with friends or family to protest the violence in Gaza.

The Communist Party was represented at all of these marches, its members and sympathizers waving red banners attesting to their affiliation. Another notable presence was made by posters and T-shirts blazoning the flag of the indigenous Mapuche—subtly calling attention not only to a people with its own place in the Chilean political landscape and imagination, but also to the struggle for land which has marked Mapuche life since their ancestral land was compartmentalized into current-day Chile and Argentina.[9] Not only did these marches foreground a form of expressive popular politics which has been employed time and again for various causes in the Chilean capital, they also highlighted a coming together of thousands of people representing a multiplicity of personal histories, ideological stances, and political causes. As the colourful assembly of people walked in slow procession down La Alameda to confront the political establishment at La Moneda, they found common ground, quite literally, in their support of the Palestinian cause.

Trawling through a space marked by the vestiges of past unrest and protest, everyone marching that day protested through a mode of expression which likewise bore remnants of this past and the contestations that it fostered. At the same time, however, the objective of this particular instance of protest was to call attention to a surge of violence occurring not in the here, but in the now.

Presence and a Politics of Palestinianness

Operation Protective Edge was of course but one extraordinarily

---

[9] For an interesting analysis of Mapuche past and present in Chile, see Joanna Crow, *The Mapuche in Modern Chile: A Cultural History* (Gainesville: University Press of Florida, 2013).

gruesome instance of violence on Palestinian soil.[10] At the heart of the conflict which has been ongoing since before the establishment of the Israeli state in 1948, is a struggle over territory and opposing claims to a homeland in historical Palestine. Indeed, according to Sari Hanafi, the 'institutionalized invisibility of the Palestinian people' goes hand in hand with what he calls the 'spacio-cidal' Israeli colonial project which 'targets land for the purpose of rendering inevitable the "voluntary" transfer of the Palestinian population primarily by targeting the space upon which the Palestinian people live.'[11] In Palestine, the struggle over physical presence on the land is and has been absolutely central to both a very real struggle for continued existence, and also to notions and narratives of everyday resistance. These notions and narratives are often tied to the concept of *sumud*; a concept which invokes a resilient Palestinianness, one of endurance and steadfastness.[12] Palestinian resistance is thus often framed as a matter of staying put, of remaining in place and continuing to make for a Palestinian presence within a highly contested space. This 'refusal to go away' can of course be understood and framed at both the physical and the metaphorical level.[13] It is a question of a sustained bodily presence on a piece of land recognized by Palestinians as their own, but it is also a question of refusing to be forgotten or left invisible. Tightly connected to the struggle for physical space, then, is the struggle for a continued and remembered presence.[14]

As such, the Palestinian struggle has much to do with what Laleh Khalili has called the 'politics of enforced visibility or invisibility.'[15] This politics, she writes, 'is about powerful state actors compelling subject populations to be visible to their own police and security forces, while preventing them from being visible to audiences not chosen by the

---

[10] Most notably, in the decade leading up to Operation Protective Edge alone, the Israel Defense Forces (IDF) conducted three large-scale and devastating military operations in Gaza: Operation Summer Rains (2006), Operation Cast Lead (2008–2009) and Operation Pillar of Defense (2012).

[11] Sari Hanafi, 'Explaining Spacio-cide in the Palestinian Territory: Colonization, Separation, and State of Exception,' *Current Sociology* 61/2 (2012), 190–1.

[12] For a recent overview and discussion of sumud and Palestinian resistance, see Anna Johansson and Stellan Vinthagen, 'Dimensions of everyday resistance: the Palestinian Sumūd,' in *Journal of Political Power* 8/1 (2015), 109–39.

[13] Julie Peteet, 'Refugees, Resistance, and Identity,' in *Globalizations and Social Movements: Culture, Power, and the Transnational Public Sphere*, eds. John Guidry et al. (Ann Arbor: University of Michigan Press, 2000), 195.

[14] Edward W. Said, 'Invention, Memory, and Place,' *Critical Inquiry* 46/2 (2000), 184.

[15] Laleh Khalili, 'Palestinians: The Politics of Control, Invisibility, and the Spectacle,' in *Manifestations of Identity: The Lived Reality of Palestinian Refugees in Lebanon*, ed. Muhammad Ali Khalidi (Beirut: Institute for Palestine Studies 2010), 126.

state.'[16] In Palestine, this politics is expressed in very tangible ways via the infrastructure of occupation: checkpoints to monitor and control the movement of Palestinians and an imposing separation barrier which in effect renders Palestinians visible almost exclusively to the Israeli state.[17] Meanwhile, the same infrastructure hinders the witnessing of Palestinian life by outsiders who rely on limited media reports and, to a higher degree following the influx of social media such as Twitter and Facebook, on images and words spilling out of Gaza and the West Bank via these more informal channels.[18]

In so many ways, then, Palestinian resistance and the Palestinian struggle is about securing presence. It is about fighting back against being pushed out of place, about struggling to maintain an enduring Palestinian presence on what is left of the land, and about making visible the trials and tribulations of the Palestinian people so as to make the Palestinian cause present in as well as beyond the old land. The centrality of space to this struggle remains a fact even outside Palestine. Palestinian resistance relies on 'spaces of appearance';[19] it relies on securing visibility in order to secure presence, especially in order to secure a continued physical presence on land that is slowly being swept up from under them. At the same time, in Santiago, this struggle for space becomes transferred and adapted to fit a diasporic context that is remarkable for its own political dynamics.

Some Palestinian-Chileans have experienced spatial exclusion in Palestine on their own bodies, and several have been very outspoken about the challenges they have faced when trying to enter the West Bank via Israeli-controlled borders. For most, however, the struggle for space in Palestine remains un-lived but vividly imagined. Meanwhile, there is a struggle for presence at play for Palestinian-Chileans in Santiago. For many of those marching down La Alameda for Gaza, the manifestation was not just one of support for Palestine; it was also a manifestation of a distinct Palestinian presence within the context of Santiago and Chile. At the same time, in both Palestine and Santiago, resistance and the struggle for presence is placed within physical spaces marked in each their particular way by past contestations and constituted as places through the practices and meanings that are tied to them. As Doreen

---

[16] Khalili, 'Palestinians: The Politics of Control,' 140.

[17] Khalili, 'Palestinians: The Politics of Control,' 126.

[18] Indeed, social media played a huge part in the mobilization around Gaza in 2014, not least in Santiago. This, however, is something that must be explored in its own right elsewhere.

[19] Hannah Arendt, *The Human Condition*, 199; Simon Springer, 'Public Space as Emancipation: Meditations on Anarchism, Radical Democracy, Neoliberalism and Violence,' *Antipode* 43/2 (2010), 528.

Massey writes, the 'identification of places as particular places, is always ... temporary, uncertain, and in process.'[20]

A Struggle for Space (Elsewhere)

As a response to Operation Protective Edge, Palestinian-Chileans and the Santiaguinos who supported their cause came out in large numbers to take temporary possession of not only wide stretches of asphalt, but also of their specific place within the contemporary political reality at La Moneda and beyond. As much as at any other marches, the processions of people walking through Santiago in support of Gaza made use of the disruptive force of their own presence within public spaces not usually designated for political activity. As seas of people slowly washed over the city's main roads from the districts of Recoleta and Providencia to the very centre of Santiago at separate instances over the course of a few weeks, they put the usual order of things on pause, stopping traffic and dominating the soundscape with the resonance of voices and objects banging against each other. As such, the protesters came together to transform 'streets and plazas into liberated territory' where they could express their collective concern, protest the state of things, and indeed explore the potential of their own presence.[21]

While these instances of protest came out of a strong tradition founded and grounded through decades of public manifestations as the go-to mode of expression for popular politics as employed from the left to the right in Chile, they also linked to a certain trajectory of engagement with the Palestinian cause among Palestinian-Chileans. According to Cecilia Baeza, the 1982 massacre of Palestinian refugees in Sabra and Shatila caused the first mass mobilization of Palestinian-Chileans.[22] It pushed internal political divisions aside and foregrounded unity among Palestinians and their descendants in the face of disaster. Soon after, students established a local chapter of the General Union of Palestinian Students, known locally as the UGEP (*Unión General de Estudiantes Palestinos*), and political engagement with Palestine from Santiago gained a new foothold. Then, after years of heightened awareness of and engagement with the conflict in Palestine and Israel, political activity came to an almost complete halt in the early 1990s when the

[20] Doreen Massey, 'Places and Their Pasts,' in *History Workshop Journal* 39 (1995), 190.

[21] Kaplan, *Taking Back the Streets*, 4.

[22] Cecilia Baeza, 'Palestinians in Latin America: Between Assimilation and Long Distance Nationalism,' *Journal of Palestine Studies* 43/2 (2014), 59–72.

Oslo peace process led many to wrongly believe that a sustainable peace was near at hand.[23]

In the wider Chilean context, an activist popular politics receded into a position of quiet observation and anticipation of the changes to come with the transition from military rule to a new democracy.[24] This transition has been characterized as a 'democratic opening' rather than the introduction of a fully functioning democracy and was kicked off with Pinochet's exit from the front lines of Chilean politics following the 1988 plebiscite which effectively paved the way for his retirement as head of state.[25] At the turn of the century, however, when Chileans and Palestinians alike failed to see the changes they had been hoping for, popular mobilization took off once again, and Santiago witnessed a return to public manifestations as a means of protest and political engagement. For Palestinian-Chileans, the years of dictatorship had a wide range of consequences, from persecution to heightened success under neoliberal rule.[26] In spite of their disparate experiences and political differences, however, the Palestinian cause came to once again make for a rallying point and source of consonance among Palestinian-Chileans in Santiago and beyond. By the time the marches of 2014 came around, then, Palestinian-Chileans of a range of backgrounds and political stances had long been active in making for a politics of Palestinianness in the Chilean capital. This politics, in turn, had been continuously formed and reformed within the realm of Chilean (popular) politics and remains emplaced within the physical and social world of public contestation in Santiago.

A couple of days after the big march for Gaza on La Alameda, I sat down with Ana for lunch and a chat about what had been going on. Ana was by no means new to Palestinian politics in Santiago. She had long been part of the UGEP and had been involved in mobilization efforts well before the initiation of Israel's Operation Protective Edge. A few weeks into this military campaign, however, she was beginning to sound exhausted. Shaken by the continued horrors in Gaza and

[23] As an important indicator of this trend, the UGEP was dissolved and only resurged in the wake of the second intifada in the early 2000s.

[24] Nicolás Somma and Matías A. Bargsted, 'La autonomización de la protesta en Chile,' in *Socialización política y experiencia escolar: aportes para la formación ciudadana en Chile*, eds. Juan Carlos Castillo and Cristián Cox (Santiago: Pontificia Universidad Católica de Chile, 2015), 207–40.

[25] Stern, *Reckoning with Pinochet*, 357.

[26] Ana and many of her peers expressed gratitude at what Pinochet and his politics had done for Palestinian-Chilean businesses, but others told stories of family members going into exile and recalled the precariousness they themselves had experienced during Pinochet's rule.

tired from working around the clock and trying to fit in her studies at university with her political organizing, Ana remained agitated as she told me that:

> We're trying to make some noise talking about this issue, trying to make everyone understand what's going on. ... Because no one talks about it. The message of these marches is clear: we want Gaza to be free. That's the message. What we're doing is that we're demonstrating that we're not going to forget.

To Ana, the most important thing was to express via protest that 'we're not going to forget,' that the Palestinian struggle would be remembered. Despite the less than bright prospects of an independent and free Palestine, promoting an active and continued focus on the Palestinian cause in the Chilean capital was at the heart of her struggle, her diasporic Palestinianness. In her Ana's case, trying to make some noise was ultimately trying to call attention to Palestine and thus to make for a Palestinian presence—in Santiago as well as in broader Chilean political life. This presence, in turn, depended and continues to depend on spaces of visibility and audibility.

Presence, understood in the widest sense of the term, is certainly crucial to the Palestinian struggle, not least in diaspora.[27] In Santiago, a politics of Palestinianness is practiced at what has been called the 'paradoxical intersections of what is there and what is not,' between the present and the absent.[28] The absences at play are many. Most obvious, perhaps, is the absence of Palestine—an absence which in certain ways facilitates and guides the marches which invoke it—but the absence of the political establishment in the Chilean capital is also significant. As the procession on La Alameda reached La Moneda, it looked impressive, imposing even, but somehow cold and devoid of life. No reaction to our presence nor a single movement could be traced inside, and the palace thus became an apt image of what conventional Chilean politics to a certain degree has come to signify; a dead space with little or no potential. In the absence of the political establishment, at this manifestation and as part of the popular Chilean political imagination more generally, the public space of the grand avenue rather than the lifeless white block at its edge became the place of protest—and indeed the

---

[27] 'Perhaps the greatest battle Palestinians have waged as a people has been over the right to a remembered presence and, with that presence, the right to possess and reclaim a collective historical reality.' (Said, 'Invention, Memory, and Place,' 184).

[28] Mikkel Bille, Frida Hastrup, and Tim Flohr Sørensen, 'Introduction: An Anthropology of Absence,' in An Anthropology of Absence. Materializations of Transcendence and Loss, eds. Mikkel Bille et al. (London: Springer, 2010), 13.

place of politics. In a way, it became a counter-site, both representing, contesting, and inverting the reality of politics in the Chilean capital.[29]

As products of 'our on-going world,' spaces and places are 'always open to the future.'[30] They are never atemporal, always in process; never self-confined, always the product of myriad and complex relations. In several ways then, the marches for Gaza that moved through Santiago during Operation Protective Edge attest to the notion that 'another world is not only possible, but that it already exists in this very space, in this exact time.'[31] The marches for Gaza came to signify the potentiality of presence within public space through what Helga Tawil-Souri has called an 'a physical, territorial and embodied *manifestation of democratic possibility*,[32] highlighting the potential inherent in the 'excessiveness of the moment' and drawing out radical imaginations of what the future might be.[33] Here, the very presence of Palestine and a (diasporic) politics of Palestinianness came into existence via its rootedness in historical trajectories of protest and resistance between Chile and Palestine and indicated a certain future in the present; a future of continued Palestinian presence, physical and otherwise, in Palestine and beyond.

In Conclusion

It remains impossible to speak of the Palestinian-Israeli conflict without speaking to the spaces and places within which it has been playing out for well over half a century. Here I have sought to give an example of how a diasporic politics of Palestinian presence came to be located within public spaces marked by their own history of contentious politics during Israel's Operation Protective Edge in Gaza. The celebratory atmosphere of the big march for Gaza which went down La Alameda in August 2014 was one, as I have sought to show, which to a large extent hinged on the victory in presence—the very presence, physical and figurative, which informs so much of the Palestinian struggle, and which creates political potency and potential.

[29] Michel Foucault, 'Of Other Spaces,' trans. Jay Miskowiec, *Diacritics* 16/1 (1986), 24.

[30] Doreen Massey, 2009, 'Concepts of Space and Power in Theory and in Political Practice,' *Doc. Anàl. Geogr.* 55 (2009), 17.

[31] Simon Springer, 'Space, Time, and the Politics of Immanence,' *Global Discourse* 4/2–3 (2014), 162.

[32] Helga Tawil-Souri, 'It's Still About the Power of Place,' *Middle East Journal of Culture and Communications* 5 (2012), 89. [emphasis in original].

[33] Colin McFarlane, 'Assemblage and Critical Urbanism,' *City* 15/2 (2011), 209.

Indeed, more than anything, the protests that I have discussed in this article came about at the intersection between a struggle for Palestinian presence—in Palestine and beyond—and a complex context of political contestation in Chile. Both the overarching struggle and the local context are constituted within dynamics to which space is central. The Palestinian struggle is one for land, for space in the physical sense on the one hand, as well as for place and presence in the wider sense on the other. At the same time, Chilean political life has seen a shift in popular political involvement from the political parties to mass mobilizations which are more often than not centred on large protests that spill through the cityscape to create awareness of a particular cause. In present-day Santiago, solidarity is put above divisive party politics. This is true for a diasporic engagement with the Palestinian struggle as well as for a wider Chilean popular politics and will most likely continue to inform and affect the dynamics of politics, space, and place in Santiago for some time to come.

In the Chilean capital, practices that serve to keep Palestine present are constantly negotiated and reshaped within the specific context of Chile. As such and as an empirical study which speaks to theoretical work on spatial justice, presence not only bears its relevance as a focal point in terms of Palestinian struggle and resistance, but also when it comes to what is made present and absent respectively in terms of all that is considered Chilean. By employing a means of protest which inverted Santiago's public spaces and turned them into the place of politics in the absence of an engaged establishment, the marchers for Gaza invoked the potentiality of space and took part in reconfiguring the political reality in the Chilean capital as such. Palestinianness in Santiago continues to be in constant movement within a distinct historical space framed by Chile as nation and state, but is also part of what moves this space. The historical and political reality of contemporary Chile, and the ways in which this reality is grappled with socially, thus remains pivotal to an understanding of how, for Palestinian-Chileans in Santiago, practices of securing presence through protest are part of a struggle for space (elsewhere). In turn, the Palestinian struggle has become part of an ongoing reformation of Chilean political life which reaches far beyond a politics of Palestinianness.

3

Political Activism, Undocumented Migrants, and Solidarity Marriage: Between Kindness and Crime?

Julia Rushchenko

Strangely, the foreigner lives within us: he is the hidden face of our identity, the space that wrecks our abode, the time in which understanding and affinity founder. By recognizing him within ourselves, we are spared detesting him in himself. ... The foreigner comes in when the consciousness of my difference arises, and he disappears when we all acknowledge ourselves as foreigners, unamenable to bonds and communities.

— Julia Kristeva[1]

Immigration law reinforces Hollywood fantasies that romantic love must be freely chosen, selfless, innocent, and naturally binding through chemistry or the irrational attraction between a man and a woman.

— Anne-Maire D'Aoust[2]

Introduction

Although the issue of cross-border marriages, including those involving 'mail-order' brides, has received broad coverage in social sciences and law over the last two decades,[3] it is a historical

---

[1] Julia Kristeva, *Strangers to Ourselves*, (New York: Columbia University Press, 1991), 1.

[2] Felicity Schaeffer, *Love and Empire: Cybermarriage and Citizenship across the Americas*, (New York University Press: New York and London, 2012), 47.

[3] Anne-Maire D'Aoust, 'Circulation of Desire: The Security Governance of the International Mail-Order Brides Industry,' in *Security and Global Governmentality: Globalization, Governance and the State*, eds. Miguel de Larrinaga and Marc Doucet (London: Routlege, 2010), 113–31; Anne-Marie D'Aoust, 'Take a Chance on Me: Premediation, Technologies of Love, and Marriage Migration Management,' in *Disciplining the Transnational Movement of People*, eds. Martin Geiger and Antoine Pécoud (London and New York: Palgrave Macmillan, 2013), 10–125 ; Nicole Constable, *Romance on a Global Stage: Pen Pals, Virtual Ethnography, and 'Mail Order' Marriages*

phenomenon with significant roots. The first American transnational 'mail-order' marriages occurred shortly after Britain and France established their colonial settlements in the early 1600s.[4] Both countries actively encouraged immigration to America but soon realized that immigration alone could not achieve the population increase needed for colonial expansion.[5] In the 1700s and 1800s, with the help of marriage agencies and catalogues, a significant number of women from Europe migrated to New Zealand and Australia in order to balance the gender ratio and create families with British settlers.[6]

In the contemporary period there are two factors that make cross-border and binational marriages a controversial field of study, highlighting the importance of focusing on the actors involved: globalization processes and punitive immigration policies. Factors such as globalization, improvements in communication technology, and ease of travel contribute to the practical 'shrinkage' of the world and intensification of cultural exchanges. As pointed out by Tomas Larsson, 'it pertains to the increasing ease with which somebody on one side of the world can interact, to mutual benefit, with somebody on the other side of the world.'[7] On the other hand, some critics argue that globalization processes invoke a necessity for migration control and surveillance. Lucia Zedner has noted that 'opposing the pull of globalization stands the counter pressure to resist the influx of migrants by strengthening borders and limiting access to citizenship in the name of security.'[8] Under these conditions citizenship becomes a privileged status. The social divisions that result from the privileges of citizenship are another outcome of globalization process. According to Katja Aas, 'rather than creating "citizens of the world," the globalizing process

(Berkeley: University of California, 2003); David Glowsky, '*Globale Partnerwahl: Soziale Ungleichheit als Motor transnationalerHeirat-sentscheidungen*' (Dissertation, Freie Universität Berlin, 2010); Nicola Piper and Mina Roces, *Wife or Worker: Asian Women and Migration* (New York: Rowan and Littlefield, 2003); Csy Chun, 'The Mail-Order Bride Industry: The Perpetuation of Transnational Economic Inequalities and Stereotypes,' U. PA. *J. INT'L ECON. L.* 17 (1996), 1155–208.

⁴ Marcia Zug, 'Lonely Colonist Seeks Wife: The Forgotten History of America's First Mail Order Brides,' *Duke Journal of Gender & Law Policy* 20 (2012), 85–125.

⁵ Zug, 'Lonely Colonist Seeks Wife,' 86.

⁶ Zoe Lawton and Paul Callister, '"Mail-Order Brides": Are We Seeing This Phenomenon in New Zealand?,' *Institute of Policy Studies*, 2011, accessed 10 October 2014, http:// igps.victoria.ac.nz/ events/completed activities/Missing%20men/ Bacground%20Paper%20-%20%20Mail%20Order %20Brides.pdf.

⁷ Tomas Larsson, *The Race to the Top: The Real Story of Globalization* (Washington D.C.: Cato Institute, 2001), 9.

⁸ Lucia Zedner, 'Security, the State, and the Citizen: The Changing Architecture of Crime Control,' *New Criminal Law Review* 13 (2010), 380.

seems to be dividing the world; creating and even deepening the "us" and "them" mentality—the national from the foreign.[9] Thus, as Sharon Pickering and Julie Ham write:

> Under conditions of globalization irregular migration has come to be constructed and responded to as one of the most pressing national and international criminal problems. Often entangled with concerns over global terrorism, increasing government and supra-government concern with irregular mobility has generated new legal, political, social and criminal justice responses that have far-reaching impacts in terms of global mobility, human rights and the rule of law.[10]

At the same time, migration stretches family life beyond and across national boundaries, and has been met by thorough legal boundaries and regulation, or 'moral gatekeeping' which generates policing and ethnic profiling mechanisms. The case study and analysis in this chapter offer one example of localized attempts at producing 'spatial justice.'[11]

Policing Marriage Migration: Relevance to Crimmigration and Citizenship Studies

Migration control and policing techniques are among many tools which the EU member states use to deal with non-citizens. I view the problem of policing non-citizens in regard to family reunification as an essential component of crimmigration discourse.[12] Crimmigration law has two sides: the expansion of immigration consequences, such as deportation and exclusion grounds that are based on criminal convictions, and the expansion of criminal law and criminal procedural tools as a way to regulate migration, particularly undocumented or unauthorized migration.[13]

[9] Katja Franko Aas, 'The Ordered and the Bordered Society: Migration Control, Citizenship, andthe Northern Penal State,' in *The Borders of Punishment: Migration, Citizenship, and Social Exclusion*, eds. Katja Franko Aas and Mary Bosworth (Oxford: OUP, 2013), 100.

[10] Sharon Pickering and Julie Ham, 'Introduction,' in *The Routledge Handbook on Crime and International Migration*, eds. Sharon Pickering and Julie Ham (New York and Abingdon: Routledge, 2015), 1–2.

[11] Helena Wray, 'An Ideal Husband? Marriages of Convenience, Moral Gatekeeping and Immigration to the UK,' *European Journal of Migration and Law,* European Journal of Migration Law 8/3 (2006).

[12] Juliet Stumpf, *'Crimmigration: Encountering the Leviathan,'* in *The Routledge Handbook on Crime and International Migration*, ed. Sharon Pickering and Julie Ham (Abingdon and New York: Routledge, 2015).

[13] Juliet Stumpf, 'Introduction,' in *Social Control and Justice: Crimmigration in the*

It can be argued that non-recognition of certain rights gives immigrants a limited status of citizenship: unlike citizens, they are 'denizens' (non-nationals whose right of residence is unlimited) and 'foreigners' (non-nationals whose right of residence or stay is limited).[14] For undocumented migrants, rejected asylum seekers or migrants whose visa is about to expire, marriage with a citizen represents a new opportunity for social advancement, and sometimes becomes the only condition of staying in a country of their choice if threatened by expulsion. Indeed, 'the question of citizenship is thus at the heart of the undocumented migrant's life.'[15] Citizenship, a status granted to full members of a community, defines bounded populations, with a specific set of rights and duties. Fortier reflects on how citizenship constitutes a 'big deal' for new applicants and becomes a site of emotional investment, arguing that naturalization practices should be understood through the politics of desire. In other words, the political realm of citizenship cannot be understood 'without bringing fantasy into the frame':

> At some level, being naturalized invests the new citizen with the same rights and responsibilities as 'native born' citizens. To 'make native' suggests that naturalization somehow entails the transferring of birthright citizenship to individuals.[16]

Some maintain that migration has already altered the perception of citizenship as a legal status that excludes rather than includes persons or groups on the grounds of their nationality.[17] Nevertheless, it is through a citizenship lens that we can better grasp complexities behind the phenomenon of transnational marriages and binational couples. In relationships of binational couples the differences in citizenship might lead to certain outcomes of marriages for the non-EU spouses such as dependence, abuse, and manipulation;[18] or, on the contrary, upward

---

Age of Fear, ed. M. João Guia et al. (The Hague: Eleven InternationalPublishing, 2013); Mary Bosworth, 'Border Control and the Limits of the Sovereign State,' *Social Legal Studies* 17/2 (2008), 199–215.

   [14] Tomas Hammar, *European Immigration Policy.* (Cambridge: CUP, 1985).

   [15] Pierre Monforte and Pascale Dufour, 'Mobilizing in Borderline Citizenship Regimes: A Comparative Analysis of Undocumented Migrants Collective Actions,' *Politics & Society*, 39/2 (2011), 203–32.

   [16] Anne-Marie Fortier, 'What's the Big Deal? Naturalisation and the Politics of Desire,' *Citizenship Studies* 17/6–7 (2013), 698.

   [17] Christian Joppke, *Immigration and the Nation-State: the United States, Germany and GreatBritain*, (Oxford: Clarendon Press, 1999); Yasemin Soysal, *Limits of Citizenship: Migrants and Postnational Membership in Europe* (Chicago: The University of Chicago Press, 1994).

   [18] Sharyne Shiu-Thornton et al., '"Like a bird in a cage'" Vietnamese Women Survivors Talk about Domestic Violence,' *Journal of Interpersonal Violence* 20/8 (2005),

social mobility, belonging, and membership.[19] By defining bounded populations, citizenship of a European industrialized state establishes the grounds for membership by granting individuals unlimited residency permits, social benefits such as medical systems or education, security and comparatively high life standards. Bill Jordan and Frank Düvell maintain that a controversial dilemma for migrants is that of 'mobility versus membership.'[20] 'Mobility' refers to the interest of migrants to pursue better life chances beyond state boundaries. The other side of the dichotomy is termed 'membership' to draw attention to the fact that host states view themselves as rightly allowing or restricting movement into their borders in order to maximize advantages for their own members. The state and the undocumented migrants are therefore seen as having two opposed self-interests and strategies 'to deal with the consequences of [complex everyday] struggles.'[21]

There are two critical narratives revolving around marriages of binational couples: the fact that a woman can be victimized by a husband abroad, and the fact that a marriage can be used for instrumental purposes such as acquiring citizenship or securing a residence permit. If the first point of view is voiced by human rights groups, social scientists and legal scholars,[22] the latter perspective is at the heart of the policing of marriage migration. In this regard 'marriage of convenience,' 'bogus marriage,' or 'sham marriage' are terms often used interchangeably by bureaucrats responsible for policy-making or monitoring immigration fraud. There are two forms of 'sham marriage': *1)* a citizen marries a non-citizen in a contract usually involving a fee with the understanding

959–76; Anita Raj and Jay Silverman, 'Violence against Immigrant Women: The Roles of Culture, Context and Legal Immigrant Status on Intimate Partner Violence,' *Violence Against Women* 8 (2002), 367–98; Cecilia Menjivar and Olivia Salcido, 'Immigrant Women and Domestic Violence: Common Experiences in Different Countries,' *Gender and Society* 16 (2002), 898–920; Marie-Claire Belleau, 'Mail-Order Brides in a Global World,' *Albany Law Review* 67/2 (2003), 595; Suzanne Jackson, 'Marriage of Convenience: International Marriage Brokers, Mail-Order Brides and Domestic Servitude,' *University of Toledo Law Review* 38 (2007), 895–922.

[19] Glowsky, 'Globale Partnerwahl'; Schaeffer, *Love and Empire*; Nicole Constable, *Romance on a Global Stage: Pen Pals, Virtual Ethnography, and 'Mail Order' Marriages* (Berkeley: University of California, 2003).

[20] Bill Jordan and Frank Düvell, *Irregular Migration: The Dilemmas of Transnational Mobility*, (Cheltenham: Edward Elgar Pub, 2002).

[21] Jordan and Düvell, *Irregular Migration*, 3.

[22] Donna Hughes, 'Human Trafficking: Mail-Order Bride Abuses,' *Subcommittee on East Asian and Pacific Affairs Senate Foreign Relations Committee*, 2014, accessed 1 January 2015, http://www.uri.edu/artsci/wms/hughes/testimony_senate_july04.pdf; Donna Lee, 'Mail Fantasy: Global Sexual Exploitation in the Mail Order Bride Industry and Proposed Legal Solutions,' *ASIAN L.J.* 5 (1998), 139–79.

that the marriage will be dissolved after the alien becomes a permanent resident; *2)* a 'unilateral' marriage where the alien deludes a citizen into the marriage and abandons the latter after obtaining permanent resident status.[23]

Before examining the notion of 'solidarity marriage,' it is important to highlight the way in which 'family,' as a value-laden determiner, is represented in EU member states. On the one hand, family has long been perceived as a stronghold against the State and 'the symbolic refuge from the intrusions of a public domain that constantly threatens our sense of privacy and self-determination.'[24] On the other hand, families where one person is a non-EU citizen from an economically weaker country are exposed to a differential treatment involving intense scrutiny of whether the relationship is 'bona fide' or 'fraudulent,' examining a suspicious marriage against a stringent set of criteria and defining the relationship as either credulous or fake.[25] The idea of companionate marriage, according to which marital ideal consists in emotional closeness, has risen to prominence in the Euro-American narrative and is usually understood as a 'modern' love as opposed to the tradition of arranged and forced marriages.[26] As sociologist Skolnick puts forth:

> In the West ... for at least two hundred years, being in love has come to be the only acceptable grounds for marriage. And love, or the emotional quality of the couple relationship, has also become increasingly important as the principal reason for staying together.[27]

In order to understand the fears behind marriages of convenience, one has to think, as suggested by Abraham and Van Schendel, as the state, examining state parlance and state perspective on the incoming

---

[23] Robert J. McWhirter, *The Criminal Lawyer's Guide to Immigration Law: Questions and Answers* (Chicago: American Bar Association, 2006), 203.

[24] Jennifer Hirsch and Holly Wardlow, *Modern Loves. The Anthropology of Romantic Courtship and Companionate Marriage* (Ann Arbor: The University of Michigan Press, 2006), 5.

[25] See European Council Resolution 4 December 1997, which directs Member States to adopt measures which will test the 'authenticity' of marriages 'of convenience': a lack of cohabitation, no financial contribution to the marriage, having a partner who speaks a different language can all be counted as evidence that the marriage may not be 'authentic.'

[26] Hirsch and Wardlow, *Modern Loves*, 2.

[27] Arlene Skolnick, 'Grounds for Marriage: Reflections and Research on an Institution in Transition,' in *Inside the American Couple: New Thinking, New Challenges*, ed. Marilyn Yalom and Laura Carstensen (Berkeley: University of California Press, 2002), 150.

migrants.[28] Policing so-called 'sham marriages' is grounded on a constellation of fears and threats represented for the Western state. As Schaeffer points out:

> For mainstream society, from Hollywood to Immigration Customs Enforcement (ICE), the marriage of convenience typifies a social contract that is not only outmoded but a threat to modern societies based on love, or the freedom of choice, individualism, and democratic governance based on equality.[29]

Besides being perceived as a threat to Western democracies—in particular values of the freedom of choice and individualism—another reason given by EU member state governments for scrutinizing suspicious marriages that lead to 'citizenship for sale' is security considerations. There have been fears articulated by scholars and security officials alike that marriage could be used as a means for terrorists and other undesired individuals to enter the country.[30] Furthermore, sham marriages are increasingly viewed as a threat because of narratives of organized crime reinforced by state officials,[31] particularly in the UK where a number of criminal networks allegedly organizing 'sham marriages' for profit have recently been prosecuted.[32]

Although most of the well-known cases of sham marriages do include monetary exchange processes and financial benefits received by an EU spouse, there are exceptions. Scholars point out that a sham marriage can be interpreted not as a criminal act, but as an example of humane behaviour, a noble act of a 'good Samaritan' seeking to help his proxy.[33]

---

[28] Itty Abraham and Willem van Schendel, eds., *Illicit Flows and Criminal Things: States, Borders, and the Other Side of Globalization* (Bloomington and Indianapolis: Indiana University Press, 2005).

[29] Schaeffer, *Love and Empire*, 3.

[30] Janice Kephart, 'Immigration and Terrorism: Moving Beyond the 9/11 Staff Report on Terrorist Travel,' CIS Paper No. 24. (Washington, DC: Center for Immigration Studies 2005); Daveed Gartenstein-Ross and Kyle Dabruzzi, 'The Convergence of Crime and Terror: Law Enforcement Opportunities and Perils,' in *Policing Terrorism Report 1* (The Manhattan Institute: New York, 2007).

[31] In the UK immigration officials besides regularly reporting about success of cracking down on immigration offenders and organized crime of sham marriages, also encourage people to participate in crime detection by collaborating with the police, see 'Report an Immigration Crime,' *GOV.UK*, accessed 10 November 2016, https://www.gov.uk/report-immigration-crime.

[32] Data from National Crime Agency, see 'Eight Arrests in Sham Marriage Operations,' *NCA*, accessed 25 October 2016, http://www.nationalcrimeagency.gov.uk/news/232-eight-arrests-in-sham- marriage-operations.

[33] Clara Kücük, 'Binationale Ehe—Schutzehe—Scheinehe—Zweckehe?' *Für Vernetzung—Gegen Ausgrenzung*, 2005, http://www.d-a-s-h.org/dossier/13 /05_binational.html, accessed 20 November 2014.

While a significant body of legal scholarship sheds light at the state-of-art of legislation regarding 'sham' marriages and marriage migration control, there is a lack of understanding of why individuals engage in such marriages and how they cope with the punitive attitudes of immigration authorities.[34] It is known that persons involved in moving objects, people, and practices across state borders may or may not share the state's view that their activities are criminal. If they consider their activities legitimate, they present yet another contradiction in defining il(licitness).[35] As Abraham and Van Schendel argue, 'what state officials view as illegal and therefore criminal behaviour may be considered well within the bounds of the acceptable by those who display this behaviour and by the communities to which they belong.'[36] Focusing on Ecuadorian labour migrants in Spain, Kyle and Siracusa argue that:

> what has been lacking from most public debates and new reporting on migrant smuggling and human trafficking is the empirical reality of how migrants themselves view their actions ... By understanding the political and moral reasoning of undocumented workers and those who aid them, we gain a better understanding of why so many non-criminals are choosing to collectively disregard some states' immigration laws prohibiting unauthorized entry and work.[37]

In a similar vein, in this article through the case study of Gabriela I pose the following questions: how do those who engage in strategies such as those framed as 'sham marriages' describe and rationalize their experiences and decisions? Do they associate themselves with lawbreakers, and if not, what kind of legitimizing discourses do they construct against the state's perception of illegitimacy? Furthermore, focusing my inquiry on the German term *Schutzehe* [literally: protection marriage], I explore how the issue of sham marriages is framed in the context of Germany.

---

[34] Marie-Claire Foblets and Dirk Vanheule, 'Marriages of Convenience in Belgium: The Punitive Approach Gains Ground in Migration Law,' *European Journal of Migration and Law* 8/3–4 (2006), 263–80; De Hart, Betty and Saskia Bonjour, 'A Proper Wife, a Proper Marriage: Constructions Of "Us" And "Them" in Dutch Family Migration Policy,' *European Journal of Women's Studies* 20/1 (2013), 61–76 and 'Introduction: The Marriage of Convenience in European Immigration Law,' *European Journal of Migration and Law* 8/3 (2006), 251–62; Hélène Neveu Kringlebach, '"Mixed Marriage," Citizenship and the Policing of Intimacy in Contemporary France,' University of Oxford, 2013, accessed 20 January 2015, http://www.migration.ox.ac.uk/odp/pdfs.

[35] Abraham and van Schendel, *Illicit Flows*, 25.

[36] Abraham and Van Schendel, *Illicit Flows*, 25.

[37] David Kyle and Christina Siracusa, 'Seeing the State Like a Migrant: Why So Many Non-Criminals Break Immigration Laws,' in Abraham and van Schendel, *Illicit Flows*, 155.

Case Study: Gabriela

In the framework of the present research I draw on semi-structured interviews and ethnographic fieldwork conducted in Germany between October 2013 and March 2014 collecting data in close collaboration with the NGOs for migrant women and courses of German languages in Hamburg. Besides interviewing foreign spouses of German citizens, I have also conducted interviews with lawyers and service providers. My analysis is guided by the analytical framework of 'crimmigration' when speaking about policing foreign spouses of German citizens and normative imaginations of family life from the state perspective, and victimization claims frequently applied in relation to women from non-EU countries. Among all the case studies I will be focusing on the story of Gabriela, as it perfectly exemplifies both tendencies, portraying *Schutzehe* in its complexity. Gabriela, whom I met at one of the language courses of conversational German in Hamburg while conducting 'snowball sampling,'[38] came to Germany 6 years ago from Ecuador. Her main objective was to gain employment and earn a reasonable wage. Although most of her relatives and friends at that time chose Spain as a country where they would not have any language problems, she opted for Germany, as she had heard it was a place with abundant economic opportunities coupled with personal security, which was lacking in her own country: 'It is more peaceful and tranquil here. Also there are more jobs available. I never regretted my choice.'

Back home in Guayaquil, a coastal city in Ecuador, she managed a small business. She describes it as a turbulent time, when once in while she would get robbed by local criminals. She had also been assaulted on the street in the middle of the day, and hence she never felt secure in her home city. The decision to move to Germany came quite spontaneously, after one of her close friends moved to Bremen. She came to Hamburg as a tourist, and decided to stay. Having found a part-time job illegally cleaning the house of a German family via some of her Ecuadorian contacts, she was trying her best to remain invisible:

> In the beginning I took all the measures of precautions. I knew: if the police catch me, I have no chance. I tried walking alone, as I knew there was a higher chance of getting caught while in a group. I also couldn't send money to my family because I knew the police was vigilant. When Ecuadorians go to send remittances, that is when they get caught. Instead,

---

[38] Snowball sampling is a non-probability sampling technique that is used to identify potential subjects in studies where subjects are hard to locate (Rowland Atkinson and John Flint, 'Accessing Hidden and Hard-To-Reach Populations: Snowball Research Strategies,' *Social Research Update*, 33/1 [2001]).

I kept money home ... Even at my own house I was quite frustrated, as I was afraid someone suddenly could enter and grab me. So I was hiding.

Living with the constant fear of detection during her undocumented stay in Germany, Gabriela considered many options. One was to marry a German man or an Ecuadorian who had an EU passport. However, she could not afford to pay one, as the usual price of the 'marriage deal' was EUR 7,000 at that time, and after paying her tickets to Europe she was completely broke. The marriage idea was a common one amongst the Ecuadorian community in Hamburg. Some had already managed to get 'papeles' or came to Germany with a Spanish passport, and were eager to help the compatriots in exchange for a sum of money. However, Gabriela was reluctant to pay for a marriage, partly because she did not have enough money and partly because she did not trust people who offered her such a deal. One night, despite all the precautions she had taken, Gabriela was arrested while walking on the street with a couple of Ecuadorian friends and brought to jail. Although it was likely a detention center and not a jail where she was taken, while narrating her story Gabriela uses the Spanish word 'la cárcel' (jail). She did not seem eager to share memories about her time in the detention center, except for the fact that she was dreading the idea of returning back home to Ecuador penniless. Since she did not have a valid visa to stay in Germany, she was threatened with deportation as soon as all bureaucratic procedures were over. Not having any alternative at hand, she decided to call Hanspeter, the only German she knew:

When he heard about my troubles ... he offered me to get married. Just like that, because he was against all the immigration system in his country, and he believed there shouldn't be any borders. He was very sympathetic about us, people 'sin papeles' (without documents). ... Eventually, it was not possible for me to stay in Germany even though he wanted to marry me. I had to go back to Ecuador, apply for a spousal visa, and come back via this route.

After Gabriela left for Ecuador, Hanspeter paid for all the visa paperwork. He went multiple times to the Alien's Office trying to find out about the rules and inquire whether their spousal visa application was ready. In just over one year, Gabriela received a clearance visa to re-enter Germany. According to Gabriela, in the beginning it was all 'for papers,' but gradually they both re-evaluated their feelings, and now it is 'for real.' The couple has a long-distance relationship, since Hanspeter works and lives with his elderly parents in Hannover, and Gabriela prefers Hamburg which is about one hour away by car. Both do not want to move in together, and instead see each other on weekends. Hanspeter mostly comes to Hamburg for a couple of days, since Gabriela does not get along with his parents. He has twice visited Gabriela's family in Ecuador—the couple having travelled there for a summer holiday. Despite being in possession of a valid visa, Gabriela still prefers working 'under the table,' since this way she can maintain free housing and does not have to pay income tax. Unlike some of her friends, Gabriela did not face any strict interrogation or surveillance of her private life related to the enquiries of whether her marriage was 'fraudulent,' even though the couple lived apart and, according to EU definitions, it could be considered as a fraud. This is how she describes her experience of dealing with authorities:[39]

> Last time I went to prolong my residence permit in the Alien's Office, it went very smooth. No one asked questions. Except for one of the ladies told me I had to put more effort into learning German. I have been here 7 years, but I still do not understand people well. I told her: yes, I will learn, I will learn [smiles]. I think it is really easy in Hannover because it is a smaller city. I have heard from other Latinos that it is not like that in Hamburg or Berlin. They are asked all sort of questions. One of my friends also got married for papers, and the Alien's Office workers were quite suspicious. They called both of them for several interviews.

As one immigration lawyer concludes, when asked about 'sham' marriages among his clientele:

> From time to time I have some clients who appear to be in a 'sham' marriage, but do not really discuss it, unless it has a direct link to the case. How do I know it? I see the couple is applying for divorce, but they do not speak a common language. Once I had a client who married his best friend so that she did not have to go back to her country after completion of studies in Hamburg. At the same time, both had 'real' partners. This does not surprise us any more. ... But I have never seen a case of a 'sham' marriage brought to the court, at least not in my practice.[40]

The right to join a spouse who is a legal resident in Germany is a basic right that is not only codified through international human rights conventions, but is also incorporated into the Constitution,

---

[39] European Council Resolutions of 4 December 1997 on measures to be adopted on the combating of marriages of convenience, see 'EUR-Lex l33063 EN,' *EUR-Lex*, accessed 10 November 2016, http://eur-lex.europa.eu/legal-content/EN/TXT/?uri=URISERV:l33063.

[40] The lawyer in this case has explained to me that few cases get prosecuted because it is very difficult to collect evidence and prove that a marriage is not genuine.

as according to the Art. 6.1 *Grundgesetz*, marriage and the family enjoy the special protection of the state.[41] Under German legislation, following a marriage to a German citizen, a spouse from outside of the European Economic Area is legally entitled to a residence permit under the Residence Act, or Aufenthaltsgesetz (AufenthG).[42] The condition is that a spouse with German citizenship has his/ her habitual residence in the Federal Territory. Notwithstanding the fact that there are criminal groups involved in organized crime linked to 'marriages for papers' in the European Union and sham marriages are framed as a threat to the state, it also happens that marriage is contracted because of pure and idealistic motivations, such as the quest for equality regardless of citizenship status, and the desire to help to undocumented migrants. My conversation with Hanspeter demonstrated that motivations for sham marriages can be linked to political ideals beyond visa regulations, and as an act of resistance against the existing governmental stance on immigration. Hanspeter belonged to a left-wing organization and volunteered in a non-profit organization that took care of refugees, and has long been sympathetic to rejected asylum seekers and undocu- mented migrants from Latin America. Speaking about his socio-political position regarding migrants in Germany, he underlines:

> I don't believe in borders, they are artificial entities created by humans. I would do what it takes to challenge existing system. ... They would have deported her [Gabriela] without any possibility of coming back to Germany, if not our marriage. I find it unjust and inhumane ... States are big machines to control our actions ... One needs to show resistance, some sort of resistance to support underprivileged ones, exploited ones.

Political Activism in Germany

On 1 May 2006, hundreds of thousands of people marched the streets of various cities in the United States to protest against the persecution of irregular migrants. The 'Day Without Immigrants' protests were part of a series of events staged in spring 2006 as a grassroots political response to the plight of the growing number of non-citizen migrant workers in the United States.[43] In an *L.A. Weekly* article entitled 'Make

[41] Can Aybek, Gary Straßburger, and Ilknur Yüksel-Kaptanoglu, 'Marriage Migration from Turkey to Germany: Risks and Coping Strategies of Transnational Couples,' in *Spatial Mobility, Migration and Living Arrangements*, ed. Can Aybek et al. (Dordrecht: Springer, 2015), 24.

[42] 'Residence Act,' *IUSCOMP*, accessed 10 November 2016, http://www.iuscomp. org/gla/statutes/AufenthG.htm.

[43] Benita Heiskanen, 'A Day Without Immigrants,' *European Journal of American*

a run for the altar,' Arellano describes how some US citizens of Latin American background residing in California take risks exercising their right to marry an undocumented migrant to protest against punitive migration legislation.[44] Such risk-taking through marriage can be understood as a kind of transnational activism. Nicola Piper shows that recent research on transnational political activism demonstrates its effectiveness is related to networking and alliance building, nationally and transnationally.[45] In Germany, a new wave of political activism aimed at support and demonstration of solidarity with migrants and undocumented individuals emerged following Lampedusa events. On the 2 November 2013, a public demonstration was held in Hamburg campaigning for the rights of West African migrants who were denied asylum in Germany and were in danger of deportation.[46] More than 10,000 people participated, and the event was followed by several other public initiatives which similarly gathered large numbers. Squats, left-wing political organizations, and even religious institutions, including St Pauli Church, opened their doors to host the refugees.[47] In Germany the topic of police investigations of binational families' private life received wide coverage by journalists and human rights activists after a German-Turkish couple, following immigration authorities' investigation, brought their case to the court in Bremen. The Alien's Office decided that it was a 'sham marriage,' because it allegedly found some disparities and inconsistencies in the spouses' answers to questions about their private lives. The couples' lawyer maintained that the interrogation and search of their home violated their fundamental right to privacy and 'informational self-determination.'[48] *Schutzehe* which,

Studies 4/3 (2009), 1–14.

[44] Gustavo Arellano 'Make a Run For the Altar,' *L.A. Weekly*, 2010, accessed 10 November 2016, http://www.laweekly.com/news/make -a-run-for-the-altar-2165879.

[45] Nicola Piper, 'Governance of Migration and Transnationalism of Migrant's Rights—An Organisational Perspective,' in *Transnationalisation and Development(s): Towards a North-South Perspective* (Bielefeld: Center for Interdisciplinary Research, 2007), accessed 10 November 2016, https://www.uni-bielefeld.de/tdrc/ag_comcad/downloads/workingpaper_22_Piper.pdf.

[46] 'Hamburg Unrest: One City, Two Sides, Thousands of Refugees,' *Spiegel*, 2013, http://www.spiegel.de/international/germany/hamburg-conflict-over-lampedusa-refugees-grow-more-heated-a-929216.html.

[47] Florian Wilde, 'Refugee Protests and the Right to the City in Hamburg,' *Transform: European Network for Alternative Thinking and Political Dialogue*, 2014, accessed 10 November 2016, http://www.transform-network.net/blog/blog-2014/news/detail/Blog/-d7bc6bebb7.html.

[48] Rolf Gösner, 'Peinliche Ausforschung der Privatsphäre. Scheinehe-Ermittlung gegen Binationale Ehepaare,' Grundrechte-Report 2013, *Internationale Liga für Menschenrechte*, accessed 1 September 2014, http://ilmr.de/wp-content/ uploads/2013/06/

to recall means 'protection marriage,' encompasses situations wherein a German national marries an undocumented person to help the latter avoid expulsion or necessity to leave the country when his visa expires.[49] Based on my media discourse analysis of Internet-based newspapers and other materials in German language regarding *Scheinehe*, I argue that in Germany this question has recently been discussed in regard to human rights, migration (particularly the concept of *Willkommenskultur*— welcoming culture) and integration of migrants.[50] The questions posed to the couples during the interrogation (e.g. Who sleeps on the left side of the bed? Does your spouse bring your gifts?) as well as the whole concept of surveillance of couples' intimate lives by government authorities are sharply criticized by human rights activists.[51] It is this context in which 'sham' marriages in the German context have been re-framed as 'protection' marriages.[52]

Reflecting on the essence of the term 'solidarity marriage,' how can this concept be explained in the German context? There are several reasons stemming from German history. From a historical vantage point, James Hollifield argues that 'the new federalism in postwar Germany and the conscious suppression of the nationalist and militarist ideals of the unitary Prussian state ... have contributed to the development of liberalism in German politics.'[53] Furthermore, as Hollifield suggests, 'German political parties, in contrast to their French counterparts, have gone to great lengths to avoid politicizing immigration policy,' with the intention of repressing nationalist senti-ments and not allowing even the hint of the racist policies of the Third Reich.[54] In a similar vein, Ellermann contends that the history of the Holocaust has given rise to a political culture shaped by a particularly profound ambivalence about the state's use of coercion. Immigration bureaucracies thus operate in highly politicized milieus characterized

Goessner-Scheinehe-Befragg-GRR-2013.pdf.

[49] '*Schutzehe*' (protection marriage) is an ironic derivation from the German term '*Scheinehe*' (sham marriage).

[50] Doris Akrap, 'Germany's Response to the Refugee Crisis Is Admirable. But I Fear It Cannot Last,' *The Guardian*, 2015, accessed 10 December 2015, http://www.theguardian.com/commentisfree/2015/sep/06/germany-refugee-crisis-syrian/.

[51] Andrea Dernbach, 'Scheinehe: Lauschangriff aufs Ehebett,' *Der Tagesspiegel*, 2012, accessed 5 February 2014, http://www.tagesspiegel.de/politik/scheinehe-lauschangriff-aufs-ehebett/6732628.html.

[52] The stories of German citizens married to non-EU nationals under the threat of deportation have received abroad coverage by mainstream mass-media channels such as 'Spiegel' and 'Taz.'

[53] James F. Hollifield, *Immigrants, Markets, and States: The Political Economy of Postwar Europe* (Cambridge, Mass., and London: Harvard University Press 1992), 203.

[54] Hollifield, *Immigrants, Markets, and States*, 200.

by sustained grass-roots mobilization against particular deportation cases.[55] Therefore, the historical legacy of the twentieth century has produced complex ambivalence toward the use of state power and coercion in contemporary German society.

The other reason consists in the fact that the construct of 'illegal migration' is relatively new in Germany, coinciding with the end of guest worker programs in the early 1970s.[56] Even though 'Überfremdung' and 'Fremdkörper' concepts have been circulating in German-speaking discourse during different historical times, they have also consolidated the left movement triggering grassroots responses in support of migrants.[57] The quest for the protection of migrants' rights, particularly the rights of foreign spouses, transnational marriages and potential simplification of legal obstacles linked to family reunification is not a new phenomenon. Its origins can be traced back to 1972 when IAF (Alliance of German Women Married to Foreigners) was founded by a group of German women married to Middle Eastern men. The main idea underpinning IAF was that emancipatory goals for women cannot be separated from German policies regarding foreigners. Foreigners' rights advocacy regarding citizenship and binational couples has remained strong since then, this strength being exemplified by the activities of NGO's and networks created for migrants such as *Verband Binationaler Familien und Partnerschaften* (Association for binational families and partnerships).[58]

Germany currently ranks as the world's third-largest migrant receiving nation.[59] The country has seen migration across its national boundaries since its founding, with an especially dramatic increase since World War II in West Germany, when immigrant labour increased

---

[55] Antje Ellermann, 'Street-level Democracy? How Immigration Bureaucrats Manage Public Opposition,' *West European Politics*, 29/2 (2006), 293–309.

[56] Heide Castañeda, 'Deportation Deferred: "Illegality", Visibility, and Recognition in Contemporary German,' in *The Deportation Regime: Sovereignty, Space, and the Freedom of Movement*, eds. Nicholas de Genova and Nathalie Peutz (Durham: Duke University Press, 2010), 245.

[57] *Überfremdung*, the idea by which excessive numbers of foreigners could threaten a national identity, was coined in Switzerland and further utilized by right-wing politicians in anti-immigration discourses, see Yvonne Riaño and Doris Wastl-Walter, 'Immigration Policies, State Discourses on Foreigners and the Politics of Identity in Switzerland,' *Environment and Planning* A 38/9 (2006), 1693–713.

[58] See 'about us,' *Verband binationaler Familien und Partnerschaften*, http://www.verband-binationaler.de/index.php?id=wir-ueber-uns.

[59] Heide Castañeda, 'Deportation Deferred: "Illegality", Visibility, and Recognition in Contemporary Germany,' in *The Deportation Regime: Sovereignty, Space, and the Freedom of Movement*, eds. Nicholas de Genova and Nathalie Peutz (Durham: Duke University Press, 2010).

following the creation of recruitment programs.[60] Hamburg is the second largest city in Germany and the second smallest Federal State. As one of the most affluent cities in Europe with many jobs linked to the port industry, Hamburg attracts many migrants from the south of Europe and from non-EU countries due to its numerous employment opportunities. According to the study commissioned by *Diakonisches Werk* Hamburg, one of the biggest non-profit service providers in Hamburg, in co-operation with *Nordelbische Kirche*, as of 2009 there were between 6,000 and 22,000 migrants residing in Hamburg without a valid residence permit.[61] The study has established that most of the paperless migrants who live in Hamburg come from Latin America and West Africa; the immigrants originally from Ghana and Ecuador are predominant. Social workers assume that these people tend to look for support within their own ethnic networks rather than from official sources or advice centers so that they are less visible. The latter fact was also confirmed in the interviews with Gabriela, since she mentioned a couple of times that before being detained she tried to avoid getting together with fellow Ecuadorians. As de Giorgi emphasizes, detention of irregular migrants occurs not due to individual crimes or behaviour, but because of their membership of an 'illegitimate' group.[62] In Germany irregular residence is a criminal offense that is usually punishable with fines and detention.[63] However, even though irregular residence is a criminal offence in Germany, irregular migrants are not usually detained under criminal law. In this way, detention has been framed as a 'safeguarding' measure, in order to protect against exclusion, rather than—as some have argued—as a punitive approach to non-citizenship.[64]

The German Residency Act makes it obligatory for authorities to report paperless individuals. This has serious consequences as it requires all public bodies to notify the Immigration Authority

---

[60] Castañeda, 'Deportation Deferred,' 247.

[61] Dita Vogel, Manuel Aßner, Emilija Mitrović and Anna Kühne, 'Living Without Papers. About the Lives of People Without Valid Residency Permits in Hamburg,' *Diakonisches Werk Hamburg*, 2009, accessed 10 November 2016, https://www.diakonie-hamburg.de/export/sites/default/.content/downloads/Fachbereiche/ME/Living-without-papers_english.pdf.

[62] Alessandro De Giorgi, *Re-thinking the Political Economy of Punishment: Perspectives on post-Fordism and Penal Politics* (Aldershot: Ashgate Publishing, 2006), 114.

[63] Anton van Kalmthout et al., eds., *Foreigners in European Prisons* (Tilburg: Wolf Legal Publishers, 2007), 64.

[64] Frieder Dünkel et al., 'Germany,' in van Kalmthout, *Foreigners in European prisons*, 377.

(*Ausländerbehörde*) of anyone who does not have a valid residency permit. The duty to report is seen by some officials as an indispensable tool in the attempt to control migration. What it means in practice is that paperless migrants avoid all contact with public bodies so as to prevent being found out.[65] Hence, partly due to the recent legislation and low level of fear among the general public regarding immigration offenders, Hamburg turns out to be a city where it is common to spot the graffiti *Kein Mensch ist Illegal* (no one is illegal) on the walls close to the port, or to discover a wide array of initiatives supporting migrants without papers under the motto *Papierlos heißt nicht rechtlos* (Paperless does not mean rightless) such as protests, language classes, yoga courses, or other empowerment practices or campaigning.[66] Some claim that Hamburg has always been an arena for political resistance, which can be exemplified by the struggle against privatization and high rental prices.[67] Besides *Diakonie* and the network *Kein Mensch ist Illegal*, many other organizations help undocumented migrants or migrants whose visa is about to expire. As one of the NGO workers informed me:

> At our NGO we are not supposed to help undocumented migrants, since there are so many other organizations that provide assistance. And yet I do it. If a woman without papers comes to seek advice, I do all my best, but don't include in the statistics that she doesn't have a residence permit. I don't believe in borders.

Hanspeter's ideas resonate with the above opinion expressed by the service provider in support of undocumented migrants. Gabriela's husband does not see himself as a lawbreaker but rather as a protector of underprivileged and marginalized individuals. Whereas a criminal law system would classify him as a 'wrongdoer,' Hanspeter views his action as morally justified rather than deviant. The debates on societal norms and perceived deviance are at the heart of 'labelling theory' that became a dominant sociological theory of crime in the 1970s. Influenced by the ideas of Durkheim, Mead, and the Chicago School, labelling theorists believe that deviance per se is not a normative concept but is heavily influenced by a dominant legal and political narrative. Howard Becker, one of the key labelling theorists, delineated the problem of

---

[65] Dita Vogel et al., 'Living without Papers.'

[66] The 'No one is Illegal' network has its parallels with 'Sans Papier' movement in France which emerged in the mid 1990s as a coalition among undocumented migrant workers and asylum seekers asserting the right to live in the country on the basis of cultural ties with France. See Anne McNevin, 'Political Belonging in a Neoliberal era: The Struggle of the Sans-Papiers,' *Citizenship Studies*, 10/2 (2006).

[67] Wilde, 'Refugee Protests.'

labelling this way:

> We [should] direct our attention in research and theory building to the questions: who applied the label of deviant to whom? What consequences does the application of a label has for the person so labeled? Under what circumstances is the label of a deviant successfully applied?[68]

Therefore, the power of those constructing the narrative by defining the nature of the label to be imposed on an act, and an agent (or 'victim') is clearly evident here. Hanspeter would be labeled as a transgressor by state officials but his own idea represents a mixture of rebellion and resistance, laying the ground for a strong rationalizing discourse and demonstrating a drastic difference between meanings attributed to deviant actions. It has been pointed out by Ferrell that labelling theories 'highlight the conflicts of meaning that consistently animate crime and deviance; they demonstrate that the reality of crime and transgression exists as a project under construction, a project emerging from ongoing negotiations of authority and reputation.'[69] Being a product of the authorities' negotiation, marriages of convenience—so-called 'sham' marriages—with undocumented migrants, motivated by political activism and a moral code, represent a site of resistance to the immigration enforcement regimes in Europe.[70]

Conclusion

Marriage enables a privileged and, some might claim, 'respectable' entry to Germany,[71] a right to move across borders and perhaps to conferring citizenship. While Western idealism that views marriage through the prism of romantic sentiments and choice dominates the discourse regulating marriage migration governance, and fears of 'citizenship for sale' available to third nationals trigger stringent immigration surveillance, the binational couples elaborate their own ways to circumvent the system. Through ethnographic study we are able to better grasp the

[68] Howard Becker, *Outsiders: Studies in the Sociology of Deviance* (New York: Free Press, 1963), 3.

[69] Jeff Ferrell et al., *Cultural Criminology: An Invitation.* (London: Sage Publications, 2008), 5.

[70] Evidently, the framework for this 'moral code' should also be subject to interrogation, as it will clearly be constructed through a non-universal, value-laden socio-political paradigm particular to each individual. It is worth considering, however, whether this is any less productive than a legal system which, though purporting to be universal, implicitly reflects a singular moral code.

[71] Schaeffer, *Love and Empire*, 14.

complexities behind the phenomenon of marriages of convenience and the way various forces and rationalization discourses coalesce. I argue that it is crucial to look beyond official discourse attempting to 'think outside conceptual and material grasp of the modern state' approaching the subject of sham marriages through the individual narratives of the individuals involved in them.[72]

The above mentioned case study demonstrated that the framework of social control generates new strategies for challenging social exclusion and acquiring membership. However, the phenomenon of 'solidarity marriage' poses a series of questions for a researcher. Besides theorizing how individuals circumvent migration law with the help of marriage, it is essential to examine how the main actors reflect on it, and what kind of contestations of criminality they utilize, as a thorough analysis 'further destabilizes these categories, and provides an important corrective to those who would distinguish too sharply between law-abiding and criminal persons and acts.'[73] Entering into a 'sham' marriage for the sake of saving a person from deportation, according to official point of view, represents a victimless crime such as prostitution, fraud, and blackmailing. While one can argue to which extent victimless crime can be considered as harmful to the society or state, neither Hanspeter nor Gabriela are inclined to think it harms anyone. Furthermore, they present powerful rationalization discourses based on the political ideology of resistance and opposition to state policies driven by the necessity to legalize Gabriela's migration status. Generating legitimizing discourses of his illicit behaviour, Hansperer contends that law itself is illegitimate, and 'borders should be abolished.' In doing so, he reinforces his political vision and his position on undocumented migrants, and uses marriage as a strategy to advance his political activism.

Although political activism in support of undocumented migrants is an international movement aimed at protesting the lack of existing options for the legalization of irregular migrants, border surveillance and selective approaches to political membership, there are several main points to be made in regard to the German context of research. Binational marriages and solidarity movement in support of undocumented migrants in Germany are closely intertwined with immigration policies and left-wing political activism. However, I argue that *Schutzehe* is a unique perspective within the German context, a lived attempt at spatial justice, which can be explained through a study of German political culture as that which rejects the use of coercion

---

[72] Abraham and Van Schendel, *Illicit Flows*, 10.

[73] Susan Coutin, 'Contesting Criminality: Illegal Immigration and the Spatialization of Legality,' *Theoretical Criminology* 9/1 (2005), 24.

by state power, promotes self-governance, and encourages critique of governmental decisions. Likewise, Germany, compared with other EU countries, boasts a high number of non-profit organizations focusing on the social services and public health, that also greatly contribute to political activism against the criminalization of migration and facilitate rationalizing narratives of 'protection marriage.'[74]

---

[74] According to Thomas Von Hippel, as of 2010 there were around 600,000 associations and 15,000 foundations in Germany ('Nonprofit organizations in Germany,' in *Comparative Corporate Governance of Non-profit Organizations,* eds. Klaus Hopt and Thomas Von Hippel (Cambridge: CUP, 2010), 200.

4

Diaspora, Space, and Tele-Biopolitics

Dafina Paca

Introduction

D iaspora and identity studies continue to increasingly occupy a
central role in social science and cultural studies discussions,
especially around increasingly politicized issues, such as nation,
immigration, asylum, borders and exile.[1] However, scholars continue
to frequently define diaspora through proposed lists or inventories of
characteristics that they apply to different diasporic groups.[2] While
current studies have extensively explored diaspora's nostalgia for the
homeland and relationship with the 'host' society, literature exploring
how the homeland constructs the diaspora is still lacking.

'Diaspora' is a contested and unstable term. As Jana Evans Braziel
and Anita Mannur note, its etymological origins are in the Greek term
diasperien, from *dia*, 'across,' and *sperien*, 'to sow or scatter seeds.'[3]
However, although this meaning is fairly mainstream in the contemporary context, its use is also problematic, suggesting clearly demarcated
geographic territories, national identity, and belonging and dislocation
from fixed nation states, territories, or countries. Such definitions may
not allow for diaspora as a self-ascription or a state of consciousness
and/or social form, and risk falling within the same outdated paradigms

---

[1] Stuart Hall, 'Cultural Identity and Diaspora,' in *Identity: Community, Culture,
Difference*, 222–37, ed. Jonathan Rutherford (London: Lawrence & Wishart, 1990);
Paul Gilroy, *The Black Atlantic: Modernity and Double Consciousness* (Cambridge,
MA: Harvard University Press, 1993); William Safran, 'Diasporas in Modern Societies:
Myths of Homeland and Return,' *Diaspora* 1/1 (1991), 83–99; Khachig Tölölyan,
'Rethinking Diaspora(s): Stateless Power in the Transnational Moment,' *Diaspora* 5/1
(1996), 3–36; Steven Vertovec, 'Three meanings of "Diaspora," Exemplified among
South Asian Religions,' *Diaspora* 6/3 (1997), 277–99.

[2] Safran, 'Diasporas in Modern Societies,' 83–4; Roben Cohen, *Global Diasporas: An
Introduction* (London: UCL Press, 1997), 26; Tölölyan, 'Rethinking Diaspora(s),' 20–7.

[3] Jana Evans Braziel and Anita Mannur, *Theorizing Diaspora: A Reader* (Oxford:
Blackwell, 2003), 1.

that referred to 'race' and ethnicity.[4] As such, experiences of the diaspora/ric, outside a territoriality of some kind, and, moreover, the relationships that homelands have with their diaspora have largely been ignored.

Kosovo and the Balkans drew much attention during the 1990s predominantly due to the nature of the conflict and the ethnic cleansing that ensued. Studies of the Kosovo Albanian diaspora, especially in the UK, have steadily emerged since the 1990s, but the number remains low and limited, mainly focusing on Kosovo Albanians as immigrants or 'new migrants.'[5] Some important work has emerged, which explores Kosovo Albanian identity and integration.[6] However diaspora research, especially that originating from Kosovo, predominantly focuses on policy, remittances, homeland development, and brain drain projects.[7] As Levitt and Glick Schiller state:

> Our analytical lens must necessarily broaden and deepen because migrants are often embedded in multi-layered, multi-sited trans-national social fields, encompassing those who move and those who stay behind.[8]

This chapter shifts the focus to examine the construction of diaspora by the Ministry of Diaspora. Most countries have established institutions and policies to enable organized institutional ties with diasporas and/or expatriate communities. For example, the UK has the Foreign and Commonwealth Office and according to a study led by Dovelyn Agunias,[9] there are 45 diaspora engagement institutions

[4] Martin Sökefeld, 'Mobilizing in Transnational Space: A Social Movement Approach to the Formation of Diaspora,' *Global Networks* 6/3 (2006), 265–84; Floya Anthias, 'Evaluating diaspora': beyond ethnicity?' *Sociology* 32/3 (1998), 557–80; Floya Anthias, 'New Hybridities, Old Concepts: The Limits of "Culture",' *Ethnic and Racial Studies* 24/4 (2001), 619–41.

[5] Zana Vathi and Russell King, '"Have You Got the British?": Narratives of Migration and Settlement Among Albanian-Origin Immigrants in London,' *Ethnic and Racial Studies* 36/11 (2013), 1829–48.

[6] Denisa Kostovicova and Albert Prestreshi, 'Education, Gender and Religion: Identity Transformations Among Kosovo Albanians in London,' *Journal of Ethnic and Migration Studies* 29/6 (2003), 1079–96.

[7] Jennifer Brinkerhoff, 'Diasporas and Conflict Societies: Conflict Entrepreneurs, Competing Interests or Contributors to Stability and Development?' *Conflict, Security & Development* 11/02 (2011), 115–43; Russell King and Julie Vullnetari, 'Remittances, Return, Diaspora: Framing the Debate in the Context of Albania and Kosova,' *Southeast European and Black Sea Studies* 9/4 (2009), 385–406; Wiebke Meyer et al., 'Who Remits More? Who Remits Less? Evidence from Kosovar Migrants in Germany and Their Households of Origin,' *Oxford Development Studies* 40/4 (2012), 443–66.

[8] Peggy Levitt and Nina Glick Schiller, 'Conceptualizing Simultaneity: A Transnational Social Field Perspective on Society,' *International Migration Review* 38/3 (2004), 1003.

[9] Dovelyn Agunias, *Closing the Distance* (Washington, DC: Migration Policy

in 30 developing countries that they carried out their research. These institutions have recently proliferated, especially in developing countries, with the aim of among others to stretch influence and attract investment for development.[10] Thus Kosovo, in common with many other countries—particularly those with recent increased migration and those relying heavily on remittances from their diaspora—has also sought to establish ties in order to benefit from its diaspora population.[11] As the Minister for Diaspora Ibrahim Makolli stated, the Kosovo diaspora is 'a community that without a doubt presents one of our strongest potentials both financially and culturally.'[12] In thinking through questions of spatial justice, there is thus a pressing need to study the role of the homeland in constructing diaspora.[13]

Etienne Balibar and Immanuel Wallerstein note that European borders are vacillating and are currently 'irreversibly coming undone.'[14] This phenomenon can be clearly observed in the simultaneous disintegration of former Yugoslavia and the integration of the European Union. Caught up in these two processes, like many former Yugoslav republics, is the former Autonomous Yugoslav Province of Kosovo.

The disintegration of Yugoslavia resulted in the largest forced migration of people in Europe since World War Two. However, throughout the twentieth century migration from Kosovo was a common occurrence. Following the end of the Balkan Wars in 1913, people migrated from Kosovo to various locations around Europe. Furthermore, migration for economic reasons was well established through the guest-worker 'Gastarbaiter' agreements between Yugoslavia and Western Europe. Kosovo was one of the poorest provinces in the former Yugoslavia

Institute, 2009).

[10] Alan Gamlen, 'Diaspora Institutions and Diaspora Governance,' *International Migration Review* 48/1 (2014), 180–217; Tjai Nielsen and Liesl Riddle, 'Investing in Peace: The Motivational Dynamics of Diaspora Investment in Post-Conflict Economies,' *Journal of Business Ethics* 89/4 (2009), 435–48.

[11] Dina Ionescu, *Engaging Diasporas as Development Partners for Home and Destination Countries: Challenges for Policymakers*, (Geneva: International Organization for Migration, 2006); Anera Alishani and Arta Nushi, 'Migration and Development: The Effects of Remittances on Education and Health of Family Members Left behind for the Case of Kosovo,' Analytical Journal 5/1 (2012).

[12] 'News: The Latest News and Updates from the Innovation Centre Kosovo,' *ICK*, accessed 10 November 2016, http://ickosovo.com/news/digitalizing-kosovos-diaspora/.

[13] FID Forum for Democratic Initiative, *Diaspora as a Driving Force for Development in Kosovo: Myth or Reality?* (FID, 2009); Behar Xharra and Martin Wählisch, *Beyond Remittances: Public Diplomacy and Kosovo's Diaspora* (Pristina: Foreign Policy Club, 2012).

[14] Etienne Balibar and Immanuel Wallerstein, *Race, Nation, Class: Ambiguous Identities* (London: Verso, 1998), 217.

and despite evidence of post-conflict development in the first decade of the twenty-first century it is still one of the poorest regions in the Balkans. Persecution of Kosovo Albanians during the Milosevic regime in the 1990s forced many to migrate, seeking political asylum around the world. It is estimated that some two million people left Yugoslavia and resettled in Western Europe.[15] As a result, in the aftermath of the disintegration of Yugoslavia, the newly emerged nation-states (although not by any means in a similar fashion) have faced challenges of constructing and sustaining national and cultural identities. In these recent endeavours to create nation states, history has been rewritten, and cultural identity fiercely debated.

Kosovo declared independence in 2008. This resulted in a movement to reclaim and redefine Kosovo origins and affiliations, which has also impacted Kosovo identity constructions and discourses of Kosovo Albanian identity inside and outside of Kosovo. Kosovo has drawn much international attention as well as international military intervention. As Tim Judah states:

> Kosovo is a tiny place with a tiny population, yet it was the reason that NATO fought its first war. Recently it has been a major subject of international discord, especially between European and American leaders on the one side and a resurgent Russia on the other. If Kosovo were in central Asia, or Africa, or in the Caucasus, this would not have been the case. Kosovo counts because it is in the middle of Europe. On February 17, 2008, it declared independence, becoming the world's newest and most controversial of states.[16]

The idea that Kosovo, although small, has an untapped resource in its diaspora is also reiterated in many reports. One such recent report, by Behar Xhara and Martin Whalisch, recommends public diplomacy through 'tapping' the diaspora. 'Kosovo's foreign Public Diplomacy could benefit greatly from an untapped resource which has not yet been fully utilized as a foreign policy tool: its diaspora.'[17] Xhara and Whalisch also launched the government-sponsored KosovoDiaspora. org online platform, which focuses on highlighting and celebrating the 'achievements of individuals, groups, and organizations related to Kosovo.' Petrit Selimi, the deputy minister for Foreign Affairs said that 'through this platform, the world will know Kosovo as a country, as

---

[15] Ulrike Ziemer and Sean Roberts, eds., *East European Diasporas, Migration, and Cosmopolitanism* (London: Routledge, 2013).

[16] Tim Judah, *Kosovo* (Oxford: OUP, 2008), xii.

[17] Xhara and Whalisch, *Beyond Remittances*, 6.

well as a thriving society.'[18] Thus using the diaspora for public diplomacy and recognition for Kosovo seems well established, and suggests that the role of diaspora is predominantly seen as an economic and or diplomatic tool for homelands to exploit. This is clearly embedded within the Kosovo Law on Diaspora, which aims to position Kosovo's visibility outside of Kosovo as well as benefit Kosovo through investments by encouraging the diaspora to send money to and/or invest in Kosovo.

Based on interviews conducted at the Kosovo Ministry of Diaspora, this chapter critically analyzes the discursive construction of the diaspora by ministry officials. By identifying and analyzing discursive and rhetorical strategies, I examine how the diaspora is constructed and how the ministry negotiate and construct their role vis-à-vis the diaspora and Kosovo. In order to consider how the Ministry of Diaspora in Kosovo circumscribe, envisage and construct diasporic space it must first be acknowledged that, as Edward Soja argues, space is not only constructed and controlled by human beings, in ways which may be 'unseen by the distant eye,' but nevertheless have profound influence on human actions and behaviour.[19] Furthermore, Edward Said states that:

> Just as none of us are beyond geography, none of us is completely free from the struggle over geography. That struggle is complex and interesting because it is not only about soldiers and cannons but also about ideas, about forms, about images and imaginings.[20]

These spatial constructions can also act as a process of partition, especially in relation to justice and punishment, as Foucault highlights, and exert important biopolitical power and discipline the body.[21] In contemporary societies, as Foucault has argued, biopolitics construct 'social order,' through the exercise of power, discipline, repression, and the construction of identities.[22] This strategy disciplines society, through governance and power while demarcating the borders and 'others' outside this group. This process creates compliance among the majority of citizens allowing for coherence between the discourses of the government and the population. Therefore, space, although seemingly distant is effectively embalmed with power and within such constructions are ideologies competing for control. Soja highlights

---

[18] 'News: The Latest News and Updates from the Innovation Centre Kosovo,' *ICK*, accessed 10 November 2016, http://ickosovo.com/news/digitalizing-kosovos-diaspora/.

[19] Edward Soja, *Postmodern Geographies: The Reassertion of Space in Critical Social Theory* (London: Verso, 1989), 1.

[20] Edward Said, *Orientalism* (New York: Pantheon Books, 1978), 7.

[21] Michel Foucault, *The History of Sexuality* (New York: Pantheon Books, 1978).

[22] Michel Foucault, *Madness and Civilization* (New York: Pantheon Books, 1965).

that this relationality stretches from 'the space of the body and the household, through cities and regions and nation-states, to the global scale.'[23] Therefore, both the Kosovo Ministry of Diaspora and the Law on Diaspora, as adopted by the government of Kosovo, are tools that are constructed to carve out particular space and power.

My critical analysis of the interviews reveals that there are four dominant discourses about the Kosovo diaspora. These include the representation of the diaspora as passive and immobilized and needing the Ministry of Diaspora to 'arouse' and mobilize them, the hegemony of the Albanian language, identity and culture, the risks and anxieties about assimilation, and the constructions of a 'good' diaspora that can be used to promote Kosovo abroad, and contribute back to Kosovo through financial investment and public diplomacy.[24]

This chapter focuses on two interviews with senior Ministry of Diaspora officials. Analyzing the discourses of officials in state institutions is important, for as Judith Butler argues 'making all human beings more like our fellow city dwellers' is a noble notion. However, what is crucial in this process is the state and state institutions: 'if the state is what binds it is also clearly what can and does unbind.'[25] Therefore, state discourses are also instrumental in constructing culture, difference, national and individual identity as well as undertaking the functional role of offering access to work and other services. Since individuals through dialogic interaction, from legal language to institutional engagement, are in constant negotiation with dominant

[23] From paper prepared for presentation at the conference Spatial Justice (Nanterre, Paris, March 2008), 2; Edward Soja, 'The City and Spatial Justice,' *JSSJ*, accessed 10 December 2016, http://www.jssj.org/wp-content/uploads/2012/12/JSSJ1-1en4.pdf.

[24] For the analysis of the language of both the Diaspora Law and the interviews with the Ministry of Diaspora officials, I employed a discourse analytical approach, namely critical discourse analysis (hereafter CDA). CDA is an intertwining and amalgamation of theory and method for the empirical study of the relations between language, discourse and social and cultural developments in different social domains (Ruth Wodak, 'Critical Discourse Analysis and the Study of Doctor-Patient Interaction,' *The Construction of Professional Discourse* 19 [1997], 173). By using a discourse analytical approach, my aim was not to search out what particular people 'truly' meant or feet, on the contrary, my standpoint here was that 'truth' is discursively constructed and achieved only through discourse, therefore discourse and discursive practices were analyzed (Norman Fairclough et al., 'Critical discourse analysis,' *Discourse Studies: A Multidisciplinary Introduction* [2011], 357–78; Louise Phillips, 'Critical discourse analysis,' in *Discourse Analysis as Theory and Method*, eds. Louise Philips and Marianne Jorgenson [London: Sage 2002], 60–95). Therefore, through CDA, I highlight the rhetorical and discursive strategies used to construct and reconstruct the diaspora Kosovo Albanians along dominant hegemonic discourses of identity.

[25] Judith Butler and Gayatri Chakravorty Spivak, *Who Sings the Nation State? Language, Politics, Belonging* (Oxford: Seagull Books, 2007), 5.

hegemonic discourses about what they should or should not be, the notion of who belongs to 'us' and who belongs to 'them' is central, both in the case of 'host' states as well as in 'the homeland.' What is at stake is dominant hegemonic discourses and governmentality, in a Foucauldian sense, that constructs a binary of insiders and outsiders. In contemporary societies, as Foucault has argued, biopolitics construct 'a social field of regulated practices,' through the exercise of power, discipline, repression and the construction of identities.[26] This strategy disciplines society through governance and power, while demarcating the borders and 'others' outside this group in a dialogical process with individuals constructing and representing populations at home and abroad, as well as influencing subjective constructions of identity.

The chapter is divided into four main sections. The first section outlines the key institutional and legal structures regarding the Kosovo Law on Diaspora. The next section focuses on the discursive strategy that depicts the diaspora as a passive community. Following on from this, the third section analyzes the use of rhetorical strategies to justify the establishment of cultural centres for the diaspora. Finally, the last section explores the focus on attracting financial investment and public diplomacy.

The Ministry of Diaspora, Diaspora Law and Policy

The Ministry of Diaspora in Kosovo was established in May 2011. The ministry was created based on Kosovo's constitution (Art. 65) and the Law on Diaspora was passed by the Kosovo assembly on 15 April 2010.[27] Art. 1 Law on Diaspora states that:

> The purpose of this law is preservation and cultivation of national identity, language, culture and education of the Diaspora members and migration and their relations with institutions of Republic of Kosovo.

The lexical choices here focus on constructing a Kosovo collective identity abroad, essentially stretching Kosovo's reach beyond its borders. Moreover, words such as 'preservation' and 'cultivation' imply an imminent threat to Kosovo's 'identity, language, culture and

---

[26] Thomas Lemke, '"The Birth of Bio-Politics": Michel Foucault's Lecture at the Collège de France on Neo-Liberal Governmentality,' *Economy and Society* 30/2 (2001), 194.

[27] 'Law on Diaspora of Kosovo, No. 03/L–171,' *Republic of Kosovo Assembly*, accessed 10 November 2016, http://www.kuvendikosoves.org/common/docs/ligjet/2010-171-ang.pdf.

education' that requires 'preservation and cultivation' through its institutions, thus arguably suggesting a certain anxiety about maintaining and advocating a sense of national identity. This discourse denotes that there is a desire to exert social and political power over individuals, including those abroad. This is a form of Foucauldian biopolitics, more specifically distance based or *tele*-biopolitics, where in this case a diasporic 'social order' is being constructed and a set of relations and identities are being constructed and manipulated from afar. This is disguised with the topoi and argumentation present in the lexicon of the Diaspora Law. The argument suggests that the diaspora is at risk of assimilation, and that Kosovo—through the Ministry of Diaspora and the Law on Diaspora—will protect it. However, what transpires in the second part of the law is a desire to control and use the diaspora through a manipulative construction of particular identities that are preferable and that can *contribute* to Kosovo. Although the second part of the law employs a vocabulary that infers help and does not provoke anxiety around assimilation, in contrast, once the anxiety is established in the first part it allows for a discourse that will enable tapping into these particular identities which are receptive to Kosovo, which will allow Kosovo to benefit from the 'inter-cultural relations between Republic of Kosovo and countries in which the Diaspora is present':

> This law, also, aims to help in organization of the Diaspora in various countries where they live and help, encourage and develop inter-cultural relations between Republic of Kosovo and countries in which the Diaspora is present.

Furthermore, the law is broad, defining 'Migrant or member of Diaspora' as 'any person dwelling or emplaced outside Republic of Kosovo and who was born or has family origins in the Republic of Kosovo.'[28] By including anyone who was born in Kosovo and has family origins in Kosovo, it legally encompasses as many people as possible and their subsequent offspring. However, although this has its benefits for Kosovo, Oliver Bakewell writes that there is a problem with casting such a broad net of self-identification:

> As governments and donors scramble to engage diasporas in development, there is a tendency to claim all who have ancestral origins in a particular country for its diaspora. This is understandable as it broadens the pool of people to whom they can appeal. However, this relationship between individuals and a 'homeland' cannot be assumed and there are dangers

[28] There is a spelling mistake present in the English version of the law, where it states 'Migration' instead of 'Migrant.'

in such assumptions.[29]

According to Bakewell, one of the problems with such assumptions is the risk of benefiting privileged, well-educated and economically wealthy transnational groups. However, it is precisely these groups that are being sought and coveted, since they are seen as potentially able to bring financial investment to enable Kosovo's development but also extend the notion of a Kosovo nation beyond Kosovo's borders. Not only does this create problems for anyone who does not conform to the dominant hegemonic identity, it also creates the potential of extending ethnonationalism, including on-going conflicts, to diasporic communities. This constructs and generalizes the diaspora as nothing more than empty vessels for homeland ideology and nationalism, and is extremely problematic as it generates discourses such as the 'schatzi' phenomenon especially targeting those who are perceived as poor or uneducated.[30] Furthermore, such generalizations imply a lack of agency within the diaspora as is demonstrated in the following section, which examines this construction of the diaspora as 'inactive' and requiring 'awakening.' Generalizations about the diaspora and the role of homelands and special ministries such as the Ministry of Diaspora in Kosovo enable the transmission and biopolitical reach of nations.

'Waking the Diaspora'

This section examines the language used by the officials at the Ministry of Diaspora in Kosovo to construct the diaspora. According to the officials I interviewed, the diaspora and migrants are not well organized and move back and forth between Kosovo and their host countries twice a year, in a 'flock-like' manner. A senior official I interviewed described the diaspora as follows :

A diaspora, which is not active, a diaspora that moves strongly twice within twelve months, regularly in summer and winter. Even in this direction we have developed policies of the Ministry, and implement, make plans and specific programs where eh migrants find themselves in

[29] Oliver Bakewell, *Which Diaspora for Whose Development?: Some Critical Questions about the Roles of African Diaspora Organizations as Development Actors* (Oxford: International Migration Institute, 2009), 1.
[30] Dafina Paca, '"Schatzi": Making Meaning of Diaspora,' *JOMEC Journal* 7 (2015), 1–17, accessed 10 December 2017, https://publications.cardiffuniversitypress.org/index.php/JOMEC/article/view/210.

various forms of activity and pursuits.[31]

Thus, the diaspora is generalized and described as inactive and instinctual, lacking agency and moving only in groups, like flocks of migrating birds. This constructs a unified and singular diaspora, one that does not reflect the hybridity and heterogeneity of diaspora that has now been formalized in diaspora theory in 'host' societies. This also suggests that previous scholarship, by focusing predominantly on diasporas in 'host' societies, have ignored the homogenizing tendencies that can be found in the discourse of 'homelands' in relation to diaspora. In contrast to such constructions, as scholars exploring diaspora and the imagined 'homeland' within 'host' country settings have demonstrated, diasporas are not passive but engaged in practices of resistance and activism. For example, in her work on mobilization and activism by the Kosovo Albanian diaspora in the UK and the US, Maria Koinova found that the diaspora are mobilized and active agents who engage in and initiate activism. She has explored four types of diaspora mobilization, and states that although the Albanian diaspora exemplifies a moderately weak mobilization after the Kosovo 1999 conflict - which resulted in a more active diaspora mobilization—the diaspora is not 'asleep' or uninterested in Kosovo. She writes that the diaspora tends to focus on specific issues, such as sovereignty. As Koinova has observed, the diaspora based in the UK is tactical and engaged when it is able to make a difference in the 'homeland':

> Diaspora entrepreneurs did not find a good reason to lobby the United Kingdom, which was mostly aligned with the sovereignty goal. Reinvigoration of diaspora networks occurred briefly after the 2004 violence in the homeland, but remained ad hoc. Processes of diaspora mobilization were primarily driven from the main secessionist elites in the homeland and not by the diaspora, but mobilization remained weak compared to that in the United States. ... Political disengagement between the Kosovo-based elites and the UK-based diaspora took place almost immediately after the warfare ended for several reasons. Political activists, mostly associated with the KLA, relocated to Kosovo. Many educated diaspora members, mostly with experience in the information technology sector, returned to Kosovo hoping to find good jobs.[32]

[31] *Një mergate e cila nuk është aktive, një mergate qe leviz fuqishem mbrenda dymbedhjet muajësh dy here, në menyr te rregult, në verë dhe ne dimer. Edhe ne këte drejtim ne kemi hartuar politikat e ministris dhe i zbatojm, bëjm plane dhe programe të caktuara ku mergimtaret eh e gjejn veten ne forma te ndryshme te veprimtarise dhe aktivitete te tyre.*

[32]   Maria Koinova, 'Four Types of Diaspora Mobilization: Albanian Diaspora Activism for Kosovo Independence in the US and the UK,' *Foreign Policy Analysis* 9/4

However, the opaque power that is demonstrated through the establishments of ministries of diaspora (where tele-biopolitics are used to control and discipline the diasporic body, without taking into account the heterogeneity of diaspora) can create disillusionment and other problems for the returning diaspora. As Koinova also notes those that returned to Kosovo were at times dissatisfied with Kosovo and subsequently returned to the UK: '[w]hile some became dissatisfied and sought their way back to the United Kingdom, others were keen on voluntary return,' but, fundamentally, 'the diaspora was disillusioned.'[33] Furthermore, such discursive practices, where the diasporic body is constructed alongside potential investment and skills for the homeland, can create a context in which the situation of diaspora in relation to social and economic wellbeing within the 'host' society is seemingly ignored. Therefore, as Koinova reports,'[i]n the words of community leaders, the government "forgot about the diaspora," and their own role as Kosovo representatives in the United Kingdom was disregarded.'[34] Thus, the diasporic body politic is bypassed and the diaspora is only represented alongside its potential to carry dominant hegemonic discourses from the 'homeland.' The emphasis on 'preservation of language, identity and culture' reverberated throughout interviews with ministry officials:

> Ministry of Diaspora is obliged to take care and to develop plans and implement such internal policies for preserving their identity abroad, to preserve the language, culture, history, then it is obliged ... draw up plans and to implement such internal policies towards educating the children of diaspora abroad, ... in many different countries where Albanians live and reside and operate.[35]

This also raises another issue. Kosovo is officially multiethnic, as it demographically consists of six main ethnic groups. Although the Albanian population makes up the majority with around 90 percent, nonetheless the remaining ethnic groups still live in Kosovo and abroad. However, the Roma, Ashkali and Egyptian (or REA) minorities, marginalized in Kosovo, are unacknowledged by the officials. Not only are they predominantly ignored and discriminated against in Kosovo although they make up a considerable part of the diaspora population, they are

(2013), 448.

[33] Koinova, 'Four Types of Diaspora Mobilization,' 448.

[34] Koinova, 'Four Types of Diaspora Mobilization,' 16.

[35] *Ministria e diaspores esht e obliguar qe qe te kujdeset dhe te hartoj plane dhe politika te atilla te zbatoj per ruajtjën e identitit te tyre jasht vendit, per ruajtjen e gjuhes, eh kultures, historis, pastaj eshte eh e obliguar qe eh të hartojë plane dhe te zbatoj politika te atilla ne drejtim te arsimimit te femive te mergates jasht vendit, eh në shume shtete te ndryshme ku jetojn dhe veprojn dhe banojn dhe jetojn shqiptaret.*

mainly ignored by the official discourse, which focuses predominantly on the dominant hegemonic Kosovo Albanian identity.[36] During my interviews with the officials at the ministry, I continuously suggested that the diaspora was not only made up of Kosovo Albanians. Although they argued that the provisions made by the ministry were for all citizens of Kosovo, and informed me that the *Serbian* minority was tended to by Serbia proper (as they did not recognize Kosovo's independence) the lexical choices and generalizations made by the officials all seemed to focus on Albanian language, identity, and culture alone. When an official stated that the ministry is developing provisions for educating the children of Albanian migrants abroad wherever they may live and I interjected that Kosovo is multiethnic, he responded, almost as an afterthought '... yes also other people who are inhabitants of the Republic of Kosovo.' This highlights the exclusion of minority and vulnerable groups, who are also then subjected to racism in 'host' societies. This is important since Kosovo is officially a multiethnic state, however, the essentialism in the official discourse is inherent and is skewed towards the dominant Kosovo Albanian identity, which is taken for granted as the most important ethnic group.

These distance-based biopolitical policies also stretch to tangible projects such as engineering physical spaces for diaspora. Whereas traditionally diasporas themselves established cultural centers and other meeting places, in the case of Kosovo, throughout the interviews the officials at the ministry were very keen to stress their aims to open and operate what they termed 'cultural centers' in different places around the world, to act as 'a home of Kosovans':

> One other policy the Diaspora Ministry is drafting, applying in fact, are the openings of cultural centres through different countries, cultural centres which have to aim to be the home of Kosovans where various forms of activities, and various layers of migrants, can attend for their culture issue, the creation of businesses, mutual recognition, to lobby for Kosovo, to promote Kosovo culture and identity in those countries where these centres are opened, according to the law for the Diaspora and Expatriates of Kosovo.[37]

---

[36] For a detailed examination of this discriminatory omission, see Nando Sigona, 'Between Competing Imaginaries of Statehood: Roma, Ashkali and Egyptian (RAE) Leadership in Newly Independent Kosovo,' *Journal of Ethnic and Migration Studies* 38/8 (2012), 1213–32.

[37] *Nje politikë tjetër që ministria e diaspores esht duke hartuar, duke e zbatuar ne fact, jan edhe hapjet e qendrave kulturore neper vende te ndryshme, qendrat kulturore te cilat kemi per synim qe të jene shtepit e kosoves ku mund te frekuentojnë forma te ndryshme te veprimtarive, dhe shtresa te ndryshme të mërgimtarëve, per qeshtje te tyre te kultures, te krijimit te bisneseve, te njohjes reciproke, te lobimit per kosoves, te*

Such constructions of cultural space enhance the legal and judi-cial distance-based biopolitical power of the Ministry of Diaspora. According to Maren Bak and Kerstin von Brömssen's research on children's diasporic practices, focusing on Kosovo Albanian children in Sweden, diasporic practices involve participation in associations or groups relating to the homeland, and 'religion and rituals, relations to the country of origin, language spoken, participation in and con-struction of transnational networks and communications.'[38] However, by engineering such projects, rather than allowing them to arise inde-pendently and also independently of ministry control, the Ministry's aim to establish cultural centres indicates a strong biopolitical power and desire to not only cultivate Kosovo Albanian diasporic identity, but also control the diasporic body, promote particular nationalistic ideology, political ideology and benefit from the diasporas potential economic power, while at the same time homogenizing the diaspora and excluding hybridity or those poor disenfranchised diaspora.[39] The perception of the diaspora as possessing economic wealth that Kosovo can tap into and attract investment to Kosovo was a major and recurrent theme throughout the interviews.

Investment: 'Those who wish to invest in Kosovo are welcome'

Kosovo is one of the poorest countries in Europe with high unem-ployment (figures range from between 40–50 per cent) therefore one of the main aims throughout the political spectrum in Kosovo is attracting investment and economic development in Kosovo. This was also the main aim represented by those interviewed at the Ministry of Diaspora in Kosovo. The extract below from the interview with a ministry official highlights the importance placed on attracting financial investment and the prevalence of this discourse. What is emphasized above all else is investment from 'highly successful migrants ... who are powerful businessmen.' This acts to alienate others who are perceived as less

---

promovimit te kultures te kosoves, te identitetit te saj ne per ato vende tu ku hapen ato qendra, dhe te kultures, sipas ligjit per diasporen dhe mergaten e kosoves.

[38] Maren Bak and Kerstin von Brömssen, 'Interrogating Childhood and Diaspora through the Voices of Children in Sweden,' *Childhood* 17/1 (2010), 116.

[39] This can also be observed in the conferences that the Kosovo Ministry of Diaspora together with the Ministry of Education in Kosovo organizes for teachers who teach Albanian in the diaspora. The conferences provide the educators with the tools to (as they state in their publications) 'preserve the Albanian national and cultural identity,' as well as providing them with instructions for teaching Kosovo Albanian Diaspora children.

wealthy members of diaspora. This is further emphasized by statements such as 'those who wish to invest in Kosova are welcome,' suggesting that if individuals from the diaspora do not have investment capital they are not as welcome, thus suggesting that the diasporic identity and space are constructed and legitimized through economic values. Further highlighting the potential impact of this on identity politics and political positions, as Doreen Massey outlines, 'issues of space, place and politics run deep. There is a long history of the entanglement of the conceptualisation of space and place with the framing of political positions.'[40]

Furthermore, the discourse is predominantly gendered and aimed at men, which suggest a patriarchal construction of diaspora alongside tradition 'homeland' Kosovo values. As the official at the ministry states:

> Also we by implementing the law, act in it and in those directions so that the policy of the Ministry of Diaspora extends in other forms, in cooperation and in different relations with migrants, for example in matters of investment, and where highly successful migrants there who are powerful businessmen can look to their capitals to bring into Kosovo to establish their own businesses either close family ones or larger projects. Well, I know about some 400 businesses of Kosovo migrants operate and are successful, and they are very good example that those who wish to invest in Kosovo are welcome and have their profits in that already, that they also help the state in the economic development of Kosovo and more.[41]

Nonetheless, Kosovo heavily depends on remittances from family members rather than 'powerful businessmen.' Remittances have been extremely important in sustaining some of the poorest families in Kosovo, as well as in infusing the local economy with billions of euros.[42]

---

[40] Doreen Massey, 'Geographies of Responsibility,' *Geografiska Annaler B*, 86/1 (2004), 5–18, 5.

[41] *Gjitheashtu ne duke zbatuar ligjin, veprojm ne ate dhe ne ato drejtime qe politikat e ministris te diaspores te shtrihen edhe ne ne forma te tjera, te bashkpunimit dhe ne relacione te ndryshme me mergimtaret, pershembul per qeshtjet e investimeve, dhe ku mergimtare shume te sukseshem ka qe janë biznismen te fuqishem dhe shikojm qe kapitalet e tyre ti sjellim ne Kosove edhe ta bëjm per ta te hapin bisneset e tyre qoft te ngushta familiare po edhe ne projekte te mdha. Eh dija qe rreth diku 400 biznese të mergimtarëve në Kosove veprojn dhe jan te sukseshem, dhe një shembul shume i mire se ata te cilet deshirojn te investojn ne Kosove jan te mireseardhur dhe kan profitet e tyre ne ate, veq se ata i ndihmojn edhe shtetit edhe zhvillimit ekonomik te gjithe e me shume te kosoves.*

[42] King and Vullnetari, 'Remittances, Return, Diaspora,' 387.

However, such contributions by the diaspora are not emphasized or coveted as much as bigger investments. Perhaps this is due to the unofficial nature of remittances, which the government has no means to control, whereas bigger investments through governmental channels such as the Ministry of Diaspora would enable clear involvement from the government.

Furthermore, a differentiation is made between 'good diaspora' that Kosovo can tap into—such as businessmen defined as 'highly successful migrants' or celebrities like the Kosovo born British Rita Ora—and the 'bad diaspora' that are involved in illegal activities and negatively depicted in western media. In fact, throughout the interviews emphasis is either placed on those with high economic and cultural capital or those with particular political struggles and connections, whereas others in manual labour and from Kosovo's ethnic minority groups are ignored. For example, those diaspora members that were involved in political struggles, either those assassinated by the Yugoslav regime or those who returned to fight for during the conflict and died in the conflict, are also positively integrated into the acceptable narrative of cultural memory. As the interviewee states:

> There have been cases when the former Yugoslavia and Serbia together with its secret services has killed political exiles in different countries such as has been Jusuf Gervalla, Kadri Zeka, Bajrush Gervalla and others. Whom and because of their political activity if within and outside the country and were executed we [can't make out] from Serbian secret services. Well hmm these migrants played a particular role, and as Minister of Diaspora we have separate treatments for those who have given specific contributions for the children of Kosovo. So as Ministry of Diaspora, the law also determines to allocate special gratitude for the special activities, whether postmortem, or whether for activities for which they have directly influenced the vision of Kosovo, and the contribution that they have given to freedom of the country.[43]

What the above extract demonstrates is the perpetuation and construction of the myths of political resistance and struggle that the

[43] *kan pas raste te renda kur ishjugaslavia bashk me Serbin dhe shperbimet e saj sekrete ka ka vra mergimtaret politike neper vende te ndryeshme siq ka qen Jusuf Gervalla, Kadri Zeka, Bajrush Gervalla dhe te tjer, cillet te eh eh me pershkak vepritaris politke dhe mrenda dhe jasht vendit jan exekutuar fisikisht ne [cant make out] nga sherbime sekrete eh Serbe. Eh kjo hmm kjo mergate politike ka lujt ni role te veqant dhe si ministria e diaspores ka tretmant te veqant per ata te cilet kan dhen eh kontribute te veqanta per bijet e kosoves. Eh prandaj eh si ministri e diaspores edhe me ligj osht percaktuar qe te ndaj qmime te veqanta per veprimtari te veqanta, qoft per postmortem qofste per veprimtari per cilat kan ndiku te drejtperdjret ne qellimin e kosoves, dhe kontributin qe kan dhan per lirin eh eh vendit.*

dominant Kosovo Albanian identity of Kosovo is based on. This enables these national myths, which are also associated with the current political elite and political factions in Kosovo, who also control various ministries, to be perpetuated and venerated. As I have described elsewhere the 'Schatzi' discourse, which also constructs the Kosovo diaspora,[44] demonstrates that those who may have migrated from Kosovo for economic reasons and were not involved in politics or seeking political asylum are constructed as less deserving. Taken together, all these elements suggest that the 'homeland' is an important and active element of constructing the spatial reach of diaspora, as institutions within the 'homeland' are instrumental in not only constructing and legitimizing diaspora, but extending the 'homeland's' power and influence.

Conclusion

This chapter has argued that the Ministry of Diaspora in Kosovo constructs a passive diaspora that requires guidance and lacks agency, a diaspora whose national identity, which is assumed as Kosovo Albanian, is threatened by 'host' society cultural and linguistic assimilation and acculturation. In contrast, one of the benefits of living outside Kosovo is the financial advantage, that the diaspora is perceived to have from economic wealth accumulated in Western Europe. Nonetheless, the diaspora is predominantly narrativized as an entity with a primary function of investing in Kosovo and positively promoting Kosovo abroad. This chapter has demonstrated the opaque power and distance based biopolitics and governmentality exercised by the discursively constructed 'homeland' through the creation of Ministries of Diaspora, Diaspora Law and institutional discourses which act to control and discipline the diasporic body as well as construct a homogenized diaspora. Taken together, all these elements suggest that 'homelands' are not passive in relation to diaspora. Despite transnational migration and fluidity, state institutions in both 'host' societies and 'homeland' continue to imagine and construct spaces in which they exert biopolitical power, which distance does not necessarily negate.

[44] Paca, 'Schatzi.'

5

Where Are We and to What End?
Marking Spaces of Bodily and Literary
Resistance in Guantanamo Bay

Melanie R. Wattenbarger

We live in the stories now.
We live in the epics.
We live in the public's heart.[1]

Contesting Spaces: Literature, Popular Culture, and State Politics

L iterature may not be the first realm to come to mind as a way to consider spaces of resistance, much less spaces which call for the necessity of resistance. Guantanamo Bay is arguably one such space that is highly problematic in its political and literal usage, a space that dominates public debate to a point of being a main fixture in American popular culture. Orange jumpsuits and black masks have, after all, become a witty choice for a Halloween costume, displaying the wearer's poor taste and insensitivity to another human's lived reality that is far from provincial games of 'Trick or Treat.' It is this very fantastical spectacle nature the 'Gitmo' detainee has taken on in American popular culture that lends their predicament to a literary analysis, namely one that intends to give the detainees' voices a platform from which to rebut such representations and offer a sobering effect to the farce and fantasy which makes their lives seem more distant than a few short miles off Florida's tip. A turn towards the relationship between the real and imaginary is exactly what a literary analysis offers this discussion of spaces of resistance among Guantanamo Bay detainees. As Ustad Badruzzaman Badr states, the detainees 'live in the stories ... in the public's heart.'

This paper examines the borders of state power and individual agency in the case of those detained in one of America's most famous

---

[1] Ustad Badruzzaman Badr, 'Lions in the Cage,' in *Poems from Guantánamo: The Detainees Speak*, ed. Marc Falkoff (Iowa City: University of Iowa Press, 2007), 28.

prisons: Guantanamo Bay. Here, the only spaces for resistance against not only global forces but also the country detaining them are the detainees' bodies and literary spaces.[2] Resistance is enacted bodily and linguistically, however even on these two planes the state intervenes and attempts control. Thus the purpose of this paper is to explore the body and poetry as sites of resistance for Guantanamo Bay detainees and in the process glean an understanding of the ties between the human body and that of literature as related spaces. The fate of the detainees, current and potential, depend upon the debates in American popular culture and media surrounding the base's closure as such public debate affects voting patterns, the setting of official policy and—less optimistically—a public rhetoric to which politicians must acknowledge in order to appease constituents and stay in office.[3] As such, this discussion is hedged within the field of cultural studies as a way to understand the function of the detainees' bodies and writing as a potentiality to enact social change and strive for spatial justice.

Situating the Detainees

Two years have passed in far-away prisons,
… O Flaij, explain to those who visit our home
How I used to live.[4]

The detainees of Guantanamo Bay are diasporics: they maintain a collective movement for return to a mythical homeland, have a 'troubled relationship with host societies' to say the least in their case, and 'a strong ethnic group consciousness sustained over a long time and based on a sense of distinctiveness, a common history and the belief of

---

[2] There has been some recourse through the American Justice system for the detainees, but this path is largely fraught as a bureaucratic quagmire which does not operate clearly as either a military tribunal nor as the penal system operates within America's borders. There seem to be no set rules which are accessible and unalienable to provide these detainees rights to judicial review. For an extended study on the legal system and Guatanamo Bay, see Jess Bravin, *The Terror Courts: Rough Justice at Guantanamo Bay* (New Haven: Yale University Press, 2013).

[3] This view is in line with Eric Hobsbawm's belief that in order to understand macro developments of nationalist ideology and policy, one must seek to understand "from below" the attitudes and interests of the common masses. As the ontology of Guantanamo Bay is highly debated and well-known across American society and politics, an analysis of a popular cultural understanding of the base and detention program is highly warranted, see Eric Hobsbawm, *Nations and Nationalism since 1780* (Cambridge: CUP, 1990), 10.

[4] Abdullah Thani Faris Al Anazi, 'To My Father,' in *Poems from Guantánamo*, 25.

a common fate.'⁵ Such categorical understandings of the term 'diaspora' have largely been challenged in the field, including by Rogers Brubaker in connection to diaspora studies defining groups rather than processes of diasporization.⁶ In *Ethnicity without Groups*, Brubaker comments that:

> 'Groupness' is a variable, not a constant; it cannot be presupposed. It varies not only across putative groups, but within them; it may wax and wane over time, peaking during exceptional but unsustainable moments of collective effervescence.⁷

Brubaker's conceptualization of the contingency of groupness on situation is especially relevant to the population of detainees at Guantanamo Bay as being from disparate states, linguistic, cultural and ethnic communities yet united under their current circumstances. This artificial homogenization that occurs when US governmental officials name the detainees as 'enemy combatants' and 'potential terrorists' is an act of erasure, not only of each detainee's personal history as if he were a blank slate retrieved from inactivity in a foreign land, but is also to erase any possibility of an alternative persona from who he is 'officially.' Detainee resistance to this act of naming is taken up later in a discussion of authorship as an act of self-appellation.

Meanwhile the attempt to strictly define the term 'diaspora' according to a categorical and group mindset maintains some utility, such as here in examining the living conditions of a population which largely go against the neoliberal humanist stance of American popular culture. In this case concerning the Guantanamo Bay detainees, Cohen's first criterion is particularly instructive. While he states a diaspora as being a 'dispersal from an original homeland, often traumatically, to two or more foreign regions,'⁸ the detainees flip this assertion, being from multiple localities and states and instead of being dispersed, they are consolidated into one locality in a forced migration that is certainly traumatic.

The collective has been artificially created into an 'ethnic' community of enemy combatants who are lawless both in terms of being outside the protection of the law as well as deviants of the law.⁹ The term

---

⁵ Robin Cohen, *Global Diasporas: A Introduction* (London: Routledge, 1997), 25.

⁶ Rogers Brubaker, 'The "Diaspora" Diaspora,' *Ethnic and Racial Studies* 28/1 (2005), 3.

⁷ Rogers Brubaker, *Ethnicity Without Groups* (Cambridge: Harvard University Press, 2004), 4.

⁸ Brubaker, *Ethnicity Without Groups*, 26.

⁹ Thank you to Emma Patchett for pointing out this Janus-faced nature of those who fall 'outside' the law.

'terror diaspora' is conceived of as the transnationalization and global proliferation of terrorist networks including the border-crossings of these networks' members or as the contribution of diasporic groups in support of terrorist modes of political activism 'at home.'[10] This paper reads 'terror diaspora' as the forced diasporization not of confirmed terrorists, but as a consolidation of suspected terrorists, a manifestation of fears personified in individuals from a plethora of countries. It is their diasporization that is full of terror. This diaspora signifies the diasporization of American sentiments of fear and a resultant 'Othering.' There is very little agency on the part of the detainees in this diasporic situation, much like the concept of forced diasporas such as applied to groups of refugees or the trans-Atlantic Black diaspora. These terms of forced and terror diaspora can be expanded to apply to the Guantanamo Bay detainees for how such configurations of diaspora relate to the concept of 'home'; as quoted above, Moazzam Begg, a former Gitmo detainee, was correct: 'Home is cage.'[11]

The text *Poems from Guantánamo Bay: The Detainees Speak* is used to frame this discussion of the Guantanamo Bay detainees and their sites of resistance; it is but one of a multitude available in the American marketplace.[12] This collection was chosen for its collaborative nature, giving voice to multiple detainees as well as the perspective of a few

---

[10] See for example Bruce Hoffman et al., *The Radicalization of Diasporas and Terrorism: a Joint Conference by the Rand Corporation and the Center for Security Studies, ETH Zurich* (Santa Monica: RAND Corporation, 2007), vii.

[11] Bruce Hoffman et al., 'The Radicalization of Diasporas,' 30.

[12] There is the Hollywood rendition from a guard's point of view in *Camp X-Ray* ('will make you question your own beliefs'), which can be tempered with documentaries such as *The Oath* ('Gripping') and *My Country, My Country*. There are memoires including *Five Years of My life: An Innocent Man in Guantanamo* by Murat Kurnaz ('compassionate, truthful, and dignified'), *Guantanamo Diary* by Mohamedou Ould Slahi ('a Homeric epic; a vision of Hell, beyond Orwell, beyond Kafka'), and Joseph Hickman's *Murder at Camp Delta* ('compelled by an inner moral code to pursue truth and justice.... The truth always matters'). The counter-point to these texts are the more academic investigations, including an analysis of the legal system and genesis of the camps in Jess Bravin's *The Terror Courts* ('a book that pulls no punches') and Lieutenant Colonel Gordon Cucullu's *Inside Gitmo* which relies heavily on the author's interviews with members of the military and Justice Department and workers of all levels from 'behind the wire' as well as his first-hand experience on the base ('facts...truth-telling' and 'tells the heroic truth about the installation'). These quotes from promotions and reviews of the texts are included here to signal the anxious nature of any work on Guantanamo Bay; such repetitious assertions of truth which are attached to such varying views of life in the detention camp signals the very anxiety that such transcendent, authentic Truth is unattainable. Just as this paper contends the poetry written by the detainees are spaces of resistance, so too can we not ignore the other commentary concerning their plight.

of the lawyers representing them. It also highlights the various ways in which detainee resistance is limited and mediated by the US government. It is my hope that this collection will give a wider platform for multiple detainees' resistance than any of the published memoirs would allow. Likewise, poetry as a medium is ambiguous and open to layers of interpretation and meaning—including various layers upon which meaning could be mediated or suppressed by those censoring the literature and the men who produce it. The fluidity of poetic language provides an intimate form in which resistance can be expressed and received.

Spaces of Resistance: The Body and the Text

> Just as the heart beats in the darkness of the body,
> So I, despite this cage, continue to beat with life.[13]

The body is the site of American control over the detainees; it is also the site where the detainees may resist. Detainees resist their conditions by living on, surviving extreme interrogation, and continued hunger strikes against their treatment in detainment. Hunger strikes are not a new form of political resistance,[14] but rather one way of using the body as material evidence of an unmoving power, displaying a deteriorated state of existence with each passing day of starvation that imposition is unyielding.

Existing literature concerning life at Guantanamo Bay outlines detainee hunger strikes and the US government's use of forced feeding methods to counteract this form of bodily resistance, what Lieutenant Colonel Cucullu calls 'asymmetrical warfare.'[15] The detainees' bodies are one of the last vestiges for resisting the control imposed on them, however with the forced feeding program,[16] the agency the detainees

[13] Shaik Abdurraheem Muslim Dost, 'Two Fragments,' in *Poems from Guantánamo*, 36.

[14] See for example George Sweeny, 'Irish hunger Strikes and the Cult of Self-Sacrifice,' *Journal of Contemporary History* 28/3 (1993), 421–37 and Patrick Anderson, '"To lie down to death for days": The Turkish hunger strike, 2000–2003' *Cultural Studies* 18/6 (2004), 816–46.

[15] Gordon Cucullu, *Inside Gitmo: The True Story Behind the Myths of Guantánamo Bay* (New York: Collins, 2009), 31.

[16] 'Behind Camp 4 ... there was another medical building, where, during the big hunger strike of 2005, they would bring detainees to force-feed them. Since there was no hunger strike going on when we arrived in March 2006, this served as the QRF staging area. The room was creepy. It was still filled with cases of Ensure, the protein drink

have is extremely limited. They are denied even the right to die. Behind the wire, suicide is deemed by some as martyrdom and others as asymmetrical warfare. It is officially prohibited.

The ill treatment of the prisoners functions as if to elicit either control of the individual through docility in the Foucauldian sense,[17] or by pushing the struggle onto the very bodies of the detainees, making them the embodiment of the 'War on Terror' struggle.[18] If the detainees were allowed to hunger strike unto death or to commit suicide, the American government would be denied their bodies as a site for engaging in war. The battlefield would be literally lost. The detainees themselves become microcosms for international struggle that is individualized into detainee-guard interactions. Hence, each exchange becomes ideologically charged as US versus Terrorism rather than guard versus detainee.[19]

The will to not only continue living, but artistically create under the pressures to control are the products of this 'war,' the poetry itself becoming a site of resisting not only detention and the conditions thereof, but the very ambiguous war under which terms they are being held. Without the agency to create much change through the use of one's own body alone, the detainees must turn towards other spaces of resistance to relieve some of the pain of their situation. Thus, a main site of resistance for the detainees is through writing as the manifestation and performance of the mind's resistance over imposed control of

---

given to detainees during forced feedings, and against one wall were piles of medical equipment, tubing, and straps used to immobilize the hunger strikers.' Joseph Hickman, *Murder at Camp Delta: A Staff Sergeant's Pursuit of the Truth About Guantánamo Bay* (New York: Simon and Schuster, 2015), 57–8.

[17] For an excellent explanation of this term and its ties to masculinist thinking and gender biases in Foucault's work, see Anderson, 'To lie down to death for days,' 828. This comparison is especially striking when considering Guantanamo Bay as all of the detainees are male and most of the interactions between guards and detainees in fiction as well as memoirs are men-to-men. The use of a patriarchal structuring of gender roles and dominating behaviours is striking as a commentary on American military interactions with these 'Others' who are so often described in the American media as 'the worst of the worst' the world has to offer.

[18] This 'ill treatment' I mention is well-documented in the memoirs of detainees and Hickman's testimonial text, so I will not elaborate in further detail here. Rather, the focus will remain on the poetry that is a reaction and protest to that treatment.

[19] Even this formulation of dialogical oppositions is an artificial construct, as the relationship between prisoners and guards does not necessitate a binary opposition and may be applied as ensurer of one's health while under state control and thus less diametrically opposed, such as how Hickman viewed his role at Guantanamo Bay. Yet, the forced feeding of detainees who hunger strike when paired with rhetoric of 'asymmetrical warfare' suggests that any more benevolent figuration of detainee-guard relationship is nonetheless ideologically charged.

the body. By writing, the detainees are engaging in another form of bodily resistance that is akin to the hunger strikes, not only because the same body can perform both types of resistance simultaneously, but as the function of resistance is similar in both cases, particularly as a re-writing of the subjectivity of the detainee as more than 'deviant,' 'enemy combatant,' or 'potential terrorist.'

These men are, discursively, defined by so many others—the Justice Department, FBI, CIA, Tiger Force interrogation teams, the media—and it is from these cages both literal and appellate that they speak. The act of writing, physically putting pen to paper and signing one's name by it is a performance of authorship, arguably naming oneself an author.[20] By naming and performing as an author, the detainee becomes more than what he is called to be by his captives. He is denying that status 'enemy combatant' or 'potential terrorist.' What is more, the publication of his texts in the public forum that is the American literary market is a public proclamation to a wider world what he is, a subjectivity that indicates a deeper identity than 'the worst of the worst' as his captors call him. The act of writing and thus constituting authorship is a resistance to the power which names, taking control through self-appellation and—while not negating what he is called by others—it at least offers a dynamic of self beyond the homogenization of groupism he is forced into as a detainee.[21]

Writing in itself is a bodily act of resistance. Not only is any group of writing commonly referred to as a 'body' or 'corpus,' but it is only through the physical motions of the body that writing comes to be. While this assertion may sound rather obvious, it is a point that has been briefly noted through literary history that deserves further explication. Gilbert and Gubar highlight this connection between the body and literature in their critique of Victorian thought on authorship, questioning 'is a pen a metaphorical penis,' and thus writing the paternalistic semination of thought to the world.[22] Similarly, Walter Benjamin measured the value of art against the distance between a

[20] See for instance Seán Burke, 'The Ethics of Signature,' in *Authorship from Plato to the Postmodern*, ed. Seán Burke (Edinburgh: Edinburgh University Press, 1995).

[21] This line of argument is largely indebted to the work of Patrick Anderson on how Turkish hunger strikers challenge the State's control over their identity through the performance of prolonged hunger strikes, see Seán Burke, 'The Ethics of Signature.'

[22] While I agree with Gilbert and Gubar that this formulation is entirely sexist, there is merit in conceptualizing writing as beginning in its germination in the body and performed on paper, thus an embodied action. This phrasing invoking the male member is quite unfortunate and debilitating for authors who feature a different anatomy. Sandra M. Gilbert and Susan Gubar, *The Mad Woman in the Attic: The Woman Writer and the Nineteenth-Century Literary Imagination* (New Haven: Yale University, 2000), 3.

work and the touch of the artist's hand and the lived experience of the piece's production.[23] The entire field of semiotics as the study of signs and the bodily expression/reception thereof further connects the body and writing as related sites not just of expression, but in this case resistance. Similarly, Judith Butler reminds that the use of language is performative, not only an expression of thought but also an affective practice that can harm.[24] Writing is far from being a strictly intellectual and imaginative endeavour; it is deeply embodied with real effects on other bodies. Thus, detainee writing is but one example of the body and literature being intimately related and performative in nature.

In addition, the writings of the detainees as objects, spaces of expressed thought, serve as an enduring form of resistance long after the pen leaves its paper. This material aspect of literary resistance will be taken up after a brief discussion exploring the significance of the writing for the detainee, in detainee relationships, and in the widest mode its relationship to a public audience. After all, as Doreen Massey reminds, space—and here literary spaces of resistance—are never set, fully constituted or closed but as continually open to shifting and interpretations, reconfigurations and as such are highly relational in nature. As Massey states, 'perhaps we could imagine space as a simultaneity of stories-so-far.'[25] These poems are spaces, 'stories-so-far' which have implications for the writer's self, his community of detainees, the institutions of power subjecting him, and the reading public.

Searching for Home

Home is cage, and cage is steel,
Thus manifest reality's unreal.[26]

It is with the mind that the detainees may escape their current confines, their sense of self being shifted to what is not here, in the

---

[23] Walter Benjamin, 'The Work of Art in the Age of Its Technical Reproducibility,' in *The Work of Art in the Age of Its Technological Reproducibility and Other Writings on Media*, eds. Michael W. Jennings, Brigid Dojerty, and Thomas Y. Levin, trans. Edmund Jephcott et al. (Cambridge: Harvard University Press, 2008), 20, 31, 35.

[24] 'Certain words or certain forms of address not only operate as threats to one's physical well-being, but there is a strong sense in which the body is alternately sustained and threatened through modes of address. ... this somatic dimension may be important to the understanding of linguistic pain.' Judith Butler, *Excitable Speech: A Politics of the Performative* (New York: Routledge, 1997), 5.

[25] Doreen Massey, *For Space* (Los Angeles: Sage, 2008), 9.

[26] Moazzam Begg, 'Homeward Bound,' in *Poems from Guantánamo*, 30.

immediate, bodily presence. In so doing they are evading the definition of active terrorist that 'enemy combatant' implies. For instance,
Moazzam Begg comments in his poem 'Homeward Bound' how
through the mind he is able to, even if briefly, leave Guantanamo and
return home:

> Still the paper do I pen,
> Knowing what, but never when—
> As dreams begin and nightmares end—
> I'm homeward bound to beloved tend.[27]

In this poem, he is a loving spouse, father, and son; he is a family man
not a terrorist or detainee. He self-appellates to something different that
challenges the violence 'enemy,' 'combatant,' and 'terrorist' imply. He
is a part of a space of security, warmth and caring; he places himself
into a space of home.

Invoking the home space, the poet shifts the reader's attention from
his present of the camp, juxtaposing what is warm, comfortable and
safe with his harsh reality. The home becomes not only a site for mental
escape but also the shadow of the detention center, the possibility of
where one could be but cannot occupy in actuality. The 'home' to
which each detainee takes flight in their dreams and psychic space is
as different as their identity, yet as a trope it remains a site for drawing
strength and a goal that is tied to their freedom.[28] Brah's concept of
'homing desire' as connected to a distinction between feeling at home
and naming a place as home suggests that home can not only be a site
for performing home, but also a performance itself in the psyche.[29] As
will be expanded upon shortly, performance implies the presence of an
audience; let us first consider the function of imagining home for the
detainee before turning towards the presence of others.

For Moazzam Begg, home is a place where he can be in the present,
find his mind wandering there and gain peace despite the condition in
a cage where his body is homed. For Abdulla Majid Al Noaimi, home
is a place not only where he can escape to in his mind, but also a place
where he can be found in ephemeral form:

[27] Begg, 'Homeward Bound,' 30.

[28] The 'homing desire' Avtar Brah writes about as 'simultaneously critiquing
discourses of fixed origins' and home and dispersal as engaged in a 'creative tension'
lends itself well to this discussion of Guantanamo detainees, not least because of
the dispersed nature of multiple origins in terms of country and placing home this
community encompasses. *Cartographies of Diaspora: Contesting Identities* (New York
and London: Routledge, 1996), 189.

[29] Brah, *Cartographies*, 194.

And when you pass by life's familiar objects—
The Beduin rugs, the bound branches,
The flight of pigeons—
Remember me.[30]

The poet's presence in places of peace, places which are familiar to him and are immediate to his loved ones proves a site—through mental travel, the mnemonic nature of places, and writing—in which he may exist as he wishes, outside the confines and degradation of his current condition. He resists his own detainment at Guantanamo Bay for his well-being by taking agency over his location through his imagination. His corporeal reality is bleak as he states:

My rib is broken,
And I can find no one to heal me.

My body is frail,
And I see no relief ahead.[31]

Yet he counters in continual resistance to the site of his reality:

Before me is a tumultuous sea;
The land continues to call me.
But I am sailing in my thoughts.[32]

Escapism is not literal, yet still possible as the imagination and poetic expression provide a way to leave the space of detention. And yet in all of these poems, home, while being a real place, is also incredibly out of reach. While these dreams and writings of home do have a power for mental escape, they remain only phantasmic spaces, spectres of life's possibility:

But is it true that one day we'll leave Guantánamo Bay?
Is it true that one day we'll go back to our homes?
I sail in my dreams, I am dreaming of home.

To be with my children, each one part of me;
To be with my wife and the ones that I love;
To be with my parents, my world's tenderest hearts.
I dream to be home, to be free from this cage.[33]

[30] Abdulla Majid Al Noaimi, 'I Write My Hidden Longing,' in *Poems from Guantánamo*, 60.
[31] Al Noaimi, 'I Write My Hidden Longing,' 59.
[32] Al Noaimi, 'I Write My Hidden Longing,' 59.
[33] Osama Abu Kabir, 'Is it True?' in *Poems from Guantánamo*, 50.

Freedom and home are synonymous spaces, those to fight for and draw strength from, but which are yet unobtainable—but not impossible. To re-phrase Butler:

> In a sense, the [return home of the detainee through his poetry] begins the performance of that which it threatens to perform; but in not quite performing it, seeks to establish, through language, the certitude of that future in which it will be performed.[34]

A wider frame in which to consider the purpose of detainee's poetry is that of performing home as a form of resistance among detainees. As the editors of the volume point out, a majority of this poetry was authored on the transient space of Styrofoam cups.[35] In this way, detainees could not only create for the self, but pass their writing among other detainees before the cups were collected and thrown out with the day's trash. The guards' initial refusal to offer proper writing materials to the detainees displays an exercise in control, an attempt to deny the space to resist with 'proper' writing implements. It was also a denial of sociability, for performance indicates an audience, and writing indicates a reader. This denial sought to further isolate detainees, individuate them into alienated submission and dependence on their captors rather than a community of detainees. Writing with imperfect materials on transient material (the cups) further resists this control, establishing the endurance of community of the detainees' making.[36]

Even when the detainees were given pens and paper, many poems were confiscated by the US government and have yet to be released to their lawyers or the wider public.[37] The precariousness of the poetry as on disposable material and its loss into the abyss of governmental scrutiny reflects the condition of the detainees, connecting their physical bodies with their bodies of work. Both are precarious material whose vitality relies on the treatment of the State and its agents.[38]

The act of continuing to write, and the collaboration of the detainees and their lawyers to publish this volume, proves a resistance to the State which denies the ability to write and have one's work received by

---

[34] Butler, *Excitable Speech*, 9.

[35] Falkoff, *Poems from Guantánamo*, 3.

[36] The communal space of literature is best described as, '[the process of literary creation] underwrites literature as a collective productive practice, as a communal undertaking. And that communal undertaking assumes a communal space in which narrative can take place.' Russell West-Pavlov, *Spaces of Fiction/Fictions of Space: Postcolonial Place and Literary DieXis* (New York: Palgrave Macmillan, 2010), 71.

[37] Falkoff, *Poems from Guantánamo*, 3–5.

[38] For more on precarity, see Judith Butler, *Frames of War: When is Life Grievable?* (London: Verso, 2010).

others. It is to resist being denied sociability with a wider public outside the prison's cages. It is to give material reality to the poets' suffering that is accessible to the wider American public. The body of poetry 'speaks' to what the detainees' bodies have been denied public witness as the material collection can travel where the poet cannot.[39] Writing as an object propels the figure of the poet, the shadow of the body as having been proximally related to a suffering and incarcerated body, out of containment, into the public arena to be witnessed, rebutted, and engaged with. In this sense, literature is relational, providing the potential space in which subjectivity can meet the world.[40]

Of course the danger in this meeting is that, as Susan Sontag warns in relation to war photography, 'they turn an event or a person into something that can be possessed' and hence fetishized.[41] What consumers are buying when purchasing *Poems of Guantánamo Bay* is the actual speech act of the detainees, a piece of their space of resistance. It is to own and in the process pay for a cathartic release a bit of another's suffering; readers can come to know 'the suspicious thrill of borrowed emotion.'[42] However, as this paper opened with an existing practice within popular American culture concerning the detainees' ontology (the Halloween costume), the publication of this volume and similar written expressions in the form of memoirs must take this risk in order to offer the detainees' voices a space to enter public debate. To deny this space would be a further violence in silencing.

Control and Spaces of Recognition

The oppressors are playing with me,
As they move freely about the world.[43]

---

[39] Butler, *Frames of War*, 9.

[40] 'Literature is written language located in potential space, the language *we* locate there. Since each of us lives out his or her own identity and its variations in interaction with social and historical circumstances, each of us brings to the literary transaction a unique style of attempting to unite inner and outer realities—our potential spaces and transitional objects are often shared but never identical.' Murray M. Schwartz, 'Where is Literature?' in *Transitional Objects and Potential Spaces: Literary Uses of D. W. Winnicott*, ed. Peter L. Rudnytsky (New York: Columbia University Press, 1993), 61.

[41] Susan Sontag, *Regarding the Pain of Others* (New York: Picador, 2003), 81.

[42] Nancy K. Miller and Jason Tougaw, 'Introduction: Extremities,' in *Extremities: Trauma, Testimony and Community*, eds. Nancy K. Miller and Jason Tougaw (Urbana and Chicago: University of Illinois Press, 2002), 2.

[43] Sami Al Haj, 'Humiliated in the Shackles,' in *Poems from Guantánamo*, 42.

The detainees' voices are highly mediated and censored. On speech acts, Foucault writes that: 'The one who uses parrhesia ... he doesn't hide anything. He opens his heart and mind to other people' and similarly, 'in parrhesia, the words, the discourse are supposed to give an exact account, a complete expression of what the speaker has in mind so that the audience is able to catch exactly what he thinks, it refers to a kind of relationship between the speaker and what he says.'[44] The public speech acts concerning Guantanamo Bay are far from this utopian form of political articulation. For one, there seems to be an inability to fully disclose the trauma the poems represent, that what is painful cannot be fully articulated not matter how dearly the poet wishes to engage in parrhesia. Some things simply cannot be stated.[45]

These poems further fall short of parrhesia in that they are all heavily charged with an anxiety over meaning and intent as if both Americans and detainees have possibly injurious ulterior motives. For instance, Mohamedou Ould Slahi's text bears over 2,600 black bars throughout, redacted portions the US government felt revealed too much for the sake of national security.[46] Similarly, the poems I share with you are in English as the US government feared their release in Arabic and Pashto, knowing many subtleties are lost in translation.[47] Of course the silence is not unilateral; surely the detainees do not write to entirely reveal themselves as is their right to edit as authors just the State maintains the

[44] Michel Foucault, 'Discourse and Truth: Parrhesia,' 10 October 2014, http://www.lib.berkeley.edu/MRC/foucault/parrhesia.html, 3:27–3:39 and 4:10, 4:20–4:28.

[45] See for example how Shoshana Felman and Dori Laub note 'the ways in which our cultural frames of reference and our pre-existing categories which delimit and determine our perception of reality have failed, essentially, both to contain and to account for, the scale of what has happened in contemporary history' in their influential study *Testimony: Crises of Witnessing in Literature, Psychoanalysis, and History* (New York: Routledge, 1992), xv.

[46] Mohamedou Ould Slahi, *Guantánamo Diary*, ed. Larry Siems (Edinburgh: Canongate, 2015).

[47] 'In addition, the Pentagon refuses to allow most of the detainees' poems to be made public, arguing that poetry "presents a special risk" to national security because of its "content and format." The fear appears to be that the detainees will try to smuggle coded messages out of the prison camp. Hundreds of poems therefore remain suppressed by the military and will likely never be seen by the public. In addition, most of the poems that have been cleared are in English translation only, because the Pentagon believes that their original Arabic or Pashto versions represent an enhanced security risk. Because only linguists with secret-level security clearances are allowed to read out clients' communications (which are kept by court order in a secure facility in the Washington, D. C. area) it was impossible to invite experts to translate the poems for us. The translations we have included here, therefore, cannot do justice to the subtlety and cadence of the originals.' Marc Falkoff, 'Notes on Guantánamo,' in *Poems from Guantánamo*, 5.

right to not engage in parrhesia concerning its acts and motivations in the space of Guantanamo Bay. Undoubtedly the stakes of transparency and power over self-disclosure are highly skewed in this comparison, thus indicating a fracture in the relationship between what is being said about Guantanamo Bay and its actors.

Like any life-writing, the memoires of detainees and Guantanamo Bay personnel fall privy to misleading and alterations of memory, taking on a fictional life all on their own. Yet, with all of this mediation and restrictions on the poet's voice, the detainees have found a way to speak to the world, to attempt to share their experiences and perspective on an issue that is a flashpoint in international politics. The fact that these poems are publicly available speaks to their tenacity and ability to resist being erased from public view during their time in detention. As Butler points out concerning this same collection: 'They are efforts to re-establish a social connection to the world, even when there is no concrete reason to think that any such connection is possible.'[48]

Conclusion

In order to contemplate a movement into potential space of literature as communal space, let us return to the relationship between literature and the body. Thus far the focus has been on the writing hand, the body that resists, and the body of literature as a material spectre of the poet's body. The aspect of body-literature relations that has thus far been ignored is that of reception: the poet's words' power to move a reader's eyes and through the rhythm of verse to alter even momentarily the movement of a reader's breath. On the interplay of text and the body as sites of resistance, consider Ariel Dorfman on the unique function of poetry:

> The origin of life and the origin of language and the origin of poetry are all there, in each first breath, each breath as if it were our first, the anima, the spirit, what we inspire, what we expire, what separates us from extinction, minute after minute, what keeps us alive as we inhale and exhale the universe. Poetry is a call to those who breathe the same air to also breathe the same verses, to bridge the gap between bodies and between cultures and between warring parties.[49]

Literature and the body are thus further intertwined. The reader's thought, if not breath as well, is transformed to match the cadence of

---

[48] Butler, *Frames of War*, 59–60.
[49] Ariel Dorfman, 'Where the Buried Flame Burns,' in *Poems from Guantánamo*, 71.

the poet's body of work, making the experience of poetry bodily and communal over space and time. The reader of the poetry must enter the performance of resistance by matching breath to breath, eyes moving over the words the hand laid on paper (or cup).

There is little doubt that the American government is 'streaking space' across the globe, laying tracks with questionable ends, some culminating in detention at Guantanamo Bay. This phrase is borrowed from Gerald Raunig's reading of Kafka's text 'Josaphine the Singer, or The Mouse Folk': 'Streaking is not brushing smooth, but rather the opposite: drawing streaks in smooth space with a streaking touch ... gently striating the space and the sociality of the multitude' and 'it is a gentle streaking of the territory, in the course of which the mouse folk [read the American public] becomes an abstract machine, fabricating singularities, events, machinic relations, and gaining its form from this streaking at the same time.'[50] Just as with Josephine's voice in Kafka's 'The Mouse Folk,' the poetry from Guantanamo Bay calls the American masses to stop for a moment and cease their endless streaking of space to contemplate something greater,[51] to consider how art can point to the significance—both brutal and beautiful—of their movements in a space that is far from empty. It is a challenge to thinking of the poet's homes as static, empty space from which terrorists in suspended animation may be lifted. The poetry is a resistance to this streaking movement as unexamined and an invitation to join in the bodily process of breathing with the detainee, reading in verse. It is an invitation to engage in the space of their resistance.

Take my blood.
Take my death shroud and
The remnants of my body.
Take photographs of my corpse at the grave, lonely.

Send them to the world,
To the judges and
To the people of conscience,

[50] Here, I do not read 'smooth space' to be empty space but rather smooth in the sense that the face of a still body of water is smooth until agitated from exterior intervention causing ripples, a tranquil home that is hardly still or empty to begin with, but is thrown into new patters when disrupted by trauma; see Gerald Raunig, *Factories of Knowledge, Industries of Creativity*, trans. Aileen Derieg (Los Angeles: Semiotext(e), 2013), 14, 10.

[51] 'Our singer is called Josephine. Anyone who has not heard her does not know the power of song. There is no one but is carried away by her singing ...' Franz Kafka, 'Josephine the Singer, or the Mouse Folk,' in *The Complete Stories*, ed. Nahum N. Glatzer, trans. Willa and Edwin Muir (New York: Schocken Books, 1971), 360–76.

Send them to the principled men and the fair-minded.

And let them bear the guilty burden, before the world,
Of this innocent soul.
Let them bear the burden, before their children and before history,
Of this wasted, sinless soul,
Of this soul which has suffered at the hands of the 'protectors of peace.'[52]

[52] Jumah Al Dossari, 'Death Poem,' in *Poems from Guantánamo*, 32.

6

Spatial Justice Through the Lens of Political Discourse, Dissecting Italian Responses to Bangladeshi and Filipino Diasporas

Le Anh Nguyen Long

> Politics is obviously fueled by word power·
> — Doris Graber[1]

A *word* both carries and imposes meaning. The use of symbolism and imagery in popular and political discourse bring messages about 'opportunity' or 'threat' and simultaneously speak to a multitude of audiences. Words are very powerful instruments. North African migrants in Italy combat a language that stereotypes immigrants as inferior, intellectually, and culturally. The adoption of the derogatory phrase '*vu compra*,' for example, assigns an identity of marginality, poverty, precariousness, and ignorance to immigrant workers from Africa.[2] The term is said to come from a *mispronunciation* of Neapolitan dialectal phrase for 'do you want to buy?' by early Moroccan migrants and typifies the immigrant as ignorant, of low education, and of low abilities.[3]

While it may have disappeared from print media, *vu cumpra* remains strongly anchored in the memory of Italians and the national groups most commonly associated with it.[4] Touching on the sensitive phrase,

---

[1] Doris Graber, *Verbal Behavior and Politics* (Urbana, Chicago, and London: University of Illinois Press, 1976), 3.

[2] Emilio Reyneri, 'Immigrants in a Segmented and Often Undeclared Labour Market,' *Journal of Modern Italian Studies* 9/1 (2004), 71–93.

[3] Bruno Riccio, 'Following the Senegalese Migratory Path through Media Representation,' in *Media and Migration: Constructions of Mobility and Difference*, eds. Russell King, Nancy Wood (London and New York: Routledge, 2001), 117.

[4] Giuseppe Sciortino and Asher Colombo, 'The Flows and the Flood: The Public Discourse on Immigration in Italy, 1969–2001,' *Journal of Modern Italian Studies* 9/1 (2004), 94–113.

Informant 795, a Moroccan businessman, recounted an incident that reflects the pervasiveness of *vu cumpra* in the Italian discourse on migration:

> They called them Macaroni. We have the rotole; rotole means all Italo-American migrants. We organized a convention which featured Italian-Americans; a convention in Pescara. ... They wrote, 'Rotoli'... on the program. I took a picture of it because it made an impression on me. They wrote, 'Macaroni and Vu Compra.' What I liked is that this gentleman from Rai who is a writer, who has been to Morocco and to Africa, to many countries, the first thing he said was, 'look, I agree with everything except with the title of the program, I disagree with this "Vu Compra".' He did not say I disagree with Macaroni. He said I disagree with vu compra. Vu compra diminishes the identity of these people who have experienced horrible things to be here.[5]

Important critical work has delved into the question of how narratives impact Italian attitudes towards immigrants and their social exchanges with immigrants.[6] However, this work overlooks the impact that popular narratives have on immigrants' engagement with Italian spaces: an oversight that misses an important variable in the equation on immigration.

In this chapter, I describe how socio-political environments shape diasporic interactions with the host society and the avenues through which they pursue their rights within the prevailing institutional environs. Migrants' engagement with Italian space critically bears upon their politicization and racialization through these narratives. Leveraging distinctions between two diasporic communities' engagement with space and society in Rome, Italy, I then illustrate how visibility through geographic clustering or through the use of space makes some migrants more susceptible to negative constructions compared to others. I describe how these narratives affect Italian understandings of migrant rights, in particular their *right to escape*, and how they may contribute to xenophobia against visible migrant groups (the manifestation of a sense of entitlement and superiority vis-à-vis the immigrant). Finally, I discuss how these constructions impact immigrant groups' relationship to their 'host.' As such, this chapter offers an empirically grounded

---

[5] Interview transcript with Informant 795, 2011.

[6] Maurizio Ambrosini, 'Fighting Discrimination and Exclusion: Civil Society and Immigration Policies in Italy,' *Migration Letters* 10/3 (2013), 313; Anna Triandafyllidou, '"Racists? Us? Are you Joking?" The Discourse of Social Exclusion of Immigrants in Greece and Italy,' in *Eldorado or Fortress? Migration in Southern Europe*, ed. Russell King et al. (Basingstoke: Palgrave Macmillan UK, 2000); Sciortino and Colombo, 'The Flows and the Flood.'

study of diasporic experiences that will be of interest to spatial justice scholars.

Narratives and the Italian Imagination on Immigration

As a country of 'new' migration, Italy serves as an ideal case study of the diaspora—that promotes spatial justice through its members' pursuit of the right to escape—in the age of globalization. To understand Italian immigration policy and politics one must necessarily see Italy as part of a region within a larger political-economic zone (the Mediterranean and Western Europe). An example is the adoption and the continued use of the term *extra-communitari* (non-European Community). In their analysis of the treatment of immigrants in over three decades of newspaper articles, Sciortino and Colombo show that the now-common term was rarely employed before 1989.[7] This disparaging descriptor is infused with connotations of belonging and exclusion and very definitively puts a box around the 'other.' *Extra-communitari* is reserved for migrants from developing countries and never used in reference to non-Europeans from North America.

In Europe, identity politics is very much alive. A European identity supplies the very basis for the formulation of the EU. Drawing the lines around who and what a European is speaks just as much to exclusion as it does to inclusion. As Cere writes:

> A dual discourse of protection of and from is intrinsic in the ideology of the European Union and its member states: the EU is caught in the dilemma of retaining its liberal ideology, at the base of which is the concept of assimilation, yet proclaiming itself as a multicultural society.[8]

The basis of inclusion (and exclusion) is space. That is, it creates a *European* space which separates and advantages those who fall within the lines compared to those who fall outside the lines. Being part of the region means that aspects of neighbouring countries' approaches are incorporated into Italian responses to immigration and immigrant. Thus, the contradictions of European ideology on immigration can be observed playing out on Italian soil. Popular narratives provide a picture of these contradictions: the espousal of universalism with limits.

Representations of immigrants in the media influence Italian opinions

---

[7] Sciortino and Colombo, 'The Flows and the Flood.'

[8] Rinella Cere, 'Globalization vs. Localization: Anti-immigrant and Hate Discourses in Italy,' *Beyond Monopoly: Globalization and Contemporary Italian Media* (2010), accessed 4 January 2015, 4. http://shura.shu.ac.uk/8161/.

of and interactions with them.[9] These narratives are multi-faceted and evolve over time. Italian narratives on immigration have shifted from one where immigrants were represented benevolently as workers seeking to escape poverty and drudgery to today's bifurcated narratives which one the one hand represent the immigrant as deserving yet penurious or as deviants and criminals, on the other hand. Immigrant visibility within the space which they share with Italians contributes greatly to this evolution. With the boom of in-migration to Italy in the 1980s Sciortino and Colombo observe:

> the Italian press discovers 'immigration' and unites the narrative threads that previously, and often for good reason, had been kept separate. For the press, immigration becomes of crucial importance for the entire social life of the country. We witness the birth of a new narrative domain, defined and fed by more generic and therefore more ecumenical vision of immigration.[10]

During this period, xenophobic undercurrents in popular writing on immigration emerged along with the coupling of immigration with criminality and deviance.[11] In the 1990s, the discourses once again shifts. We begin to see an association between immigration and security.[12]

Navigating Space: Visibility and the Diaspora

Italian perceptions of immigrants vary according to each national groups' visibility. While Italians may be willing to tolerate immigrants so long as they attend to those needs and services that are promote the preservation of Italian quality of life, once immigrants become visible they begin to be perceived as a threat.[13] Immigrants' visibility hinges

---

[9] Nicola Mai, *Myths and Moral Panics: Italian Identity and the Media Representation of Albanian Immigration* (Farnham: Ashgate, 2002); Nancy Wood and Russell King, 'Media and Migration: An Overview,' in *Media and Migration: Constructions of Mobility and Difference*, ed. Nancy Wood and Russell King (New York and London: Routledge, 2001), 1.

[10] Sciortino and Colombo, 'The Flows and the Flood,' 102.

[11] Mahmoud Mansoubi, *Noi, stranieri d'Italia: immigrazione e mass-media Vol. 2* (Lucca: Maria Pacini Fazzi, 1990); Marcello Maneri, 'Lo straniero consensuale. La devianza degli immigrati come circolarità di pratiche e discorsi,' in *Lo straniero e il nemico. Materiali per l'etnografia contemporanea*, ed. A. Dal Lago (Genova: Costa & Nolan, 1998), 236–72.

[12] Giuseppe Campesi, 'Migrazioni, sicurezza, confini nella teoria sociale contemporanea,' *Studi sulla questione criminale* 7/2 (2012), 7–10.

[13] Ambrosini, 'Fighting discrimination and exclusion.'

on numerous factors including their phenotypical distinctiveness, the differences between their cultural practices and host practices, and their numbers. Diasporic use of space also impacts their visibility. Migrants engage space for their livelihood, for shelter, and for recreation. In other words, visibility has a spatially contingent aspect. To demonstrate how this spatially-contingent social construction takes place, the stark contrast that can be found in the treatment of the dispersed and invisible Filipino diaspora and the geographically concentrated (and therefore visible) Bangladeshi diaspora, whose notable presence across the *Tor Pignattara* neighbourhood has earned that borough the nickname 'Bangla-Town,' is explored.

There are patterned differences in the Filipino and Bangladeshi diaspora's engagement with Italian institutions and in their efforts to seek political representation.[14] The law grants documented immigrants equivalent access to social programs as Italians. Compared to Filipinos, there is a higher reliance on Italian government among Bangladeshis. Perhaps this is attributable to the longer stay and (thus) greater stability within the Filipino community. Alternatively, an apparently higher visibility makes the Bangladeshi community easier to approach and recruit in an effort to serve (and to regulate) them.

In many cases, however, migrants work through intermediaries when accessing government programs. In Rome, there are a mélange of intermediaries that dually complement and compete with government

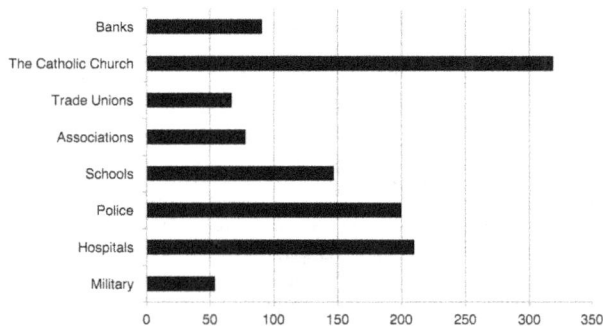

Fig. 1 Entities Associated with Migration Policy Implementation

[14] Le Anh Nguyen Long, 'Institutions, Information Exchange, and Migrant Social Networks in Rome,' *Ethnic and Racial Studies* 38/15 (2015), 2722–37; Kristine Crane, 'Governing Migration: Immigrant Groups' Strategies in Three Italian Cities—Rome, Naples and Bari,' FEEM Working Paper 37/04, 2004, accessed 10 November 2016, http://dx.doi.org/10.2139/ssrn.523362.

agencies in providing public services to immigrants. Eight general categories of intermediaries often associated with immigrant policy making and program implementation were identified (see Fig. 1).

Italian intermediaries have been instrumental in facilitating diasporic migrant integration. Some intermediaries purposively sought to bring migrants into their organizations. Informant 849 of an Italian labour union spoke of the efforts that were undertaken to build relationships with the Sikh in the Latina region:

> It has been eight years that we seek to get to know the Indian community because in the beginning language was the obstacle: they speak five and we one and a half; therefore, we communicated a bit in English but they spoke absolutely no Italian. The first time we met them, and by meeting them I mean we went into the camps where they work and then we discovered that there were many temples where they pray in Latina. And we spent four years praying with them within the temples. We got to know them. And now their community trusts us. In fact, the first words in Italian for many was 'FLI-CGIL' and this fills me with pride.[15]

ONLUS stands for *Organizzazione Non Lucrativa di Utilita' Sociale* (Not for Profit Organization of Social Uses). Many of the registered Italian associations that deal with migrants fall under this category. Compared to ethnic associations, Italian associations have better access to state resources. Caponio found that Italian associations were favored over immigrant associations in accessing public funds.[16] When asked if they ever participated in competitions for government funds, ethnic association heads who were interviewed often responded negatively. For them, applying for state support was seen as a waste of time:

> Alright, the bando pubblico, let's say to fund associations, if the association is a migrant association it is already outside the competition because a majority of these contests are run by Italian associations. And, of course, the contests organized by the mayor, province, regions, well in these, of course the province, region and mayor, all of these prefer their own associations. Therefore since immigrants cannot vote these people into office, why should the region give money to Association X [his association], there is no return, do you see?[17]

Public funds permit Italian associations to employ staff and to 'do

---

[15] Interview transcript with Informant 849, 2011.

[16] Tiziana Caponio, 'Policy Networks and Immigrants' Associations in Italy: The Cases of Milan, Bologna and Naples,' *Journal of Ethnic and Migration Studies* 31/5 (2005), 931–50.

[17] Interview transcript with Informant 790, 2011.

more' than migrant associations. Commenting on the work accomplished by migrant activists in Rome, Informant 799, an immigrant representative elected to serve on Rome's consultative body for migrants, made the following observation:

> They promote a lot of change because they work a lot on immigration and on social programs. First, because they have the necessary awareness and also because for them it is a job. It's not as it is for me—I don't earn anything from this. Many people who attend meetings at the consultative body come from their associations. That is, their time is paid for by these associations.[18]

Trade unions actively seek to engage the diaspora. 25 per cent of Filipinos and 35 per cent of Bangladeshis prefer to work with trade unions over the various ONLUS. The recognition of migrant labour through the Martelli Law 1990 placed migrant rights under the purview of labour movements. Migrant rights have been integrated into the mission of the many labour unions especially those that serve sectors that employ a large share of migrant workers, like APICOLF (*Associazione Professionale Italiana Collaboratore Familiare*), the union for domestic helpers.

The *Confederazione Generale Italiana del Lavoro* (Italian General Confederation of Labour, CGIL) was among the first to champion migrant rights under the leadership of Antonio Pizzinato (then National Secretary of CGIL). His advocacy for immigrant workers goes back to the 1970s when he encouraged the inclusion of immigrant workers in the trade union and established service offices. The CELSI (*Centro lavoratori stranieri*) was a pioneer office that provided immigrant workers with assistance with documentation and advocacy on other labour related needs. Two years before the enactment of the Martelli Law, the CELSI of Rome already began to mobilize for the political and social recognition of migrants. Many of the migrants trace their relationship back to CELSI's charismatic ex-manager, Simonetta Dandoli. When she was alive and in charge of the office, the services in the office went beyond labour into policy, 'When Simonetta was in charge,' one of the Buonarroti employees observed, 'we had more stringent relationships with immigrant leaders. Those days, each ethnic association used to have a representative to CGIL. The CIELSI office had structured relationships with every national community. CGIL was a 'training ground' for these organizations.' Some of the formal relationships of the past remain, though. Filipinos have a particularly strong

---

[18] Interview transcript with Informant 799, 2011.

relationship with CGIL.[19] One of its most active leaders, the president of one of the two Filipino activist groups, Informant 714 is also a union representative for the union. Her relationship with CGIL predates the first Italian law on migration, the 1990 Martelli Law. 714 continues to bring Filipinos into CGIL where she works as a representative every Thursday afternoon.

Italian intermediaries make powerful allies for diasporic groups. One caveat of this *representation by proxy* is that it may incorrectly or incompletely represent the migrant condition. Moreover, it makes the migrant reliant on others for access to their rights. Politics requires presence that communicates the authenticity of the migrant experience. The wish to give a face to the 'alternative' reality in Italy provides a strong motivation for participation.[20] As Informant 799 comments:

> You have asked me why I decided to work at the consulta and to participate in politics, it was exactly for this. I seek to, well, tell the story, no? From the point of view of someone who lives it.[21]

The displacement of host institutions by intermediaries (Italian or not) may further isolate the most vulnerable immigrants from the mainstream. This isolation makes immigrants more vulnerable to exploitation and abuse by co-nationals, from other migrants, and also from Italians.[22] Previous work has documented the exploitation of migrants that may occur through the organization of migration chains or at the hands of their employers.[23] One's position and reliance on others dictates who one meets and the ability of one to leverage those relationships for his/her benefit. In most cases, important interpersonal relationships are missing:

> Let's say that we are isolated from this social life. ... Contact depends on seeing. But those who make laws, who organize things, they organize them for ... who? Because once it was all for immigrants and after that period, immigrants have nothing left, they don't even have the rights they had to begin with.[24]

[19] Crane, 'Governing Migration.'
[20] Gaia Danese, 'Participation beyond Citizenship: Migrants' Associations in Italy and Spain,' Patterns of prejudice 35/1 (2001), 69–89.
[21] Interview Transcript of Informant 799, 2011.
[22] Long, 'Institutions.'
[23] John MacDonald et al., 'Chain Migration Ethnic Neighborhood Formation and Social Networks,' The Milbank Memorial Fund Quarterly 42/1 (1964), 82–97; Franca Van Hooren, 'When Families Need Immigrants: The Exceptional Position of Migrant Domestic Workers and Care Assistants in Italian Immigration Policy,' Bulletin of Italian Politics 2/2 (2010), 21–38.
[24] Interview transcript with Informant 795, 2011.

In large part, Filipinos in Rome work in the domestic services, as maids or in child or elderly care. The first wave of Filipino migrants were women whose work contracts were brokered through the intervention of the Catholic Church.[25] It is not uncommon for Filipina domestics to live in the homes of their Italian employers, and therefore the diaspora is dispersed throughout Rome. When they live separately from their employers, Filipinos are spread out along the metro-lines (A and B), which allows them to traverse the city quickly for work.

Although many of them live with their employers or rent relatively small apartments, Filipinos convene in large groups on their days off. When Filipinos gather, they avoid public spaces (with the exception of the central station, Termini). Instead, Filipinos congregate at Catholic churches or at the embassy.[26] The activities in both spaces are overseen by embassy employees and so-called community leaders, leaders of Catholic associations who operate in direct consultation with the Filipino diocese in Rome. Both of these institutions have an interest in maintaining the positive reputation of Filipinos as meek, quiet, and well-behaved.

Remittances by Filipino overseas workers account for a substantial 10 percent of the nation's GDP (World Bank). In fact, the push to export labour from the Philippines was part of an initiative by the Marcos government aimed at finding new sources of taxable income to be used to pay down the national debt. This effort was institutionalized through the 1974 Labor Code which introduced a government administered recruitment and placement program 'to ensure the careful selection of Filipino workers for the overseas labour market to protect the good name of the Philippines abroad.' The continuation of key programs instituted during the Marcos era is indicative of a continued willingness to leverage Filipino labour to pad the nation's GDP. As such, leaders of these institutions keep a watchful eye on the community and try to solve its problems so that it does not become a nuisance to Italians.[27] At a meeting of Filipino association and community leaders at the embassy, embassy staff were observed discussing drug use by Filipino youth. One of the central themes in this discussion was on how such drug use would affect the reputation of the Filipino community in Rome. The embassy and churches then become places where Filipino migration-related problems are discussed and dispatched. As a result,

[25] Charito Basa and Rosalud Jing de la Rosa, *Me, Us and Them: Realities and Illusions of Filipina Domestic Workers—A Community Research Project by the Filipino Women's Council* (Rome: FWC, 2004).

[26] Crane, 'Governing Migration,' 5.

[27] Long, 'Institutions.'

in many ways, the community is self-contained.

Consequentially, while quite large, the Filipino community is tolerated and accepted by Italians. Indeed, the work that Filipinos do is necessary for preserving the Italian way of life and as such, the domestic worker continues to be supported within the realm of Italian policy-making.[28] This support also finds itself in the narrative on the caregiver and the domestic. In a piece entitled, 'I thank the caregivers, the silent army,' della Ragione writes:

> We must not tire of giving thanks, every day, to a silent army consisting of more than two million units, which permits Italy to continue walking in its selfishness, the son of the consumer society. Our women now aspire only to work outside the home and they unload on the household staff, almost all foreign, tasks which until a generation ago they saw to happily, the management of the house, the 'education of children and the' commitment more heavy, the 'elderly care.' The arrival of a flood of care givers of different races and cultures is readily accepted by the families, it is tolerated even in the most senseless dictates of the Northern League and can be an opportunity to gradually change costumes. In severe cases they lend their valuable assistance constantly at home, often, however, they go out for a walk with the person entrusted to them and furnish us images of great tenderness as they sit thoughtfully together on a bench in the gardens or lovingly help during a brief morning walk, to convince the 'assisted' to continue to live. The old and the caregiver seem light years away, conversely they almost always are able to understand one another at a glance, both are very wise, one due to experience accumulated over the years, the other because living away from home makes now mature. They are both fragile as glass due to illness and the poor protection of their rights. They dream of the distant family, and suffer from an incurable loneliness: the foreigner has his loved ones thousands of kilometers away, the old still more distant, although their in-laws live a scant few blocks away.[29]

Filipinos work inside Italian homes, take care of their children and parents, and often times live alongside their Italian employers. Such relationships require trust and faith. Popular narratives of Filipinos tend to depict them as upstanding, mild mannered, hardworking, and deserving. This deservingness is heightened by the poverty commonly associated with the Filipino. An example of the narratives associated with the Filipino is shown below. The picture (taken by Joyce Giles Girofranca) was published in La Reppublica in July 2015. It was

[28] Van Hooren, 'When Families need Immigrants,' 22.
[29] Della Ragione, Achille, 'Ringrazio Le Badanti Un Esercito Silenzioso,' la Repubblica, 13 August 2011.

captioned:

> The symbolic and powerful image has circulated the world within a few hours. It shows a Filipino child, kneeling on a sidewalk in front of a stool, without electric light at home, doing his homework diligently by the light of a street lamp.[30]

However, Filipino integration within the Italian social landscape is anything but complete. Although it is one of the oldest Diasporas in Rome, there is very little mixing between Filipinos and Italians outside the employer-employee relationship; intermarriage is rare as are friendships between members of the two groups. Moreover, despite the reliance of Italians on Filipino (and other) domestic workers, these workers enjoy very few protections. They are often asked to make sacrifices for the families and often work on the edge of informality.[31]

Filipinos are tolerated so long as they maintain their subservient position. Poverty is a key aspect of invisibility. Italians are willing to accept those who are escaping from poverty within their space, so long as this exodus is continuous. In interview, one Filipino recounted how another Filipina lost her job as a childminder:

> Flor (name redacted) felt a strong affection for the children of the family she had served for ten years. She invited the children to accompany her to the Philippines one year. When they returned, the children were full of stories about Flor's home and possessions. She was summarily fired. Flor believes that she was fired out of spite. She feels that her employers could not accept that a maid—their maid—might not live a life of abject poverty.[32]

To have a Filipino in the house also brings status to Italians. In interviews, Filipinos living in the diaspora demonstrate an elevated awareness of how Italians perceive them, one even jokingly referring to Filipinos as 'the Mercedes Benz of the domestic services industry.' They understand that the perseverance of such imagery hinges on Filipinos visibility within Italian society. The diaspora serves as a mechanism of discipline for Filipinos. It enables the continued and expansive exercise of the Filipino of their right to escape through the purposive deployment of norms that promote invisibility and the strategic engagement of Italian public space. Which is why, when the Filipino community engages the Italian public it rarely does so through protest (indeed,

---

[30] Adriano Sofri, 'Daniel che studia alla luce di un lampione,' *la Repubblica*, 3 July 2015.

[31] Van Hooren, 'When Families need Immigrants,' 23–25.

[32] Interview transcript with Informant 650, 2011.

participation in protest is explicitly forbidden by a number of Filipino associations like the Guardians) and demonstrations—behaviour which Italians may interpret as subversive. Instead, Filipinos prefer to engage in cultural exchange through film, state sponsored events, and media. They call these efforts 'sensibilization,' an effort to expose their Italian neighbours to the more desirable (and thus, easily exotified) aspects of Filipino culture.

Lately, Filipinos are becoming more visible. One factor that affects their (in)visibility is gender. The Filipino woman is seen as deserving but weak, her male counterpart less so. The composition of the Filipino community is shifting. Early Filipino migration waves were dominated by Filipino women. With the institution of the Martelli Act 1990, family reunification was made possible. Slowly, Filipino men and children trickled in and currently make a more significant part of the Filipino community in Rome. With the arrival of their families, Filipinos began to have more extensive contacts with Italian institutions and public spaces like schools and hospitals. These interactions have increased their visibility and Italian concern with Filipino behaviour. Over the past ten years, reporting on Filipino criminality has increased, especially male, youth criminality. But these reports are rare and innocuous compared to those associated with the Bangladeshi.

Unlike Filipinos, the Bangladeshi community was established by male-driven migration chains many of whom worked as labourers for other immigrants, like the Chinese or as street vendors.[33] Over time, the first group of Bangladeshis in Italy set up 'travel agencies' through which they recruited co-nationals, frequently from their own provinces.[34]

By means of travel agencies, Bangladeshi leaders set up visas, living arrangements, and employment opportunities for their co-nationals. These activities established and strengthened Bangladeshi migration chains. The Italian media has speculated extensively not only on the legality of these arrangements, but on the possibility that exploitation is widespread within the Bangladeshi community. In November 2015, the police blotter of the Rome edition of *la Reppublica* reported on the arrest of a Bengali man who was caught trafficking false documents to refugees for 600 Euros. The report connects the illegal activities to a 'network of the Bengali … with whom the Senegalese man was linked in recent weeks.' A few weeks later, similar activities were linked

---

[33] Nicholas Demaria Harney, 'Transnationalism and Entrepreneurial Migrancy in Naples, Italy,' *Journal of Ethnic and Migration Studies* 33/2 (2007), 219–32.

[34] Melanie Knights, 'Bangladeshi Immigrants in Italy: From Geopolitics to Micropolitics,' *Transactions of the Institute of British Geographers* (1996), 105–23.

to the terrorist events in Paris.[35] In Italy, all foreign born residents are supposed to register their address at a registry of the Ministry of Internal Affairs.

Because most Bangladeshis rely primarily on co-ethnics for employment, the Bangladeshi community tends to be geographically clustered. This clustering has contributed to the emergence of an enclave economy. The neighbourhood of Tor Pignattara is home to numerous businesses that serve the Bangladeshi community, including a language school where Bangladeshi children may learn Bangladeshi on the weekend, restaurants and grocers, a handful of video stores, and apparel stores where Bangladeshi women may buy *Sharee* or the less formal *salwar kameer*. Also contributing to their visibility is the sizeable engagement of Bangladeshis in commerce. Bangladeshi businessmen have also began to run small businesses across the city, taking over shops that were previously run by Italians. Their visibility has engendered considerable resentment among Italians.

In the majority of crimes involving immigrants that have been reported in the press, immigrants are usually the perpetrators. In the case of Bangladeshis however, a disproportionate number of crimes reported involve acts of violence committed against Bangladeshis. This despite the fact that other national groups are just as visible as the Bangladeshi, the Chinese for example have a notable presence in the Esquilino neighbourhood where they operate numerous wholesale apparel stores, restaurants, bars, and grocery stores.[36] The level and frequency of violence suggest that Bangladeshis safety is not considered of equal value as other groups. A newspaper report recorded the following incident:

> Late Wednesday three Italian youths allegedly attacked a 39-year-old Bangladeshi who was selling T-shirts in Via dei Baullari, close to the popular tourist zone of Campo de' Fiori in central Rome. According to media reports the victim claimed he was surrounded by the youths, who began calling him a 'dirty nigger,' as they proceeded to destroy the makeshift stall. Later, the youths savagely kicked and punched the immigrant and allegedly stole the man's mobile phone. Dozens of people witnessed the attack, but police have not found those responsible for

[35] Annie Phizacklea, 'State Security Versus the Security of Migrants: The Unbalanced Contest,' in *Security, Insecurity and Migration in Europe*, ed. Gabriella Lazaridis (London and New York: Routledge, 2016), 287.

[36] Russell King and Jacqueline Andall, 'The Geography and Economic Sociology of Recent Immigration to Italy,' *Modern Italy* 4/2 (1999), 135–58; Uma Kothari, 'Global Peddlers and Local Networks: Migrant Cosmopolitanisms,' *Environment and Planning D: Society and Space* 26/3 (2008), 500–16.

the violence.[37]

A 2011 report by Human Rights Watch found that, despite evidence of increasingly violent attacks on Bangladeshi business-owners and street vendors:

> Public authorities tend to minimize the extent of racist violence in Italy, calling such crimes episodic and rare, and the racist or xenophobic dimension of events—such as the targeted attacks on sub-Saharan African seasonal migrants, gangs that target immigrants for extortion and beatings, and attacks on Roma settlements—is often minimized or excluded.[38]

Some of this scorn may stem from the phenotypical differences between Bangladeshis and Italians. Another source of conflict may be religious identity, which is exacerbated through the media representation which centers on 'Otherness,' as Rinella Cere observes:

> Prejudice and stereotyping have reached new proportions in the constant association between Islam and terrorism and the consequent criminalization of Muslim. Immigrants from Muslim countries, or mixed faith countries (Kurdish people from Iraq and Turkey, Northern and Sub-Saharan Africans, especially Senegal, Eritrea, Somalia and in recent times more frequently from Asia, especially Bangladesh) make up the largest immigrant group in Italy. These communities are often in the news due to anti-Islamic feelings constantly been whipped up by the Lega Nord and other centre-right forces alongside sections of the Catholic Church. … Issues covered often revolve around the building of new mosques and activities in mosques, what may appear to be 'non-events' in news and informational culture. The opposition to mosque building is an ongoing trope in Italy as mosques are increasingly seen as terrorist centres rather than places of worship. Over the years research has shown that in Italy as elsewhere much news coverage has centred on 'fears of mosques,' 'Islamic invasions' and 'threats to civilization.'[39]

---

[37] AKI, 'Italy: Bangladeshi ambassador alarmed at migrant attacks,' *adnkronos*, 12 February 2014, accessed 1 January 2015, http://www1.adnkronos.com/AKI/English/Security/?id=3.0.3009839575.

[38] Human Rights Watch, 'Everyday Intolerance: Racist and Xenophobic Violence in Italy,' *Human Rights Watch*, 2011, accessed 10 November 2016, https://www.hrw.org/report/2011/03/21/everyday-intolerance/racist-and-xenophobic-violence-italy.

[39] Cere, 'Globalization vs. localization,' 8. See also Cere, Rinella. '"Islamophobia" and the Media in Italy,' *Feminist Media Studies* 2/1 (2002), 133–36; Chantal Saint-Blancat and Ottavia Schmidt di Friedberg, 'Why are mosques a problem? Local politics and fear of Islam in northern Italy,' *Journal of Ethnic and Migration Studies* 31/6 (2005), 1083–104.

These incidents hint at a sense of entitlement on the part of Italians regarding who deserves to be safe, who deserves to be free, who deserves to have a good life. Visible diasporic migrants are perceived as less than human: as such they merit disdain. They need not be acknowledged. To acknowledge them is to recognize their right to share in that space that was once occupied exclusively by Italians and other desired individuals. Those who are less than human may be exotified in their cultural and physical form. They invite contempt and their life and safety may be considered of less value.

In response the Bangladeshi diaspora protests. It makes the language of the public square felt. It uses public space as a stage where it shouts its right to escape. Discussing the political organization of the Bangladeshi community during an interview with Informant 790, an important association leader, declared:

> The institution only knows one language. This is the power of the public square. They don't understand Italian, Bangladeshi, or Pakistani. Nothing. Nothing. If we are many in the square, in movement, they understand. That is, this is a language that they are familiar with.[40]

Spatial Justice, Social Constructions and the Right to Escape

Spatial (in)justice employs 'an intentional and focused emphasis on the spatial or geographical aspects of justice and injustice. As a starting point, this involves the fair and equitable distribution of space of socially valued resources and the opportunities to use them.'[41] This analytic framework provides an important lens through which we may view contemporary diasporic migration.

The very same globalization that has contributed to the free movement of goods, has promoted the imposition of artificial constraints on the free movement of people.[42] This trend has led to an intensification of distributional (injustice) between the global core and periphery. In other words, globalization has effectively reorganized global and local communities so that the spatial distribution of power and opportunity has intensified and is maintained through control over human physical and social mobility. This is an injustice which migrants actively seek to combat through efforts to overcome the imposition of national confines

---

[40] Interview transcript with Informant 790, 2011.
[41] Edward Soja, 'The City and Spatial Justice,' Spatial Justice 1 (2009), 3.
[42] Sandro Mezzadra, 'The Right to Escape,' *Ephemera* 4/3 (2004), 272.

upon their own spatial identities.[43] Diasporas, then, bely the absolutism assigned to the migrant condition through the tight control of access to space.

David Harvey employs a relational view of space. In his conceptualization, space is a social construction which engages in and is engaged by social processes.[44] Social constructions are assignments of membership through particular affiliations with a set of determining characteristics.[45] They furnish societies with a fast, easy to deploy, and simple way to frame policy preferences. There is a multiplicity in migrants' engagement with space, and therefore in the social constructions they encounter.

In his treatise on contemporary migration, Mezzadra expresses a deep dissatisfaction with the nature of rhetoric on immigration flows disseminated by immigration's supporters and detractors, alike.[46] Immigrant detractors vilify the immigrant. The intensity, dynamism, and elevated numbers of human mobility brought about by globalization have aided the rise to power of nationalist movements concerned with securing borders and promoting the 'preservation' of national identity.

After its explosion in the early 1980s, Italian in-migration was characterized in the dominant discourse as a social disease from which the nation must cleanse itself.[47] Fear and dislike of immigrants runs across classes because immigrants—and diasporic migrants in particular—are seen as a threat to a cohesive national identity:

> I am telling you, the pride of the Romans, Romans [emphasis], that pride inside that with the arrival of immigrants says, 'they will ruin the purity of the genetics of the Roman people.' There is that pride that even today remains. If you take a Roman, one from Lungotevere, Trastevere, and he will respond in a rude way saying, 'Ehhhh, the Italian race is mixing. This is not right. I am a Roman from Rome.' The pride of the Ancient Romans remains ingrained.[48]

Over the years, the symbolism of security has overtaken that of

---

[43] Suzanne Hall, 'Migrant Urbanisms: Ordinary Cities and Everyday Resistance,' *Sociology* 49/5 (2015), 853–69.

[44] David Harvey, *Social Justice and the City* (Athens: University of Georgia Press, 2010).

[45] Anne Schneider and Helen M. Ingram, *Deserving and Entitled: Social Constructions and Public Policy* (New York: SUNY Press, 2005).

[46] Mezzadra, 'The right to escape.'

[47] Norma Bouchard, 'Reading the Discourse of Multicultural Italy: Promises and Challenges of Transnational Italy in an Era of Global Migration,' *Italian Culture* 28/2 (2010), 104–120.

[48] Interview transcript with Informant 651, second generation Bengali woman.

disease in the Italian imagination on immigration. This symbolism was crafted and promoted through media outlets, in popular writing, and by political leaders.

The 2009 Security Act is Italy's standing policy position on immigration. It was aimed at reinforcing and moving Italy further along a path that was set with 2002's Bossi-Fini Law (Law No. 189). Both laws were designed and adopted by Silvio Berlusconi's Center-Right coalition government and signaled a new phase in the Italian state's approach to immigration which reflected the dominance of discourses on immigrant deviance within the ruling party and its supporters.

The 2009 Security Act was promoted using three general justifications: economic security, physical security, and national security. These discourses were powered by the political opportunism of Berlusconi's Forza Italia and along with the ethno-centric populist party, La Lega Nord (the Northern League). La Lega established itself as *the* anti-immigration party.[49] It adopts a strategy of blame and fear. Among the tropes commonly employed by the party involves terrorism and jihad and the suggestion that migrants are a source of unfair economic competition that threaten Italian households. In this view, the immigrant is a scourge, a deviant, and a criminal. The immigrant is less than human.

In contrast, advocates for immigrants bring forth issues of poverty, precariousness, and desperation. New human movements have given rise to an active and energetic migrant advocacy. Unfortunately, the discourses adopted by these groups, in large part, impose a paternalistic view of the immigrant, a dependent. Immigrant allies tend to dress immigrant groups in the garb of deserving (often noble) but weak individuals. Often couched in universalistic ideology, their arguments characterize immigrants as helpless and in need of saving, specifically, through the intervention of public authorities. As an object rather than a subject of discourses, immigrants are further stripped of their power. Once again, the immigrant is less than human.[50] Both pro- and anti-migration narratives converge upon the main theme of poverty. Indeed, the central debate has become about the right to escape poverty

---

[49] Daniele Albertazzi and Duncan McDonnell, 'The Lega Nord in the Second Berlusconi Government: In a League of Its Own,' *West European* Politics 28/5 (2005), 952–72.

[50] 'Within any system of stratification, people with power and authority are prone to undertake boundary work to define one or more out-groups and them frame them as lacking basic human attributes of warmth and competence.' Massey, S. Douglas, and Magaly Sánchez, *Brokered Boundaries: Immigrant Identity in Anti-Immigrant Times: Immigrant Identity in Anti-Immigrant Times* (New York: Russell Sage Foundation, 2010), 14.

in light of the *equivocal nature* of migrant purposes.[51] While poverty is a main focus, both accounts underplay the role of purpose. Thus, they ignore the migrant's agency.

Mezzadra offers us an alternative view of the migrant who, in choosing to ignore the constraints of space, indeed, in choosing to directly to engage space is simply exercising every human being's *right to escape*. He describes contemporary migration flows as 'globalization from below' which:

> In absolutely every sense, it is through the migrations that millions of women and men have materially organized their own existence, their own social relations, their own production and reproduction, giving no thought to the boundaries between states and constructing new 'transnational social spaces.'[52]

In other words, through immigration, migrants engage space and wrest power back for themselves. By cementing the relocation of cultures, traditions, belief systems, and physical bodies the diaspora is the physical manifestation of human agency, of every immigrant's 'expression of a series of subjective movements of escape from the rigidities of the international division of labour.'[53] Immigration is thus a form of resistance, and the diaspora the core of such resistance to the spatial power of the word.

[51] Cere, 'Globalisation vs. localisation.'
[52] Mezzadra, 'The right to escape,' 272.
[53] Mezzadra, 'The right to escape,' 274.

7

Racial and Spatial Injustices and the Tower Hamlets Coup

Nadine El-Enany

Introduction

'LET JUSTICE BE DONE THOUGH THE HEAVENS FALL,' Deputy High Court Judge, Richard Mawrey declared as he delivered a recent ruling which voided Lutfur Rahman's reelection as mayor of the London borough of Tower Hamlets on 22 May 2014 (para. 527).[1] Almost 37,000 people voted for Rahman in an election which saw a record turnout. Lutfur Rahman was born in Bangladesh (at the time, East Pakistan) and came to Britain as a child, growing up in Tower Hamlets. Rahman was first elected as mayor of the borough in 2010, becoming Britain's first Muslim mayor. He was reelected in 2014. Under Rahman's mayorship, schools in Tower Hamlets went from being among the worst-rated in the country to being among the best.[2] While other boroughs closed their libraries, Tower Hamlets' expanded and the availability of social housing increased.[3] In a 200-page judgment delivered on 23 April 2015, Mawrey found Rahman guilty of a series of corrupt and illegal practices. However, the verdict rested on a failure to understand the meaning and extent of racism in Britain today, and is based on racist, and specifically Islamophobic reasoning. It cannot therefore be said to be just. How can Muslims in Britain have faith in a legal system that produces a judgment such as this one? This chapter draws on the work of Avtar Brah on diasporic communities to argue that this legal judgment not only deprived Rahman of his mandate to rule, but has also put in jeopardy a more promising socio-economic

[1] *Erlam and Others v Rahman and Another* April 23 2015 [2015] EWHC 1215 (QB)
[2] Helen Crane, 'How Tower Hamlets Transformed Its failing Schools,' *The Guardian*, 11 December 2013, accessed 26 January 2016, http://www.theguardian.com/teacher-network/2013/dec/11/tower-hamlets-transforming-failing-schools-ofsted.
[3] Paul Thomson, 'Tower Hamlets: A Victory for Democracy or a Neocolonial Coup?' *Open Democracy*, 22 June 2015, accessed 26 January 2016. https://www.opendemocracy.net/ourkingdom/lutfur-rahman-victory-for-democracy-or-neocolonial-coup.

future for Tower Hamlets' Bangladeshi community, rendering it more precarious and contingent. Further, drawing on the work of Sara Ahmed and Sarah Keenan on whether and how spaces can be re-oriented or reshaped towards justice, it is argued that to be concerned with spatial justice demands an engagement with the way in which spaces of injustice are often racialized.

Tower Hamlets as a Space of Racial Injustice

Avtar Brah has emphasized the importance of identifying the 'regimes of power' that 'inscribe the formation of a specific diaspora.'[4] According to Brah, the means through which a diasporic community 'comes to be "situated" in and through a wide variety of discourses, economic processes, state policies and institutional practices is critical to its future.'[5] It is in the course of determining the 'relational positioning' of diasporic communities that we begin to be able to 'deconstruct the regimes of power which operate to differentiate one group from another; to represent as similar or different; to include or exclude them from constructions of the 'nation' and the body politic; and which inscribe them as juridical, political, and psychic subjects.'[6] The Muslim Bangladeshi diasporic community residing in Tower Hamlets has a history imbued with resistance to imperialism and struggle for independence from colonial rule, with first generation migrants being active in the mass independence movement in Bangladesh resisting the Pakistan government in the 1960s and 70s through participation in protests, fundraising and lobbying of the British government.[7] According to David Garbin, this 'politicization of Bangladeshi migrants through the independence struggle paved the way for the institutionalization of an ethno-national identity based on secular, nationalist and socialist values,' which 'had a key role to play in the maintenance of a diasporic collective memory linking the "Liberation War" in Bangladesh to strategies of resistance to racism and discrimination in the British Bangladeshi urban enclaves.'[8]

In the course of removing Rahman from office and declaring the

[4] Avtar Brah, *Cartographies of Diaspora: Contesting Identities* (New York and London: Routledge, 1996), 182.

[5] Brah, *Cartographies*, 183.

[6] Brah, *Cartographies*, 183.

[7] David Garbin, 'A Diasporic Sense of Place: Dynamics of Spatialization and Transnational Political Fields among Bangladeshi Muslims in Britain,' in *Transnational Ties: Cities, Migrations, and Identities*, eds. John Eade and Micheal Peter Smith (New Brunswick and London: Transaction Publishers, 2009), 150.

[8] Garbin, 'A Diasporic Sense of Place,' 150.

2014 mayoral election result void, Deputy High Court Judge Mawrey denied that Bangladeshis are a 'beleaguered ethnic minority' due to their relatively large size (32 per cent) within the borders of Tower Hamlets.[9] Further, he deduced that Bangladeshis are therefore not subject to 'hostile racial prejudice.'[10] Yet it is not the number of individuals belonging to a particular group in a borough that makes them a minority, but their presence as a racialized community within a broader political context of oppression. As Jan Mohammed has argued, a minority 'can be defined only in "political" terms—that is, in terms of the effects of economic exploitation, political disenfranchisement, social manipulation, and ideological domination.'[11] Much evidence exists demonstrating that the Bangladeshi community is subject to extreme economic and other forms of structural oppression.[12] In economic terms, Bangladeshi males face significant discrimination and disadvantage, earning on average 21 per cent less than white males.[13] A 2010 study found that the families of 73 per cent of Bangladeshi seven-year olds were living on less than 60 per cent of the average national household income.[14] Tower Hamlets suffers from the highest levels of poverty in Britain.[15] Further, Muslims continue to be portrayed in an overwhelmingly negative manner in the media which contributes to the hostility and violence meted out against them.[16] One study found that 91 per cent of 352 randomly selected articles about Muslims in a one week period in 2007 were 'negative.'[17] Metropolitan Police Service figures show that between April 2012 and September 2014, 100 'Islamophobic' hate crimes were recorded in Tower Hamlets, more than in any other London borough.[18]

[9] *Erlam and Others v Rahman*, para. 179.

[10] *Erlam and Others v Rahman*, para. 179.

[11] Abdul Jan Mohammed and David Lloyd, *The Nature and Context of Minority Discourse* (Oxford: OUP, 1990) in Brah, *Cartographies*, 188.

[12] Simonetta Longhi and Lucinda Platt, *Pay Gaps Across Equalities Areas* (Colchester: Institute for Social and Economic Research, 2008).

[13] Longhi and Platt, *Pay Gaps*, ix.

[14] Alice Sullivan et al., *The Consequences at Age 7 of Early Childhood Disadvantage in Northern Ireland and Great Britain* (London: IOE Centre for Longitudinal Studies, 2010), 27.

[15] Ben Gray, 'Social Exclusion, Poverty, Health and Social Care in Tower Hamlets: The Perspectives of Families on the Impact of the Family Support Service,' *British Journal of Social Work* 33/3 (2003), 361–80; End Child Poverty Commission, *London's Poverty Profile* (London: New Policy Institute, 2013).

[16] Adrian Cousins, 'When Is a Minority Not a Minority? When They're Bangladeshis Living in Tower Hamlets,' *Counterfire*, 13 May 2015, accessed 13 January 2016 www.counterfire.org/articles/analysis/17777-when-is-a-minority-not-a-minority-when-they-re-bangladeshis-living-in-tower-hamlets.

[17] Sara Ahmed, 'A Phenomenology of Whiteness,' *Feminist Theory* 8 (2007), 25.

[18] TELLMAMA (2014), 'Anti-Muslim Hate Crimes, 2012–2014 in London: An

Mawrey's downplaying of racism against the Bangladeshi community in Tower Hamlets seems not merely to be a matter of ignorance, but to connect to a broader political agenda, manifested in his discussion of institutional racism. The 1999 Macpherson report defined institutional racism as:

> The collective failure of an organisation to provide an appropriate and professional service to people because of their colour, culture, or ethnic origin. It can be seen or detected in processes, attitudes and behaviour which amount to discrimination through unwitting prejudice, ignorance, thoughtlessness and racist stereotyping which disadvantage minority ethnic people.[19]

Mawrey expresses sympathy for the view that 'the imputation of "institutional racism" made by the Macpherson Inquiry, albeit 16 years ago, still dogs the [Police] Force' and acts as a hindrance to the proper carrying out of their work.[20] For a judge to regret that the police force, or any organization, might be concerned about institutional racism is dangerous. The origins of the Macpherson report lie in the Met police force's failure to competently investigate the racially motivated murder of Stephen Lawrence. Mawrey's comment therefore is not only reckless in its dismissal of the importance of identifying and tackling institutional racism, but is also entirely out of touch with reality. Allegations of police racism have not subsided in the 16 years since the Macpherson Inquiry.[21] In 2013, the Metropolitan Black Police Association declared that the force was still 'institutionally racist.'[22] Black people are six times as likely to be stopped and searched, and Asian people twice as likely, as their white counterparts.[23] In 2013, Stephen Lawrence's brother, Stuart Lawrence, lodged a racism complaint after having been

Analysis of the Situation,' 11 November 2014, accessed 26 January 2016, tellmamauk. org/anti-muslim-hate-crimes-2012-2014-in-london-an-analysis-of-the-situation/; See further Saied Reza Ameli and Arzu Merali, *Environment of Hate: The New Normal for Muslims in the UK* (Wembley: Islamic Human Rights Commission, 2015).

[19] Home Office (1999) *The Stephen Lawrence Inquiry: Report of an Inquiry by Sir Willian Macpherson of Cluny* (Cm 4262-1) [*The Macpherson Report*], para. 6.34.

[20] *The Macpherson Report*, para. 610.

[21] Paul Lewis, 'Eleven Met Police Cases of Alleged Racism,' *The Guardian*, 16 April 2012, accessed 26 January 2016, www.theguardian.com/uk/2012/apr/16/met-police-cases-alleged-racism.

[22] Hugh Muir, 'Metropolitan Police Still Institutionally Racist, Say Black and Asian Officers,' *The Guardian*, 21 April 2013, accessed 26 January 2016, www.theguardian.com/uk/2013/apr/21/metropolitan-police-institutionally-racist-black.

[23] Niamh Eastwood et al., *The Numbers in Black and White: Ethnic Disparities in the Policing and Prosecution of Drug Offences in England and Wales* (London: Release, 2013).

stopped in his car by police 25 times.[24] Mawrey not only believes that the existence of racism is overplayed, but also that those who 'call out' racists, are merely 'playing the race card.'[25] He characterizes the 1993 election of British National Party (BNP) councillor Derek Beackon as having elicited a reaction 'bordering on hysteria' amongst Tower Hamlets politicians and was 'used, for decades afterwards, to justify the claim that racism stalked the Borough and that only constant vigilance would prevent Tower Hamlets from becoming a fascist, not to say Nazi, outpost.'[26] Mawrey deems 'the BNP and later the EDL' (English Defence League) to have been 'a very useful bogeyman with which to affright the citizens, especially the non-white citizens, of Tower Hamlets,' asserting that 'in reality the political support for these organizations has long been negligible.'[27] Yet there is much cause for Tower Hamlets residents to maintain a vigilant attitude towards racism. The EDL have three times marched through the borough. Beackon was the first of scores of BNP candidates to achieve electoral success. His win came shortly after the murder of Stephen Lawrence. After the BNP established their head-quarters in South East London, the area saw a spate of racist murders, including that of Lawrence. Considering this context, for Mawrey to sneer at 'hysterical' anti-racist campaigners is not only facetious, but also significantly underplays the prevalence of racism in the borough. This glib and insinuating tone runs throughout the judgment and is indicative of Mawrey's systematic trivialization of racism.

Thus, Mawrey disparages dog-whistle politics, congratulating the 'wise folk of the Oxford English Dictionary' (OED) for not deigning to define it.[28] He turns to Wikipedia instead and notes that dog-whistle politics is 'political messaging employing coded language that appears to mean one thing ... but has another additional, different or more specific resonance for a targeted subgroup.' 'The advantage of the cliché,' he opines, 'is that one may take a completely innocent, indeed anodyne, statement of a political opponent and claim that it contains a 'coded' message often ... of a racist nature.'[29] For Mawrey, to accuse a politician of dog-whistling is always to cry wolf. In the face of the increasing popularity of anti-immigration parties such as the United Kingdom Independence Party (UKIP) and the number of its members

[24] Shiv Malik and Sandra Laville, 'Stephen Lawrence's Brother Lodges Racism Complaint against Met Police,' *The Guardian*, 9 January 2013, accessed 26 January 2016 http://www.theguardian.com/uk/2013/jan/09/stephen-lawrence-brother-racism-police.

[25] *Erlam and Others v Rahman*, para. 529.

[26] *Erlam and Others v Rahman*, para. 191.

[27] *Erlam and Others v Rahman*, para. 191.

[28] *Erlam and Others v Rahman*, para. 196.

[29] *Erlam and Others v Rahman*, para. 197.

who are suspended for making racist remarks, it is naive to deny the existence of dog-whistle politics, a point even the right wing press has acknowledged.[30] Most disturbing is Mawrey's adoption of racist reasoning. The perception that Muslims are of inferior mind runs throughout the judgment. On finding Rahman guilty of 'undue spiritual influence,'[31] Mawrey draws a comparison with the use of this offence to overturn the votes of Irish Catholics in the 1800s:

> Time and again it was stressed that the Catholic voters were men of simple faith, usually much less well educated than the clergy who were influencing them, and men whose natural instinct would be to obey the orders of their priests... This principle still holds good.... a distinction must be made between a sophisticated, highly educated and politically literate community and a community which is traditional, respectful of authority and, possibly, not fully integrated with the other communities living in the same area...it is the character of the person sought to be influenced that is key to whether influence has been applied.[32]

From this he concludes that 'it would be wrong ... to treat Tower Hamlets' Muslim community by the standards of a secular and largely agnostic metropolitan elite.' The suggestion is that the typical Muslim voter is not capable of the rational judgment and circumspection of her 'White-British' counterpart.[33]

Mawrey cannot claim ignorance of the meaning of racism. He includes the OED definition in the judgment, stating that racism is:

[30] Kevin Rawlinson, 'Ukip Suspends Election Candidate Jack Sen over Racially Charged Comments,' *The Guardian*, 1 May 2015, accessed 26 January 2016, www. theguardian.com/politics/2015/may/01/ukip-suspends-election-candidate-jack-sen-over-racially-charged-comments; Anthony Bond et al., 'The UKIP Leader and the Facebook Racist: Nigel Farage Shakes Hands with Party Candidate Who Says Discrimination Is "Just Ethnic Banter" and Supports Extreme Right,' The Daily Mail, 27 April 2013, accessed 26 January 2016, www.dailymail.co.uk/news/article-2315656/ The-UKIP-leader-Facebook-racist-As-UKIP-leader-Farage-pictured-shaking-hands-English-Defence-League-supporter-candidates-embroiled-homophobic-row.html; Graeme Archer, 'Ukip's Extremists Might Not Represent the Party, but Their Dog-Whistle Mood Music Sets the Tone Nonetheless,' 29 April 2013, accessed 26 January 2016, blogs.telegraph.co.uk/news/graemearcher/100214210/ukips-extremists-might-not-represent-the-party-but-their-dog-whistle-mood-music-sets-the-tone-nonetheless/.
[31] The High Court has recently granted Rahman permission to apply for judicial review of this aspect of the judgment. See further on the guilty verdict for the offence of undue spiritual influence, Giles Fraser, 'The Lutfur Rahman Verdict and the Spectre Of "Undue Spiritual Influence,"' *The Guardian*, 29 April 2015, accessed 26 January 2016, www.theguardian.com/commentisfree/2015/apr/29/ lutfur-rahman-tower-hamlets-mayor-verdict-undue-spiritual-influence.
[32] *Erlam and Others v Rahman*, para. 159.
[33] *Erlam and Others v Rahman*, para. 178.

a belief that one's own racial or ethnic group is superior...also a belief that the members of different racial or ethnic groups possess specific characteristics, abilities, or qualities which can be compared and evaluated. Hence prejudice, discrimination, or antagonism directed against people of other racial or ethnic groups (or, more widely, of other nationalities), esp. based on such beliefs.[34]

Mawrey's reasoning that Tower Hamlets' Bangladeshi community, like the 19th century Irish, have a 'natural instinct' to obey orders, are 'less well educated' and not 'politically literate,' and should be treated according to different standards than a 'secular and largely agnostic metropolitan elite,' fits comfortably within the OED definition of racism.[35]

Mawrey did not include the OED definition of racism in order to be judged against it himself, but in order to test the allegation that Lutfur Rahman made 'false statements' contrary to s. 106 of the Representation of the People Act 1983 that John Biggs, the rival Labour mayoral candidate, was a racist. Mawrey sees no racism in Biggs' claim that, 'all [Rahman's] councillors are from the Bangladeshi community and the primary focus of his policy making has been on the Bangladeshi community ... what we don't want to have is small communities that are separate from each other and are very inward looking because the world will pass them by.'[36] Mawrey found the statement not to be 'racially insensitive' and this laid Rahman open to a guilty verdict. Yet if we consider the reality of everyday racism—subtle, commonplace forms of discrimination—and of dog-whistle politics, we can identify the racism in Biggs' comment.[37] It plays to a stereotype of the Bangladeshi community. The message is that Bangladeshis are the problem: their leaders are corrupt, their failure to 'integrate' is a result of their preference for an 'inward looking' lifestyle, they are ignored by the world because of their own deficiencies rather than because they are victims of structural discrimination and Islamophobia.[38] This is the very same reasoning about Bangladeshi Muslims that is reproduced in Mawrey's judgment and that made this community's votes so expendable.

---

[34] *Erlam and Others v Rahman*, para. 380.

[35] *Erlam and Others v Rahman*, paras 159 and 561.

[36] *Erlam and Others v Rahman*, para. 394.

[37] On the reality of everyday racism, see Alvin Alvarez and Linda Juang, 'Filipino Americans and Racism: A Multiple Mediation Model of Coping,' *Journal of Counselling Psychology* 57/2 (2010), 167–78.

[38] Alvin and Juang, 'Filipino Americans and Racism.'

Conclusion: Towards Spatial Justice?

In the judgment which secured the removal of Lutfur Rahman from office, Mawrey not only expresses the view that the existence of racism is overplayed, but he also employs racist reasoning. With this in mind, it is difficult not to draw the conclusion that Mawrey should not have been trusted to ascertain the guilt of a Muslim and to determine allegations of racism. While this case concerns local politics, its implications stretch far beyond the borough of Tower Hamlets. The reasoning deployed in the judgment is indicative of an Islamophobia which Hamid Dabashi has described as 'unabated and growing' in Europe and North America.[39] That a judge can expound the view that the 'natural instinct' of Muslims is to defer to their religious leaders and that Bangladeshis are a 'less sophisticated' and 'less well-educated' people begs the question as to whether the accusation of institutional racism that Mawrey so derides cannot also be laid at the door of the judiciary and the legal system it is tasked with upholding.[40] In view of the judgment and its wider implications, the question remains as to whether justice is possible for Muslims in Britain, whether the space in Tower Hamlets, and Britain more widely, can be 'reshaped' or 're-oriented' towards justice, or at the least, a different outcome yielded than that dealt by the law in this instance.[41] The Electoral Petition which succeeded before Mawrey followed multiple attempts by the media and political establishment over the course of several years to smear Lutfur Rahman.[42] The ease with which Rahman was removed from office, by a Deputy High Court judge sitting alone, with barely a voice of protest discernible in the media, and left with no avenue for appeal, save judicial review, creates a sense that Rahman's time in power was somehow always up, always time-limited, that Tower Hamlets was never really 'available [to him] as a space for action,' as a Muslim from Bangladesh living in Britain today.[43] As Ahmed writes, 'bodies are shaped by histories of colonialism, which makes the world "white", a world that is inherited, or which is already given before the

---

[39] Hamid Dabashi, *Brown Skin White Masks* (Pluto Press, 2011).

[40] *Erlam and Others v Rahman*, para. 159.

[41] Sarah Keenan, *Subversive Property: Law and the Production of Spaces of Belonging* (Abingdon and New York: Routledge, 2015), 11; Ahmed, 'A Phenomenology of Whiteness,' 149–68.

[42] Ashok Kumar and Richard Seymour, 'The Lutfur Rahman Verdict and the Spectre Of "Undue Spiritual Influence,",' *The Guardian*, 30 May 2014, accessed 26 January 2016, http://www.theguardian.com/commentisfree/2014/may/30/lutfur-rahman-tower-hamlets-mayor-smear-campaign.

[43] Ahmed, 'A Phenomenology of Whiteness,' 153.

point of an individual's arrival.'[44] While colonialism makes the 'world "ready" for certain kinds of bodies' and 'puts certain objects within their reach,'[45] it puts those objects, places, institutions out of reach of other bodies. Institutions, including political institutions, such as offices of local government 'take the shape of "what" resides within them.'[46] If 'institutions become given, as an effect of the repetition of decisions made over time, which shapes the surface of institutional spaces,' then Lutfur Rahman, as a Bangladeshi Muslim mayor with progressive socio-economic goals, was perhaps always 'out of place,' 'improper,' always acutely, especially at risk of being 'repelled, unsettled or realigned.'[47] While Tower Hamlets might be home to a Bangladeshi community, the judgment and its effects suggest that the borough is not *for* them. Though they might inhabit the borough, the legacies of colonialism have meant that they neither inherited 'the reachability' of crucial resources, nor the power to determine their management and material distribution.[48] Through his administration's policies, Lutfur Rahman had been working towards achieving a fairer allocation of socio-economic resources within Tower Hamlets. In this way, Rahman's policies were directly pitched against the production of 'unjust geographies' by the incumbent Conservative government's economic policies entailing deep cuts in spending on sectors such as welfare, housing, and healthcare.[49] In the course of giving his ruling, Mawrey censured Rahman for having concentrated rehousing projects in wards with a higher proportion of Bangladeshis. Yet these are the areas in which there is the highest level of poverty and overcrowding, the effects of which are borne primarily by racialized communities. The judgment thus not only accomplished the confiscation of Rahman's mandate to govern Tower Hamlets, but also secured the erasure of his progressive policies and the further disenfranchisement of the most marginalized in the borough. It is not only their votes which have been discarded, but along with them, a more promising socio-economic future for the poorest in Tower Hamlets.

If race can be understood as a 'question of what is within reach, what is available to perceive and to do "things" with' and space understood as 'taking shape by being oriented around some bodies, more than

---

[44] Ahmed, 'A Phenomenology of Whiteness,' 153.
[45] Ahmed, 'A Phenomenology of Whiteness,' 153–4.
[46] Ahmed, 'A Phenomenology of Whiteness,' 157.
[47] Keenan, *Subversive Property*, 13.
[48] Ahmed, 'A Phenomenology of Whiteness,' 154.
[49] On 'unjust geographies,' see Edward Soja, *Seeking Spatial Justice* (Minneapolis: University of Minnesota Press, 2010), 8.

others,'[50] then to be concerned with spatial justice demands an engagement with the way in which spaces of injustice are often racialized. To understand spaces of injustice, to begin to think of ways of making those spaces just, there is a need to begin 'with the body that loses its chair.'[51] Lutfur Rahman's unseating and the disenfranchising effects for the Bangladeshi community of Tower Hamlets will continue to be felt for some time to come. As local organizers gathered outside the venue for a rally in support of Rahman shortly after the judgment was delivered, they tried to hand leaflets to those passing by. One Bangladeshi man, on refusing a leaflet, said sadly, 'democracy in Tower Hamlets is dead.'

[50] Ahmed, 'A Phenomenology of Whiteness,' 154 and 157.
[51] Ahmed, 'A Phenomenology of Whiteness,' 160 [emphasis in original).

8

Ethiopian Diasporic Community Networks and Practice of Homemaking in Sweden

Tekalign Ayalew

Introduction

Ethiopian diasporic communities in Sweden are said to have divided along political, ethnic, and religious lines.[1] But even though Pan-Ethiopian community organizations are rare in Sweden there are several interest groups and community organizations built around Christian churches, profession, political opinion, cultural self-help institutions known as *Iqqub* (a semiformal rotating saving and credit association) and *Iddir* (migrants' association for burial services and emotional and financial support for a grieving person) so as to fulfill the community social and economic needs in Sweden and maintain connections to Ethiopia.[2] Based on Rogers Brubaker's notion of diaspora as a category of practice and using the broader perspective on the concept of 'home' as a place where one is emotionally attached and practically engaged in continuous political, social, familial, and economic projects,[3] I will explore community homemaking activities in relation to countries of destination and origin as well as other dispersed national communities elsewhere. As Bill Ashcroft writes:

[1] The division is the result of diversity back in the 'homeland.' Ethiopia is a multiethnic country with more than 80 languages, and many religious groups. Different regimes have historically used and abused this diversity historically to capitalize their political powers in the country. This has evidently significantly affected Ethiopian origin community organizations in diaspora. See Dereje Feyissa, 'The Transnational Politics of Ethiopian Muslim Diaspora,' *Ethnic and Rational Studies* 35/11 (2012), 1893–913; and Walle Engedayehu, 'The Ethiopian Orthodox Tewahedo Church in the Diaspora: Expansion in the Midst of Division,' *African Social Science Review* 6/1 (2013), accessed 10 November 2016, http://digitalcommons.kennesaw.edu/assr/vol6/iss1/8.

[2] Aredo Dejene, *The Informal and Semi Formal Financial Sectors in Ethiopia: the Study of Iqqub, Iddir and Savings and Credit cooperatives, Research Paper 21,* (Nairobi: African Economic Research Consortium, 1993).

[3] Rogers Brubaker, 'The "Diaspora" Diaspora,' *Ethnic and Racial Studies* 28/1 (2005), 1–19.

Scattering leads to a splitting in the sense of home. A fundamental ambivalence is embedded in the term diaspora: a dual ontology in which the diasporic subject is seen to look in two directions—towards a historical cultural identity on one hand, and the society of relocation on the other.[4]

Diasporic practices of homemaking are manifested when community networks are mobilized for economic and social opportunities by way of overcoming structural challenges such as access to the labour market, welfare systems and permanent residence/citizenship rights in destination country.[5] In other words, money, information, and knowledge; other resources are generated via networks to confront socio-economic and political/jurisdictional barriers and establish a life and livelihood in Sweden. Networks are also mobilized to build churches, in order to facilitate religious and cultural practices in the host land. Community organizations and interest groups are also frequently mobilized to support social and political changes in the country of origin, in collaboration with diasporic groups in other national spaces. Even though there are internal political rifts, envies, or competitions and there is at times exploitation in the community-based ethnic enclaves, people engage in networks instrumentally by *contracting and expanding* one's identity frameworks for a particular purpose at particular moments. Hence I will argue that one dimension of the diasporic practice of homemaking is a dynamic process of negotiating one's connections and disconnections as well as exclusions and inclusions in both the country of origin and that of destination, via solidarity generated through a particular form of shared experiences consolidated during the process of migration.[6]

In the first section of this chapter I will elaborate on the notion of diaspora and 'home.' In the second section the process of Ethiopians emigration to Sweden and community formation will be discussed briefly. The third section traces the establishment and role of Ethiopian Christian church organizations in everyday homemaking activities in Sweden, and through practices of transnational engagement. The fourth section discusses the organizational role of the Ethiopian Sport and

[4] Bill Ashcroft et al., *The Post-Colonial Studies Reader* (London: Routledge, 1995), 425.

[5] Sofie Fredlund-Blomst, *Assessing Immigrant Integration in Sweden after the May 2013 Riots* (Washington, DC: Migration Policy Institute, 2014).

[6] Avtar Brah, *Cartographies of Diaspora: Contesting Identities* (New York and London: Routledge, 1996); Minoo Alinia et al., 'The Kurdish Diaspora: Transnational Ties, Home, and Politics of Belonging,' *Nordic Journal of Migration Research* 4/2 (2014), 53–6.

Culture Federation and the Ethiopian Radio in Sweden in facilitating socioeconomic and cultural needs in Sweden and facilitating cross border solidarity with Ethiopians in diaspora. Section five explores the purpose and role of cultural self-help associations (*Iqqub* and *Iddir*) in settling community day-to-day social and economic challenges. The sixth section discusses the association of Ethiopian Health professionals in Sweden and its members' individual and collective engagement in community related development projects in Sweden and Ethiopia. The last part offers concluding remarks by elaborating how homemaking in the diasporic setting is an ongoing process of extending solidarity and establishing connections in spaces of destination and origin, where both locations can be read as 'home.' The chapter thus provides an empirically grounded study of issues related to the concept of spatial justice.

The Notion of Diaspora and 'Home'

The notion of diaspora has been widely contested when it is applied to explain the dispersal of people across multiple localities, and the subsequent development of a shared consciousness.[7] Scholars such as Rogers Brubaker critically elaborate on the three core elements in diasporic phenomena: dispersion in space, orientation to 'homelands,' and boundary maintenance.[8] It is argued that the dispersal can be forced, or exist in the paradigm of labour movement or trade. Orientation to the 'homeland' is also not only about longing and the concept of return, but also maintaining multiple ties to both 'hostland' and 'homeland.' Diasporic communities are discernable through their maintenance of distinctive cultural and social forms from 'host societies.' However, maintaining original cultural forms, religious practices, and other values may not contradict with migrants' incorporation or adaptation to 'host societies.' Rather both practices may coexist and complement each other: cultural innovations and hybridity is, therefore, also part of these experiences and practices.[9] Diasporization does not necessarily

---

[7] Thomas Faist, *The Volume and Dynamics of International Migration and Transnational Social Spaces* (Oxford: OUP, 2000); Steven Vertovec, 'Three Meanings of "Diaspora," Exemplified by South Asian Religions,' *Diaspora* 6/3 (1997), 277–300.

[8] Brubaker, 'The "Diaspora" Diaspora.'

[9] Thomas Faist, 'Diaspora and Transnationalism: What Kind of Dance Partners?' in *Diaspora and Transnationalism: Concepts, Theories and Methods*, eds. Rainer Bauböck and Thomas Faist (Amsterdam: Amsterdam: Amsterdam University Press, 2010), 12; Homi Bhabha, *The Location of Culture* (New York: Routledge, New York, 1994).

contradict with acculturation and adaptation to receiving societies.[10]

To understand the complex and dynamic conditions resulting from transnational migration, many scholars approach the concept of diaspora in two main ways: some attempt to explain the features of diasporic phenomena by describing the context of cross-border solidarity in diaspora.[11] Others attempt to understand diaspora as an ongoing process of affiliation with a 'homeland' (real or imagined), 'hostland,' and other diasporics.[12] In this paper I will follow the second perspective, which takes a social constructivist approach of identity.[13] Kim Butler argued that 'rather than being viewed as ethnicity diaspora should be studied as a specific process of community formation,' and Avtar Brah also suggested the need for examining the historicity of diasporic experiences, as 'each empirical diaspora must be analyzed in the historical specificity.'[14]

Diasporic conditions are manifested when a population dispersal is followed by collective efforts to adapt a new environment, while retaining a commitment to a country or a place of origin, through mobilizing various types of loyalty and claiming a distinctive collective identity.[15] Diasporic communities may be built around certain kind of imaginations, narratives, memories, practices, and affiliations based on a specific form of shared experience which has emerged during the process of migration and settlement in distant lands.[16] Martin Sökefeld

[10] Öncel Naldemirci, 'Caring (in) Diaspora: Aging and Caring Experiences of Older Turkish Migrants in a Swedish Context' (PhD thesis, University of Gothenburg, Gothenburg, 2013), 37.

[11] William Safran, 'Diasporas in Modern Societies: Myths of Homeland and Return,' *Diaspora*, 1/1 (1991), 83–99; Robin Cohen, *Global Diasporas: An Introduction* (London: UCL Press, 1997); Jan Abhink, 'Slow Awakening? The Ethiopian Diaspora in the Netherlands, 1977–2007,' *Diaspora, A Journal of Transnational Studies* 15/2–3 (2006), 361–80.

[12] James Clifford, 'Diasporas,' *Cultural Anthropology* 19/3 (1994), 302–38; Parreñas, Rhacel and Lok C. D. Siu, *Asian Diasporas: New Formations, New Conceptions* (Stanford, California: Stanford University Press, 2007).

[13] For details about the methodological, conceptual and ontological debates surrounding the constructivist perspectives, see Peter Berger and Thomas Luckmann, *The Social Construction of Reality* (London: Penguin Books, 1991); Vivien Burr, *Social Constructionism*, 2nd Ed. (London: Routledge, 2003).

[14] Kim Butler, 'Defining Diaspora, Refining a Discourse,' *Diaspora: A Journal of Transnational Studies* 10/2 (1994), 194; Brah, *Cartographies*, 183.

[15] Steven Vertovec, 'Three Meanings of "Diaspora"; Martin Sökefeld, 'Mobilizing in Transnational Space: A Social Movement Approach to the Formation of Diaspora,' *Global Networks* 6/3 (2006), 265–84.

[16] Steven Vertovec and Robin Cohen, 'Introduction,' in *Migration, diasporas and transnationalism*, ed. Steven Vertovec and Robin Cohen (Cheltenham: Edward Elgar Publishing, 1999).

described diasporas as 'imagined transnational communities [whereby the] assumption of a shared identity ... unites people living dispersed in transnational space thereby becomes the central defining feature of diasporas.'[17] A particular sense of 'belonging' can be developed among immigrant communities based on a shared geographic origin or history of migration; a common language; religion; ethnic or tribal background. This sense of 'belonging' can be mobilized for economic collaborations and political engagements to overcome marginalization in destination or advocate for social change in the 'homeland.'[18] Hence, the rhetoric of community is activated by diasporas through the establishment of associations and interest groups, cultural events, commemorations, religious institutions and the performance of traditional rituals.[19] Furthermore, there is the practice of maintaining active transnational connections via the Internet, establishing and consuming various satellite television broadcastings that target the community in destination and significant others in other locations. Khachig Tölölyan termed this contemporary diasporic practice as 'exemplary communities in transnational moments.'[20]

However, as critical scholars of diaspora have argued, diasporic belonging and identities are not natural consequences of emigration from an origin and settlement in distant lands: a specific process of mobilization in immigrant communities has to take place for diaspora to emerge.[21] Rogers Brubaker argues that counting or estimation of members of a specific diaspora risks essentializing diasporas as bounded homogenous units, ignoring the complexities of identity politics and the diversity of people's relation to place.[22] Brubaker suggests that diaspora should be studied as claims, projects, and category of practice used to mobilize energy for a cause in the immigrant community in the 'hostland' or across the diaspora. The practice of making and using different types of networks in fulfilling community needs are, therefore, an essential element in diasporic life. Indeed, a national diasporic community may have diverse sub-groups based on religion, ethnic or tribal backgrounds, political opinion or other interests,[23] which demonstrate the

---

[17] Sökefeld, 'Mobilizing in Transnational Tpace,' 280.

[18] Sökefeld, 'Mobilizing in Transnational Space.'

[19] Jennifer Brown, 'Expressions of diasporic belonging: The divergent emotional geographies of Britain's Polish communities,' *Emotion, Space and Society* 4/4 (2011), 229–237; Engedayehu, 'The Ethiopian Orthodox Tewahedo Church.'

[20] Tölölyan, 'The Nation-state and Its Others: In Lieu of a Preface,' *Diaspora: A Journal of Transnational Studies* 1/1 (2011), 5.

[21] Sökefeld, 'Mobilizing in Transnational Space.'

[22] Brubaker, 'The 'Diaspora' Diaspora.'

[23] Munzoul Abdalla M. Assal, 'Somalis and Sudanese in Norway-Religion,

way in which individuals use identities and 'belonging' instrumentally, contracting and expanding one's identity frameworks for a particular purpose at a particular moment. Ali Eminov argues that 'members of a given community have multiple identities, each activated upon appropriate circumstances pragmatically.'[24] First generation Ethiopian migrants in Sweden have various types of networks and interest groups based on political opinion, religion, ethnicity, hometown, and other shared experiences, which have resulted during immigration to Sweden. Individuals are members of several networks simultaneously, and engage and benefit from each network depending on their prevailing needs. Several interest groups have emerged in the last few decades and various types of economic and social resources have mobilized to adapt the Swedish systems as well as maintain ties with Ethiopia and Ethiopians elsewhere. Many of community members are constructing 'home' and 'belonging' in Sweden and Ethiopia simultaneously. It is therefore important to ask the question: what is 'home' for this kind of community?

The concept of 'home' is a highly contested concept within diaspora studies, as 'home' and 'homeland' is viewed and defined in multiple ways. In broader perspectives 'home' can represent either the immediate domestic sphere, as well as a national geographic space, or a place where one feels safety and security. Avtar Brah writes that 'home' is both the 'lived experiences of locality and a mythical place for diasporic imaginations.'[25] Alinia et al. argue that 'home not only offers shelter in a physical sense but is also a place where we create and attach personal, political and social meanings.'[26] It can be argued that, although 'home' can be considered as a narrative of nostalgia, or myths of a lost or imagined land, it can also *simultaneously* reflect lived everyday experiences of connections and disconnections, inclusions and exclusions, in both the 'homeland' and 'hostland.'[27]

In this section I will use this broader perspective of 'home' as a place where one is emotionally attached *and* practically engaged in political, social, family, and economic projects. In many instances making 'home' in a diasporic setting is about the continuous struggle to overcome traumas of separation and dislocation by establishing a new life in the

Ethnicity and Clan in diaspora,' in *Diasporas Within and Without Africa: Dynamism, Heterogeneity and Variation*, ed. Leif Manger and Munzoul Abdalla M Assal (Stockholm: The Nordic Africa institute, 2006).

[24] Ali Eminov, 'Social Construction of Identities: Pomaks in Bulgaria, European Centre for Minority Issues,' *JEMIE* 6/2 (2007), 1.

[25] Brah, *Cartographies*.

[26] Alinia et al., 'The Kurdish Diaspora,' 54.

[27] Brown, 'Expressions of Diasporic Belonging,' 233.

present location, and making reconnections with the country of origin individually and collectively. Community networks are mobilized to overcome social, economic and cultural challenges, performing one's religion and culture in the new land as well as extending mobilized resources to the country of origin. For many first generation Ethiopian migrants, like other contemporary African migrants, the 'country of origin' is not just a mythical place where one's ancestors once lived, but a very real place where family, kin members, friends, and property are located. Hence many live what can be termed a 'transnational' life by sending remittances, travelling back and forth, engaging in online social networks, and participating in collective efforts so as to bring social and political reforms.[28] The diasporic space is also, however, importantly constructed by those owning assets and businesses in the 'host' country; constantly negotiating their double presence and double absence in both of origin and destination countries continuously re-shapes the meaning of 'home.'[29] The process of immigration and specific socioeconomic and political circumstances engaged in both sending and receiving migratory flows shapes the processes of 'belonging' and shaping space.

Crossing Nations?

Ethiopian emigration to Sweden is part of broader transnational migration processes in both countries. Although Sweden contributed to and benefited from the European colonial powers' prejudice, domination, and exploitation directly and indirectly, through missionary activities, colonial relations were not the sole cause of emigration.[30] The Ethiopians emigration to Sweden was initiated by the coming of Swedish Missionaries in the late 19th century who paved the way for a diplomatic relationship between the two states, particularly between the 1930s and 1960s.[31] Swedish missionaries first arrived in

[28] Feyissa, 'The Transnational Politics of Ethiopian Muslim Diaspora'; Anne Kubai, 'Being Here and There: Migrant Communities in Sweden and the Conflicts in the Horn of Africa,' *African and Black Diaspora*, 6/2 (2013), 174–88.

[29] Nina Glick Schiller, Linda Basch and Cristina Szanton Blanc, 'From Immigrant to Transmigrant: Theorizing Transnational Migration,' *Anthropology Quarterly* 68/1 (1995), 48–63.

[30] See Mai Palmberg, 'The Nordic Colonial Mind. Complying with Colonialism: Gender, Race and Ethnicity in the Nordic Region,' in *Complying with Colonialism: Gender, Race and Ethnicity in the Nordic Region*, ed. Suvi Keskinen et al. (Farnham and Burlington: Ashgate, 2009).

[31] Viveca Halldin Norberg, *Swedes in Haile Selassie's Ethiopia, 1924–1952* (Uppsala: The Scandinavian Institute of African Studies, 1977).

Massawa in 1886. Later in 1904 pastor Karl Cedevqvist—the first Swedish missionary—reached Addis Ababa and he was followed by extensive missionary activities in the country. The missionaries engaged in education and health care sectors and facilitated ways for state-to-state relations. The high level state to state cooperation began after emperor Haile Selassie I visited Sweden in 1924 and crown prince Gustav Adolf made a reply visit to Ethiopia in 1935. The establishment of Swedish embassy in Addis Ababa in 1946 and the Ethiopian embassy in Stockholm followed in 1947. From 1930s to 1960s the Ethiopian government recruited many Swedes as army and police officers, medical staff, lawyers, air force personnel, teachers, telecommunication and technical assistants.[32] This early missionary and development encounters reproduced Sweden and Swedish images in Ethiopia as the case of other missionary practices and processes in Africa.[33]

It is possible to divide the immigration process into three phases. During the first phase (1940s–1974) mainly students, adopted children, spouses of Swedish volunteers and Ethiopian embassy personals arrived. This was followed by early emigration of Ethiopians for higher education and shorter professional trainings. Many Ethiopians and Eritreans came to Sweden to study during the reign of Emperor Haile Selassie I between 1930s and 1960s.[34] Some Ethiopians stayed in Sweden as refugees when the political and economic situation worsened immediately after the end of the emperor's rule in Ethiopia. In the second phase (1970s to 1993) many Ethiopian refugees entered Sweden during the economic and political crises and civil wars in Ethiopia that became acute mainly after the 1974 Ethiopian revolution.[35] When the military regime, led by Colonel Mengistu Haile Mariam, began to persecute Ethiopian students and young generations who challenged his dictatorship in 1970s and 1980s students and other refugees migrated en masse, and many settled in the United States, Australia, Canada, and in Europe, with 9,000 Ethiopian refugees settling in Sweden.[36] During

---

[32] Norberg, *Swedes in Haile Selassie's Ethiopia*, 103–60.

[33] Robert Strayer, 'Mission History in Africa: New Perspectives on an Encounter,' *African Studies Review* 19/01 (1976), 1–16.

[34] Norberg, *Swedes in Haile Selassie's Ethiopia*.

[35] Aaron Matteo Terrazas, *Beyond Regional Circularity: The Emergence of an Ethiopian Diaspora* (Washington, DC: Migration Policy Institute, 2007).

[36] For a detailed discussion of the refugee crises in Ethiopia in 1970s and 80s, see Assefaw Bariagaber, *Conflict and the Refugee Experience: Flight, Exile, and Repatriation in the Horn of Africa* (Aldershot, UK: Ashgate, 2006); 'Statistics,' *Migrationsverket* (Migration Agency, Stockholm), 2014, accessed 10 May 2014, http:// www.migrationsverket.se/English/About-the-Migration-Agency/Facts-and-statistics-/ Statistics.html.

this phase many Ethiopian and Eritrean students attending courses in fellow communist countries in Eastern Europe and Russia also moved to Sweden and other West European countries and sought asylum after the fall of communism in the region.

In the third phase (1993 to the present time) a mixed migration flow of family, refugees, students and labor can be observed. After Ethiopian People's Revolutionary Democratic Front (EPRDF) took power in Ethiopia in 1991, refugees and other migrants started to bring their families, via the Swedish immigration provisions that allow family (re) unifications for documented immigrants from their respective 'homelands.' Hence, the third and forth phases of immigration to Sweden is characterized by the relaxation of immigration provisions in Sweden for refugees, family and labor migration from developing countries.[37] From the 1980s to 2014 as much as 5528 Ethiopian immigrants settled in Sweden through family reunification, and nearly 2000 Ethiopian entered as students.[38] In 2008 Sweden allowed employers to hire non-EU labor migrants. Currently there are 15,494 Ethiopian born people residing in Sweden and a third of them are resident in Stockholm. However, one has to be careful in attempting to differentiate between Swedish Ethiopians and Eritreans, as before 1990s many Eritrean refugees registered themselves as Ethiopians because the Eritrean state was not formally founded,[39] and now many Ethiopians self-identify as Eritreans partly to minimize the risk of deportations in case their asylum application is rejected. More importantly these official statistics never included those who are waiting for residence permits and others undocumented for various reasons and the number of undocumented is estimated to be equal with those who are documented.[40]

Gradually, following these different waves of immigration, many Ethiopian diasporic community organizations emerged in Sweden.[41]

[37] Scholars put modern immigration to Sweden into four phases. Phase one (1938–1948) is the refugee immigration from neighboring countries; second phase (1949–1971) is Labor immigration from Finland and Southern Europe. The third phase (1972–1989) characterized by family reunification and refugee flow from developing countries and final phase is asylum seekers from southeastern and Eastern Europe (1990–present) and the free movement of EU citizens within the European Union and labor immigration outside Europe since 2008 (see Fredlund-Blomst, *Assessing Immigrant Integration in Sweden*; Charles Westin and Sadia Hassanen, *People on the Move: Experiences of Forced Migration, with Examples from Various parts of the World* (London: Red Sea Press, 2014).

[38] 'Statistics,' *Migrationsverket* (Migration Agency, Stockholm).

[39] Agnarson, Laris. 'The Integration Experinces of Ethiopian Immigrants in Sweden,' (Masters thesis, Stockholm University, Stockholm, 2006).

[40] Kubai, 'Being Here and There,' 177.

[41] Kubai, 'Being Here and There.'

The first active Ethiopian community organization was the Ethiopian Student Union in Sweden, which played an active role in mobilizing the community to support the revolutionary movement in Ethiopia that later overthrew the imperial autocracy in 1974 and the subsequent struggles against military dictatorial regime in Ethiopia in the 1980s.[42] The other earliest and still active Ethiopian community institutions in Sweden are church organization, such as the Ethiopian Jerusalem Evangelical Church in Sweden. In the 1970s and early 1980s all religious groups (including Muslims) from Ethiopia would gather in this church in Stockholm every Sunday to perform their religious rituals whilst socializing as fellow exiles with shared emigration experiences. As Abbink suggests, when the population of the community increased many splinters then emerged, as groups started to establish their own associations and church organizations based on specific denominations.[43]

Ethiopian Christian Church Organizations in Sweden

Community members with shared hometowns such as Addis Ababa, Gondar, Mekele; Ethnicities (Oromo, Amhara, Tigrigna); a common political opinion (pro or anti EPRDF regime in Ethiopia) or friends working in the same profession formed a coalition of their own Christian church organizations in and around Stockholm.[44]

---

[42] Bahru Zewde, Gebre Yntiso, and Kassahun Berhanu, *Contribution of the Ethiopian Diaspora to Peace-Building: A Case Study of the Tigrai Development Association*, DIASPEACE Working Paper No. 8 (Jyväskylä: University of Jyväskylä, 2010).

[43] Abbink, 'Slow Awakening?'; The first Ethiopian Christian church branch became independent was Medhanealem Ethiopian Orthodox Twahido Church which was followed by Ethiopian Mekane Eyesus Church and many other protestant denominations sprang up subsequently in Stockholm and other bigger cities where sizable Ethiopian communities are found.

[44] For instance in Stockholm areas there are numerous Ethiopian Orthodox Tewahido Churches (EOTC) and Protestant Church organizations. The most vibrant protestant Church congregations are: Ethiopian Evangelical Mekane Eyesus Church in Skärholmen, Ethiopian Jerusalem Evangelical Church in Älvsjö, and Full Gospel Eritrean and Ethiopian Church Stockholm in Solna. There are 3 Ethiopian EOTC: Debreselam Medhanialem EOTC in Högsätra, Silassie OETC in Hötorget, St. Mary Ethiopian OETC in Kallhäll, Silassie EOTC in Nacka. There are many other similar churches in other bigger cities such as Lund, Malmo and Gutenberg. EOTCs expansion in Sweden is also related to the division of Ethiopian Holy Synod into two: one in Ethiopia and the other in diaspora, which is known as exiled synod. Individual EOTC in diaspora in turn is divided into three groups: affiliated with the Exiled Synod, affiliated with the Home Synod and Neutral (Engedayehu, 2014). Sweden is in fact the hub of the expansion of EOTC in Europe since it hosts Abune Eliyas, who was former archbishop of Europe and

Church organizations in Sweden are formally registered with the Swedish Tax office as immigrants' associations and get state subsidizes provided for multicultural organizations. Swedish state support is provided in the form of grants administered by the Swedish Commission for Government Support to Faith Communities (SST), (*Nämnden för statligt stöd till trossamfund*) under the Ministry of Culture. Faith based associations are considered voluntary organizations which promote the 'fundamental values' of Sweden. This is in fact related to the long process of secularization in Sweden while using and supporting Faith Based Organizations (FBOs) as partners in building Sweden's secular and multicultural self-identity. This in turn enabled the FBOs such as Ethiopian church organizations to have voices in the community and in relation to the state.[45] State supports are provided to encourage ethnic, language, and religious minorities to maintain and develop cultural and religious group identities of their own in co-existence with the Swedish system.

The role of religion in the transnational migration process has historically been given little attention in academic literature.[46] Church congregations have acted as community organizations connecting people from different ethnic, class and gender backgrounds, offering various types of financial, material, and counseling support for members. They play a particularly key interventionist role in assisting undocumented migrants. Aber and her 15 year old daughter were undocumented for 10 years in Sweden after their asylum applications were rejected:

> A member of Jerusalem Church subcontracted me an apartment. I got childcare work in households through friends in the church. The church also covers some of bills for my daughter. She is performing very well in school. I am very happy now. I would have been mad if there had been no support from thee Jerusalem Church.

Africa and now EOTC's representative in Europe for the exiled Holy Synod of Ethiopia in USA (Engedayehu, 'The Ethiopian Orthodox Tewahedo Church in the Diaspora'). The bishop approves and opens new churches for Ethiopian migrants in Europe.

[45] For details on the role of religion in the development of Swedish welfare state as well as the power dynamics in the history of church state relations in Sweden,

see Tobias Harding, 'Faith-Based Organizations and the Secular State: The Establishment of a Muslim Study Association in Sweden,' *Journal of Muslim Minority Affairs* 33/3 (2013), 341–55 and Karen M. Anderson, 'The Church as Nation? The Role of Religion in the Development of the Swedish Welfare State,' in *Religion, Class Coalitions, and Welfare States,* eds. Kees van Kersbergen and Philip Manow (Cambridge: CUP, 2009), 210–35.

[46] Levitt, Peggy and Jaworky Nadya. 'Transnational Migration Studies: Past Developments and Future Trends,' *Annual Review of Sociology* 33 (2007), 140.

Her testimony demonstrates the ways in which social capital is generated through churches for individual members to overcome legal and economic barriers in order to survive in Sweden. It is also apparent from the above story that religious identities are reactivated as a survival strategy in the absence of state welfare supports for undocumented migrants.[47]

Under the umbrella of large church organizations there are dynamic sub groups and networks, which perform collaborative roles in finding jobs, accommodation, and social activities.[48] Ethiopian Christian Churches in diaspora act as a space of 'home/homing,' within which migrants may maintain Ethiopian identities by practicing religious rituals and socializations as they are practiced in Ethiopia: in some cases mass, songs, and other services are even provided in Amharic and Geez languages, creating an emotive connection to Ethiopia;[49] the churches are also designed to reflect the architecture and artifacts of Ethiopia. Hence the 'sacred' space of the 'homeland' is reproduced in diaspora:[50]

> When we are in the church and the Kedase (Mass/liturgy) is held and songs are sung in Amharic and in Geez language; the way priests and singers are dressed up make you feel like you are in 'Hager bet' or back in Ethiopia. ... Churches are also living museums for us to teach our children born in Sweden about Ethiopian languages and culture. When we take them for holidays to Ethiopia nothing is new for them.

For more than 60 per cent of Ethiopians Christian religious practices are part and parcel of everyday social and cultural life in Ethiopia.[51]

---

[47] For details on the challenges and survival strategies of undocumented migrants in Sweden, see Khosravi Shahram 'An Ethnography of Migrant "Illegality" in Sweden: Included Yet Excepted?' Journal of International Political Theory 6/1 (2010), 95–116.

[48] These include: elderly prayer council, women sisterly networks known as ye Ehitoch Hebret, Men Brotherhood Networks known as Ye wondimoch hibret, youth singers, bible study groups, Sunday School Students, a saint's friend association known as ye Tsewa Mahiber (for members of EOTC). Ye Ehitoch Hibret is instrumental particularly in sharing experiences of good care and supporting educational achievements and religious values in children born in Sweden.

[49] Al-Ali and Koser, 'New Approaches to Migration'; Brown, 'Expressions of Diasporic Belonging.'

[50] Heldman Marilyn, (2006) 'Creating Sacred Space: Orthodox Churches of the Ethiopian American Diaspora,' Diaspora, a Journal of Transnational Studies 15/2–3 (2006), 285–302.

[51] Orthodox Christianity has shaped the culture, tradition, people's identity and history of Ethiopia for centuries and until now. Ethiopians brought this institution into diaspora as an important cultural and identity marker. For details of the EOTCs history in diaspora and its internal divisions and politics, see Engedayehu, 'The Ethiopian Orthodox Tewahedo Church,' 116.

Migrants brought this practice to diasporic spaces in the West.[52] Thus church organizations are important social and physical spaces where members reproduce 'home' and practice 'belonging' in everyday bases in Sweden. Christian religious institutions function, then, as a dual space: not only acting in Sweden alone but instituting several outreach programs and development projects for social reforms implemented back in Ethiopia via mobilizing support from relevant organizations for funds in Sweden.[53]

In addition, Ethiopian church organizations in Sweden exist within a financial, pastoral, administrative, and technical network with member churches in Europe, the United States, and elsewhere. Church leaders meet in actual and virtual spaces to discuss how to translate common church principles into local contexts. Funds to build new churches or for other purposes are usually contributed from members in other churches across the diaspora;[54] famous singers and renowned religious figures from Ethiopia or in diaspora frequently travel transnationally to provide their services. Lay members of Ethiopian churches in Sweden in turn travel in groups to other countries to attend religious festivals organized by each church in Europe and United States every year. They also travel to Ethiopia to visit and financially support known shrines and monasteries and also contribute money to build new churches in the 'homeland.' Hence, these Christian religious networks perform an instrumental role in constructing the contours of the space through which diasporics connect emotionally and practically with Ethiopia, Sweden, and significant others in other diasporic spaces. However, this is not to imply smooth functions of church organizations in Sweden and beyond. There are internal power competitions, gender hierarchies and at times corruption allegations and abusing of power positions for personal and political gains. But the organizational behaviors and power dynamics within the church organizations are beyond the scope of this paper and deserve further study.

Cultural Collectivity in Diaspora

Another association that attempts to collectivize people based on their Ethiopian origin is the Ethiopian Sport and Culture Federation,

---

[52] Engedayehu, 'The Ethiopian Orthodox Tewahedo Church.'
[53] Sökefeld, 'Mobilizing in Transnational Space.'
[54] For instance, the Debreselam Medhanealem EOTC in Stockholm is building a new church with the capital of 35 million SEK. It managed to raise more than a million SEK from EOTCs in United States.

founded in 1996. In this case, Ethiopian origin is the sole defining membership trait. Its objective is to teach children born to families of Ethiopian origin about the language and culture of Ethiopia, thereby facilitating 'their double integration to Ethiopian systems and Swedish systems.' The organization tries to confront everyday challenges of identity and questions of origin by black children born in Sweden. This is partly because sometimes children face severe racist discrimination from the settled, largely native Swedish society; in many instances they are frequently asked the question, 'where are you from?' even though they were born and grew up in Sweden, because of their black skin. In common with many diasporic generations, children usually ask their parents about the culture and history of Ethiopia. The association aims to therefore construct a narrative about 'homeland' culture, *in absentia*.[55]

In collaboration with the Ethiopian Radio in Sweden the Federation organizes cultural events during Ethiopian New Year (*Enqutatash*) celebrations every September in Stockholm, widely disseminated via the radio and online social media. Though the radio mainly disseminates opposition to the current regime in Ethiopia, it also serves the community by announcing association meetings, music, or other cultural events in Sweden and beyond. The Ethiopian Radio in Sweden, the Internet, and Ethiopian Satellite Television (ESAT) play a key role in mobilizing the community in Sweden to participate in public protests in Sweden. The community usually extends support across the diaspora in different ways: through remittances; organizing public protests in support of political activists who are working to bring social and economic reform in Ethiopia; or publicly opposing human rights violations. For instance, when Saudi Arabia deported more than 160,000 Ethiopian migrants in 2013, thousands of Swedish Ethiopians and other migrants organized rallies in front of the Saudi embassy in Stockholm carrying slogans criticizing both the Saudi and Ethiopian regime, a message which was disseminated to other Ethiopians across the diaspora via social media, diaspora based satellite television, and radio. Similarly, in April 2015 a large number of people of Ethiopian and Eritrean origin gathered around the central station in Stockholm protesting against the ISIL massacre of Ethiopian Christian migrants in Libya, as well as

---

[55] Anastasia Christou, 'Deciphering Diaspora–Translating Transnationalism: Family Dynamics, Identity Constructions and the Legacy Of "Home" in Second-Generation Greek-American Return Migration,' *Ethnic and Racial Studies* 29/6 (2006), 1040–56; Hagar Salamon, 'Misplaced Home and Mislaid Meat: Stories Circulating Among Ethiopian Immigrants in Israel,' *Callaloo* 33/1 (2010), 165–76; Russell King et al., '"Diverse Mobilities": Second-Generation Greek-Germans Engage with the Homeland as Children and as Adults,' *Mobilities* 6/4 (2011), 483–501.

the xenophobic attacks and lootings of Ethiopian migrants in South Africa. Community leaders and religious representatives condemned both ISIL and the EPRDF regime in Ethiopia, as well as expressing resistance to the brutal measures taken against Ethiopians holding similar demonstrations in Ethiopia.

Diasporic media channels, like ESAT and Ethiopian Radio, keep Ethiopian diasporic communities connected all over the world through the dissemination of resistance, including the voices of activists and protest groups, and its news and programs transmit daily from Stockholm, Amsterdam, and Washington DC. During a big fund raising event in Stockholm to support ESAT in 2012, for example, vocal anti EPRDF activists such as the artist Tamagn Beyene from the USA and representatives of Ethiopian Radio in Sweden participated in the event, and more than SEK 300,000 was raised from those gathered in the crowd. Hence the two institutions are organizing and connecting the community in Sweden and in Ethiopia simultaneously, as well as working hard to make the community visible in both locations. The other most specific culture based institutions that organize the community for on a more practical, daily, and integrationist basis are *Iqqub and Iddir*.

Iqqub and *Iddir*

Iqqub is a long established traditional saving and self-help institution in Ethiopia.[56] It is a rotating saving and credit type of association whose members make regular contributions to a revolving loan fund. Unlike saving and credit cooperatives, it does not bear interest on the money saved. *Iqqub* enables a family to obtain the necessary funding for activities such as weddings, building a house, or starting a micro-business. Migrants brought this institution to Sweden and use it to solve everyday social and financial problems in their destination country.[57] These institutions have a double purpose: firstly as a means of providing practical financial support outside the 'host' system since it is more flexible than state sanctioned financial systems, yet also acting as an opportunity to socialize in *Habesha* (Ethiopian) restaurants in Stockholm, so that individuals can collect *Iqqub* money while enjoying the cuisines of typical Ethiopian national dishes, whilst listening to

---

[56] Aredo, *The Informal and Semi Formal Financial Sectors.*

[57] In Stockholm, local businessmen gather in Ethiopian or Eritrean restaurants at the end of every month to contribute money, and the collected sum is given to a member usually based on a lottery system.

Ethiopian music. As several scholars have demonstrated, food and music have powerful emotional roles in reactivating memories about the 'homeland' and constructing 'home' and 'belonging' in diasporic spaces.[58] These activities not only maintain a sense of belonging and emotional attachments to the 'homeland' but also new friendships and ties are established and existing ones are reactivated. People update and exchange information on issues concerning the community such as socioeconomic and political circumstances in Ethiopia as well as changing policies and regulations of employment or welfare benefits or sharing information about changing family reunification and asylum procedures in Sweden. As Sökefeld argues, this institution is also one arena where social mobilization for the community causes such as pubic protests that was mentioned earlier are initiated.[59]

Iddir is one of a range of indigenous voluntary organizations and associations involved in self-help and other social activities in Ethiopia. Traditionally its aim was primarily to provide mutual aid in burial matters and other community concerns. Households become members of an *Iddir* and pay fixed contributions monthly. Whenever death occurs among members, the association raises an additional amount of money (depending on the specific bylaws) and handles the burial ceremonies. In addition, certain members are assigned to stay at the house of the bereaved for two to three days to assist the household.[60] As in the case of *Iqqub,* immigrants brought this institution to Sweden where it functions through member contributions as an important social network. Members are usually drawn from shared ethnic back-grounds or hometowns or are members of a church congregation. It is a semiformal saving and credit association work side by side with state sanctioned financial systems. Unlike the banking systems it does *not* require members to show legal residence status documents. Membership is based on trust, which offers a great opportunity for undocumented migrants to have a flexible credit and saving service. So it is an indigenous institution *modified and adapted* to thrive in diasporic spaces. One informant stated that:

> In Sweden you need friends in your own group from your community, true friends of course, to take care of your bills and maters related to

[58] Brown, 'Expressions of diasporic belonging'; Iain Walker, 'Ntsambu, the Foul Smell of Home: Food, Commensality and Identity in the Comoros and in the Diaspora,' *Food and Foodways,* 20/3–4 (2012), 187–210.

[59] Sökefeld, 'Mobilizing in Transnational Space.'

[60] Alula Pankhurst and Damen Haile Mariam, 'The Iddir in Ethiopia: Historical Development, Social Function, and Potential Role in HIV/AIDS Prevention and Control,' *Northeast African Studies* 7/2 (2000), 35–57.

> tax office or migration board when you go for holydays or for business trips to Ethiopia or other places for some longer time. … You also need someone you trust to share your problems and anxieties when you are in difficult situations. There are many challenges here (he means Sweden). Sweden is a lonely country. You easily get depressed when something happens mainly during the dark and long cold season (winter) when everyone stays behind doors and you are lonely. You may loose jobs or your wife or partner may abandon you unexpectedly. It is not like Ethiopia when some crack happens in family people get involved and mend social/family relations. Of course you also need friends to raise *Iqqub* together and borrow money when you need it for instance while you are investing in housing in Ethiopia.

Sweden is usually portrayed as having the most generous welfare policies and successful integration programs to help migrants' education and political and economic participation in the labour market.[61] However, evidence shows that on the ground immigrant communities perform at markedly lower rates when it comes to education, in the labour market, and in levels of political participation.[62] My informants told me that all the policies, programmes and benefits are available but remain inaccessible because many migrants lack the language and other skills needed to access the system. Hence Ethiopian immigrants usually depend on one another to learn how to negotiate Swedish systems. It can be argued that the community networks are in fact life-saving for asylum seekers and others while adapting to destination systems and maintaining transnational relations.[63]

Such community practices should not be read as a reflection of absolute solidarity in the community in the process of their adaptation to sociocultural systems in the 'Hostland.' Inevitably there is some mistrust and exploitation and there are some divisions, tensions, and abuses (in ethnic enclaves) in the community. The ethnic nationalism that plagues current Ethiopia and divergent political ideologies are some of the reasons behind the conflicts and divisions, as well as inter-generational tensions. Informants of different generations stated that those who came during the Ethiopian revolution see themselves as exiles and heroes who contributed to the removal of the military dictatorship in Ethiopia, and look down on recent arrivals who take

[61] Anders Hellström and Tom Nilsson, '"We Are the Good Guys": Ideological positioning of the nationalist party Sverigedemokraterna in contemporary Swedish politics,' *Ethnicities* 10/1 (2010), 55–76.

[62] Fredlund-Blomst, *Assessing Immigrant Integration in Sweden.*

[63] See also Glick Schiller, 'From Immigrant to Transmigrant' and Faist, *The Volume and Dynamics of International Migration* for detail elaboration of the role social networks in transnational migration processes.

risky journeys for economic betterment when there is a chance of social mobility in Ethiopia. Thus, some recent arrivals distance themselves from established migrants who want to actively engage in 'homeland' politics. In addition, many members of civic and advocacy organizations hope to preserve their relations with the EPRDF regime back in Ethiopia, despite their anti-government advocacy activities. Because of these internal ethnic, political, and religious divisions pan-Ethiopian community organizations never last long in Sweden. However, people engage in networks instrumentally by *contracting and expanding* one's identity frameworks.[64] When one network fails to serve as a form of support, then he/she moves to another one so that both cooperation/solidarity and conflict/competition exist simultaneously.

I Am 'Here,' and I Am 'There'

The Ethiopian diaspora became involved in peace building and 'homeland' development activities in different ways mainly after 1991.[65] Some associations have water and sanitation programmes in rural and urban Ethiopia. Individuals have been supporting many Ethnic based development associations such as Tigray Development Association (TDA)which has chapters in Sweden and other places. Others engage in health and education related development projects in Sweden and Ethiopia. Doctors of Ethiopian origin residing in Sweden have been providing volunteer services training young medical staffs at Addis Ababa Black Lion Hospital and, for example, the first Cardiac hospital in Ethiopia via associations such as the Association of Ethiopian Health and Health-related Professionals in Sweden (AEHHPS), one of the non-religious and non-political organizations primarily concerned with humanitarian activities in Ethiopia.

Recently the EPRDF regime in Ethiopia designed several policy incentives to attract its population in diaspora to engage in the country's development programs.[66] The Ethiopian government extends civic, investment and national rights to its population in diaspora by offering the Ethiopian Origin ID Card known as the Yellow Card, which is almost equal to having an Ethiopian passport. Many Swedish

---

[64] Myria Georgiou, Diaspora, *Identity and the Media: Diasporic Transnationalism and Mediated Spatialities* (Cresskill, N.J., United States: Hampton Press, 2006).

[65] Feyissa, 'The Transnational Politics of Ethiopian Muslim Diaspora.'

[66] Seilgel Melissa & Kuschminder Katie, 'Diaspora Engagement and Policy in Ethiopia,' in *Emigration Nations: Policies and Ideologies of Emigrant Engagement*, ed. Collyer Michael (Harvard: Palgrave Macmillan, 2013), 50–74.

Ethiopians have the Yellow Card and built businesses and assets in Sweden and in Ethiopia. The rights and benefits extended to Ethiopian origin people in diaspora encourage remittances and facilitate return migration and investment, as well as for the transfer of knowledge and skill.[67] The Yellow Card offers benefits and rights in exchange for political partnership or neutrality. One informant who is Swedish Ethiopian and recently built a four-star hotel in Dukem, a small town at the southern border of Addis Ababa, stated:

> Ethiopia is doing good now. … Ethiopians abroad can use this opportunity. I built a hotel and started modern farming near by the city of Hawassa. The government have several incentives and support programs and inviting Ethiopians in abroad to come and invest.

There are hundreds of similar Swedish Ethiopian entrepreneurs who own businesses and assets 'here' and 'there.' Still others have strong transnational kinship ties and fulfill cross border family obligations by sending remittances or facilitating emigration of other family members to Sweden or other places. They move back and forth frequently for holidays, to manage businesses enterprises, and to visit family. Thus having these rights, benefits, and assets in Ethiopia and in Sweden means both locations can be both literally and figuratively 'homes' for those in diaspora. In contemporary diasporic settings homemaking is a continuous process and practice of implementing economic, social, cultural, and family projects both in origin and destination localities by mobilizing resources via community networks and interest groups at local and transnational levels.[68]

Conclusion

This discussion demonstrates the ways in which community identity frameworks are mobilized, and several networks and interest groups are established across the diaspora. For many first generation migrants both the location of origin and destination are their 'homes' as they are emotionally attached and practically engaged in social, economic,

---

[67] See Siegel & Kuschaminder, 'Diaspora Engagement and Policy in Ethiopia.'

[68] Akhil Gupta and James Ferguson, 'Beyond "culture": Space, Identity, and the Politics of Difference,' *Cultural Anthropology* 7/1 (1992), 6–23; Faist, 'Diaspora and Transnationalism'; Ash Aminy, 'Spatialities of Globalisation,' *Environment and Planning A* 34/3 (2002), 385–400; Nadje Al-Ali and Khalid Koser, 'New Approaches to Migration? Transnational Communities and the Transformation of Home,' in *Transnationalism, International Migration and Home*, eds. Nadje Al-Ali and Khalid Koser (London: Routledge, 2002), 1–14.

and religious projects. They own assets, maintain family connections, and build churches and working for social and economic betterment both 'here and there.' Thus, homemaking in the diaspora is revealed as an ongoing process of negotiating one's inclusions and exclusions, connections and disconnections; a diasporic 'home' is not just about longing to return to the 'Homeland' when experiencing exclusions in the 'Hostland,' but rather mobilizing identities and networks to maintain connections and establish ongoing projects in multiple settings.

These everyday homing practices are shaped by prevailing legal/political and social circumstances back in Ethiopia as well as in Sweden. One way of increasing understanding of the diasporic construction of 'home' is exploring the specific empirical realities of how diasporic communities are formed by 'triadic relationships': between *1)* country of origin, *2)* country of destination, and *3)* 'globally dispersed yet collectively self-identified ethnic'/national groups.[69] Rather than try to define spatial justice this chapter has offered an empirical study of an attempt to find it. Making 'home' in diasporic space is, therefore, about engaging across networks and interest groups in diaspora, *contracting and expanding* one's identity frameworks to adapt the space to the needs of the broader community.

[69] Vertovec, Steven, 'Three Meanings of "Diaspora".'

9

Diaspora Space and Nomadic Legality? *Tribe* and the Criminal Justice and Public Order Act 1994

Emma Patchett

T his chapter will examine the historical context of legislation and policy in the construction of space for the Gypsy and Traveller community, as a framework through which to explore questions of spatial justice and legitimacy in the case of the Dale Farm evictions in 2011. This case study will be analyzed through a reading of the novel *Tribe* by John F. McDonald, a work of fiction tracing the complexities of being an 'itinerant Gypsy' in contemporary society. This interdisciplinary approach enables a focus on the concept of spatial justice as it exists beyond a scalar reading of law, by offering a critique of the narrative of a minority rendered permanent 'outsiders' in the demarcation of marginalized spaces, in order to ask wider questions about foundational concepts of ownership and belonging in contemporary Britain.

In socio-legal terms, the Gypsy and Traveller community in the UK are defined paradoxically through the concept of nomadism, despite the fact that around 200,000 of the estimated 300,000 population now live in settled housing.[1] As Helen O'Nions notes, the condition of 'mobility' has become the key concept in the construction of this particular minority, so much so that 'for centuries legislation has sought to eradicate this aspect of their culture as it is seen to pose a direct challenge to the glue that holds the sedentary society together.'[2] Thus, as O'Nions acknowledges, an emphasis on movement paradoxically authorizes the need for legislation designed to control movement. Such self-justifying rhetoric means that prohibition relies on its own narration to *legitimize*

---

[1] Heaven Crawley, *Moving Forward, the Provision of Accommodation for Travellers and Gypsies: A Consultation Paper* (London: CLG, 2004), 6.

[2] Helen O'Nions, *Minority Rights Protection in International Law—The Roma of Europe* (Aldershot and Burlington: Ashgate, 2007), 7.

the prohibition.[3] This paradox is explored in McDonald's novel *Tribe*, where the anti-hero Owen inhabits a liminal space moving between different identities, from the 'tinker' looking for work on roadside sites with other 'Gypsies,' to living in a 'poky little flat' with a girlfriend who likes to pretend he isn't a Traveller.[4] McDonald's novel is fundamentally about what it means to 'settle,' and an exposure of the conceit that 'settling down' represents a transition to a 'real' life.[5] Owen bears a hatred of being confined, and only feels as if he's *coming back to himself* when he's on the move again; however, this is no endorsement of a narrative of transition in which the Gypsy and Traveller community must simply learn to 'adapt' to the modernities of bricks and mortar. McDonald writes that as he 'covers the miles I feels as if I'm becoming part of something again,' and yet it is movement with a 'head full of confusions and contradictions.'[6] This shifting of identities could be seen to be a refraction of uneasy discourses which have sought to prioritize movement, despite the fact that after shifts in the post-war economy there was a reduction in seasonal work and a gradual elimination of traditional stopping places. Although the Caravan Sites Act 1968 meant local authorities were obliged to address this, the prohibition itself remained unchallenged, partially through the provision of specified 'sites' across England.

Romany Gypsies and Irish Travellers are legally recognized as ethnic groups, and protected from discrimination by the Race Relations Act (1976, amended 2000) and the Human Rights Act (1998).[7] However, despite a raft of domestic and international obligations ostensibly in place to protect the rights of this minority group, including European Court directives to 'facilitate the Gypsy way of life' (Connors v UK at para. 84), access to culturally acceptable accommodation is still out of reach for a considerable number of Gypsies and Travellers.[8] The Committee of Social Rights found that the situation in the United Kingdom was not in line with Art. 16 European Social Charter—the right of the family to social, legal and economic protection—on the grounds that the right to housing was not being effectively secured.[9]

---

[3] O'Nions, *Minority Rights Protection*, 41.

[4] John F. McDonald, *Tribe* (1) (Dublin: Wolfhound Press, 2000), 17.

[5] John F. McDonald, *Tribe* (2) (Douglas Isle of Mann: MP Publishing, 2002), 22.

[6] McDonald, *Tribe* (1), 65.

[7] Problematically, with regard to the Race Relations Act, legal definition as an ethnic minority was legitimated through nomadism.

[8] Connors v. United Kingdom [2004] 40 EHRR 189; Jo Richardson, *Providing Gypsy and Traveller Sites: Contentious Spaces* (York: Joseph Rowntree Foundation, 2007), 9.

[9] Thomas Hammerberg, 'Letter to The Rt Hon Eric Pickles, Secretary of State for

Indeed, O'Nions points out obligations under Art. 8 European Convention on Human Rights—the right to protection of private and family life—are simply not enough, as she argues that 'the limited protection of cultural identity offered under the provision [demonstrates the lack of] awareness of the importance of minority identity when balanced against the planning interest of the state.'[10] After the Cripps report in 1977 suggested that three quarters of the Gypsy population had nowhere to lawfully reside, the government invested money in council schemes to provide sites for suitable accommodation. However, the Criminal Justice and Public Order Act 1994 instituted a framework in which forced eviction and regulated spaces were given legitimate precedence over the notion of public access to space. Furthermore, this Act took away the duty to provide sites, and simultaneously authorized the police to force trespassers to leave private land, which, along with the Anti-Social Behaviour Act 2003 ensures the power to evict is defiantly and distinctly enshrined in law. This legislation therefore began the process of containment and criminalization reflected in the novel, whereby local 'settler' vigilantes perceive the travelers as illgitimate 'cannibals and child-stealers [and would come] down at night with their guns and their fucking petrol bombs.'[11] This, I argue, is the crux of the paradox: the Public Order Act revealed the relationship between property, ownership, and law as a justification of both an exorcism of illegitimate—nomadic—occupancy, whilst explicitly intoning 'that every Traveller family must find an approved place.'[12] This can be read, therefore, as a powerful display of law's foundations in the violence of authorized possession, for as Austin Sarat and Thomas Kearns write, 'law is a creature of both literal violence, and of imaginings and threats of force, disorder, and pain ... in the absence of such imaginings and

---

Communities and Local Government,' *Council of Europe*, 2012, accessed 1 January 2013. https://wcd.coe.int/ViewDoc.jsp?id=1919233&Site=COE.

[10] O'Nions, *Minority Rights Protection*, 81. It must be acknowledged that the right to housing is guaranteed under international law CESER general comment 4 identifies this right as a prerequesite for numerous other entitlements: 'The human right to adequate housing ... is of central importance for the enjoyment of all economic, social and cultural rights.' However, this right is sufficiently muted in practice through policy and legislation that validates the paradigm of ownership rather than residence. Similar provisions on the right to adequate housing are contained in the Convention on the Elimination of All Forms of Racial Discrimination, the Convention on the Elimination of Discrimination Against Women, the Convention on the Rights of the Child, the International Convention on the Suppression and Punishment of the Crime of Apartheid, and the International Convention Relating to the Status of Refugees.

[11] McDonald, *Tribe* (1), 71.

[12] McDonald, *Tribe* (2), 51.

threats there is no law.'[13] This Act was not, then, an aberrant anomaly, but rather can be read as legislation that exposes the ways in which 'the establishment or redefinition of regimes of property is often predicated upon the mobilization of violence.'[14] As Nicholas Blomley writes, it is important to stress the role of power in constructions of spatiality through the matrix of particular configurations of planning and property ownership, for as he emphasizes: 'prevailing arrangements of property in land have important implications for social ordering.'[15] Thus, although subsequent legislation can be seen to place the emphasis back on obligations for provision of sites, such as The Housing Act 2004, research commissioned by the Equality and Human Rights Commission found that, whilst planning permission had increased, overall progress on providing adequate sites was slow.[16] This was not due to limited funding, as over GBP 97 million had been set aside through a grant intended for Gypsy and Traveller site provision,[17] but rather as a result of an unimaginative and limited planning framework, which often refused permissions or declared land unsuitable for development, as well as significant opposition from the surrounding community that was rarely dealt with by the authorities.[18] The issue of *illegal occupancy* is in fact relatively minor—despite media perceptions of illegitimacy—as about 75 per cent of Gypsies and Travellers live on authorized encampments, and yet the shortage of adequate accommodation is widespread.[19] The battle is turned into one of criminal

[13] Austin Sarat and Thomas Kearns, *Law's Violence* (Ann Arbor: University of Michagan Press, 1992), 1.

[14] Nicholas Blomley, 'Law, Property, and the Geography of Violence: The Frontier, the Survey, and the Grid,' *Annals of the Association of American Geographers* 93/1 (2003), 126.

[15] Blomley, 'Law, Property, and the Geography of Violence,' 122.

[16] Government circular 01/2006 para. 12 identified the need 'to create and support sustainable, respectful, and inclusive communities where Gypsies and Travellers have fair access to suitable accommodation, education, health and welfare provision; where there is mutual respect and consideration between all communities for the rights and responsibilities of each community and in which they live and work,' whilst '[protecting] the traditional travelling way of life while respecting the interests of the settled community,' which included acting to 'reduce the number of unauthorized encampments'; Philip Brown et al., *Assessing Local Authorities' Progress in Meeting the Accommodation Needs of Gypsy and Traveller Communities in England and Wales* (Manchester: Equality and Human Rights Commission, 2010), 4, 6.

[17] Alexandra Topping and Hugh Muir, 'Dale Farm Battle Highlights Funding Black Hole for New Traveller Sites,' *The Guardian*, 28 September 2011.

[18] Brown et al., *Assessing Local Authorities*, 7.

[19] Pat Niner, *The Provision and Condition of Local Authority Gypsy/Traveller Sites in England* (London: Office of the Deputy Prime Minister, 2002); Margeret Greenfields, 'Accommodation Needs of Gypsies/Travellers: New Approaches to Policy in England,'

misappropriation or illegitimate occupation, when in fact the focus should be on the lack of provision, the gradual and wide-ranging restriction of access to land and the ongoing privatization of public space. As Blomley writes:

> Property also offers an important means by which we assign order to the world, categorizing and coding spaces and people according to their relationship to property ... When we talk about land and property, we are not simply talking about technical questions of land use, but engaging some deeply moral questions about social order.[20]

As a Traveller facing eviction recently stated, 'the camps we used to pull in to have been closed and barricaded up. Travelling life is finished.'[21] McDonald evokes this sense of nostalgia for a life that has been taken away in the text, when he describes a scene of sedentarized living using romantic language imbued with references to nature as the only vibrant, moving entity within a static space, following the erosion of former nomadic practices, in which 'Winter flowers hanging in coloured wooden baskets from the fences and grass growing tall round the wheels of a few ornate vardas ... will never see the road again.'[22] McDonald's theme is frequently the death of nomadism or 'the old ways,' characterized through the internal and external re-drawing of space.[23] Owen often feels claustrophobic, hemmed in by the 'poky little flat' he lives in with his girlfriend, remarking that a 'Traveller can't hold himself together in a small confined space.'[24] Owen's predicament can be read as emblematic of a politics of stasis, a liminal space in the ambiguous temporality of a past long gone: he feels distant from the Travellers, and repeatedly rejects the idea of living in a road-side camp, but he simultaneously rejects the alternative 'settled' world of 'gavvers,' the authorities and the council.[25] Owen's extensive tirade against these bodies of power is reflected in a diatribe against institutions he sees himself as pitted against:

> Hounded by town councils and district councils and county councils and borough councils and rural authorities and urban authorities and

---

Social Policy and Society 7/1 (2008), 73–89; David M. Smith and Margaret Greenfields, *Gypsies and Travellers in Housing* (Bristol: Policy Press, 2013).

[20] Blomley, 'Law, Property, and the Geography of Violence,' 122.

[21] Quoted in Rachel Stevenson, 'Dale Farm Travellers: 'We Won't Just Get up and Leave,' *The Guardian*, 27 July 2010, accessed 13 January 2013, http://www.theguardian.com/society/2010/jul/27/dale-farm-essex-travellers-eviction.

[22] McDonald, *Tribe* (2), 354.

[23] McDonald, *Tribe* (1), 18.

[24] McDonald, *Tribe* (1), 17, 157–58.

[25] A word in Romani dialect, meaning 'the police.'

sanitary inspectors and agents and landowners and vigilantes and local residents' committees and an assortment of wobs and gavvers and muskras.[26]

The way in which Owen lists these bodies as a combined whole reflects a system of disciplinary governmentality that has failed; failed because although on the one hand, in semantic terms, it is a story of fragmentation and destruction, of stoppage and attempts to generate order, and yet, on the other hand, the enjambment of the sentences, limited punctuation, and stream-of-consciousness form replicate a sense of a chaotic disorder, the impossibility of flight but simultaneously, the impossibility of containment. It is a space modified continuously by its own failure to set limits. McDonald's use of untranslated dialect and Romani vocabulary, interspersed deliberately to interrupt the smooth enjambment of the sentence, reflects a form of dialectical tension in which multiple tongues are colluding on the space—this time in a collision of terse sentences and aggressive consonants—acknowledging:

> A milieu of other cunts around me now ... Some a sort of black colour and others off-white. Brown and half-baked. Slushy skinned and shite stained. The air full of Shelta and Cant and Gamon and Romany and spitting on the ground.[27]

Here, McDonald disrupts the idea of the site as one of provision or containment. The narrative troubles this reading of space as so easily segmented, even when the weight of criminalization and the power play of 'order vs disorder' is used to legitimize this thematic bias. The text achieves this by shifting the focus not simply onto the site in question—therefore reifying the idea of this as a 'problem' space, a dangerous 'other' marginal territory—but by subverting the contention that there is an 'inside' and 'outside' at all. Owen's doubting questions about the nature of his belonging to a defined and delineated world are reflected in the questions he asks: 'Why not some other world? Why this particular one? ... Why here? And now.'[28] For McDonald, all space is implicated in a process of chaotic disorder; he makes us 'step out into the long back yard with isolated islands of gaunt grass fighting for survival in the desolation of sand and gravel and pigeon shite' and recognize it for its simplistic dystopia as well as its inherent complexities (in this instance, the convergence of multiple substances in a single framed space) as a perversion of the idea of the sedentary

---

[26] McDonald, *Tribe* (1), 32–3.
[27] McDonald, *Tribe* (1), 23–4.
[28] McDonald, *Tribe* (1), 96.

vs the Gypsy and Traveller community, or the centre vs the marginal.[29] McDonald relates the Roma to the 'American Indians,' inciting the spaces of reservations used to sedentarize and cauterize America's indigenous population as a comparison with the fatal erosion of rights in the campsites for Gypsies and Travellers: 'They've taken everything away from us ... gradually, like a creeping death.'[30] This comparison is also acknowledged by Spencer, who draws on the parallels between the nomadic Métis culture from Canada and the Gypsy and Traveller community of the UK in an overview of legislation designed to offer better living conditions and to sedentarize, and the groups' resilience and maintenance of their own minority culture despite this pervasive interference.[31] Spencer advocates drawing on this comparison in order to construct a more adequate system of protection for the Gypsy and Traveller community. However, it can be argued, that whilst drawing on similarities through the emphasis on nomadic identities may be useful—particularly through the way in which indigenous practices demonstrate contested claims on the space—it also persists in reifying a majority/minority culture and forms of protection which have so far proven largely inadequate.

The site of Dale Farm, on the outskirts of Basildon in Essex, became well known following reports of the legal battle against eviction, and the protests and campaigners which drew support and condemnation from both sides. Home to around 1,000 residents and 90 families—mainly Irish Travellers—it had been a site of residency since the 1960s, gradually swelling to accommodate greater numbers following a reduction in the number of halting sites and other stopping grounds. The council began to take legal actions against the Travellers in 2005 under s. 127 Town and Country Planning Act. In 2008, the High Court ruled that evictions could not take place until alternative accommodation could be found. However, in 2009 this was overturned following an appeal by the council, and finally in 2010 bailiffs were appointed to evict the residents from the plot. Basildon council argued that illegal development of green belt land had necessitated eviction, although reports of village residents claiming abusive behaviour, adverse affects on property values and a decrease in academic results at the local schools were also heavily prominent in contemporary media reports.[32]

[29] McDonald, *Tribe* (1), 97.
[30] McDonald, *Tribe* (2), 587.
[31] Siobhan Spencer, 'To Be a Gypsy and Not Be A "Gypsy": That Is the Question,' *Travellers' Times*, 28 February 2012, accessed 1 January 2013, http://travellerstimes.org.uk/Blogs--Features/To-be-a-Gypsy-and-not-be-a-gypsy-that-is-the-quest.aspx.
[32] Stephen Bates, 'Essex Council Criticized over £8m Plan to Evict Travellers,' *The Guardian*, 15 March 2011.

Despite an intervention from the UN Special Rapporteur on the right to adequate housing, who in a statement urged 'the UK authorities to halt the evictions process and to pursue negotiations with the residents until an acceptable agreement for relocation is reached in full conformity with international human rights obligations,'[33] the evictions that took place in 2011 were demonstrably violent, with police clashes between protestors and evidence of the use of tear gas.[34] Indeed, broadcasters were saved from being forced to hand over incriminating footage of the police actions during evictions only following a judicial review by the High Court.[35] Only three pitches were temporarily protected by court order, and those who moved to a nearby legal site soon faced evacuation due to the council's claim the site had become 'overcrowded.'[36] The attempt to regulate these spaces is a disciplinary practice positioned as a necessary protection against an excess of disorder, but one must recognize the disciplinary practices of these bodies within these space are not passively subjectified. They have *marked the space* as their own, indeed, to be 'taken with them,'[37] and this is what the Criminal Justice and Public Order Act fails to account for. This resistance is potently made explicit through Owen's vituperative monologue, in which he catalogues an inventory of disciplinary punishment and hostile acts levied at his community, through syntax that is both fluid and yet like a rallying battle cry, reciting an endless series of offences as a torrent of unstoppable noise:

> And ethnic cleansing is a fucking euphemism in which language disguises official violence—like holocaust and apartheid and clearances and final fucking solution. And Travellers over the years has been subjected to everything that could be thrown at us. Murder and enslavement and imprisonment and extermination and sterilization and seizure of the chavvies and expulsion and laws restricting intermarriage and forced conscription and the banning of our languages and them all hoping we would just disappear altogether from the face of the fucking earth. And the Travelling races is an ethnic minority—a mobile community surviving

---

[33] United Nations, 'UN Rights Experts Urge UK to Resolve Eviction Threat for Irish Travellers,' UN News Centre, 5 August 2011, accessed 12 July 2012, http://www.un.org/apps/news/story.asp?NewsID=39241&Cr=housing&Cr1#.U2tXI15mLwI.

[34] Joe Turner, 'Governing the Domestic Space of the Traveller in the UK: "Family," "Home" and the Struggle over Dale Farm,' *Citizenship Studies* (2016), 1–20.

[35] *BSkyB and others v Chelmsford Crown Court and Essex* Police [2012] EWHC 1295.

[36] Alexandra Topping, 'Dale Farm Travellers Face New Eviction Battle after Moving to Nearby Site,' *The Guardian*, 19 January 2012.

[37] Sarah Keenan develops the concept of 'taking space with them' in the context of migration, see Sarah Keenan, *Subversive Property: Law and the Production of Spaces of Belonging* (Abingdon and New York: Routledge, 2015).

in a settled world. On the receiving end of an endless series of fucking bye-laws and acts of parliament and private bills and codes of good practice and all kinds of other legislation.[38]

For some critics, such as Carol Rose, 'force and violence are the nemesis of property and their frequent use is a signal that a property regime is faltering.'[39] This is true in some sense, but the violence McDonald evokes here reveals law's narrative qualities as a different and more complex reading of property and space: as the residents were legal owners of the land, the issue was not one of *ownership* as a flawed concept, but of a planning system which is incapable of acknowledging ways in which space can be adapted, enacting instead a grid of belonging into which they could not fit. Thus legislation, despite the international frameworks established to protect minority rights, can be seen to fall invariably on the side of eviction. In the novel, McDonald replicates this constant narrative of eviction as a consequence of policy, writing that 'legislation forced us off the tramp so we had to be given a hatch.'[40] Owen does not romanticize a nomadic past nor demonstrate longing for what he calls 'the shit-heap site' where he grew up,[41] nevertheless he disrupts the construction of deprivation with a recognition of a different reading of the site for the people who inhabit it which resonates strongly with testimonies from the Dale Farm residents, evincing an alternative politics of location, as wandering about, Owen observes:

> An atmosphere of private pride and public squalor—like a ghetto. Forced to live in these gudgell conditions and it's us Gypsies who considers the Gorgios to be the dirty ones—with their shitty cities and their slums[42]

McDonald is dismissing the binary and exposing everything, everywhere, all at once, as mutually implicated in a polluted and chaotic space: the disorder is mutually imposed and reciprocated. Here then, as Blomley writes, we can read law as resting:

> on the definition of a violent world of nonlaw ... the very existence of that deemed property has long relied upon a distinction to a domain of nonproperty. Inside the frontier lie secure tenure, fee- simple ownership, and state-guaranteed rights to property. Outside lie uncertain and

---

[38] McDonald, *Tribe* (2), 555.
[39] Carol Rose, *Property And Persuasion: Essays On The History, Theory, And Rhetoric Of Ownership* (New York: Westview Press, 1994), 296.
[40] McDonald, *Tribe* (1), 22.
[41] McDonald, *Tribe* (1), 22.
[42] McDonald, *Tribe* (1), 23.

undeveloped entitlements, communal claims, and the absence of state guarantees to property. Inside lies stability and order, outside disorder [and] violence.[43]

Within such a definition, propriety is a key determinant of legitimacy, yet there is no attention according to what a site at the limit or frontier would contain, if it was neither lawless nor liminal.[44] McDonald would suggest it complicates the idea of a frontier altogether: everything is not infinite nor is it a state of exception: ownership is striated but not through the grid-like matrix of possession. Spatial justice may provide a framework in which it is possible to configure this space differently, if we reject the very basis of a proprietorial doctrine, where temporal sovereignty confirms all owned space as within the realms of legitimacy—but only if owned so that, 'in the beginning, all the World was America'?[45] To question this singular framework of space in which one can be excluded is to question the basis of law itself, to take account of Bentham's contention that 'property and law are born together, and die together.'[46] Ownership, without this symbiotic relationship, would actually exist beyond the rhetoric of planning policy and hierarchies of governance, at an originary site of natural law. If we adapt Locke's philosophy through a turning towards spatial justice as a radical critique of the myth of legitimacy, then, there is a distinct possibility of acknowledging the shaping of space. McDonald's text theorizes ownership within a broader critique of space:

> Somewhere back there is a marker on the turnpike between the open roads and my little flat. And I knows there's no going back. Heritage and history fades fast in the swirling mainstream of this gobbling grunting hog of a world. I knows that eventually I'll step finally over the line you've drawn on the ground.[47]

This sense of a devouring violence and the metaphor of the whirling, enveloping current has connotations of a disruptive space between order and disorder, through its juxtaposition with the strictly delineated markers of spatial cartography. Such juxtaposition is frequently

---

[43] Blomley, 'Law, Property, and the Geography of Violence,'124.

[44] Peter Fitzpatrick, *The Mythology of Modern Law* (Routledge: New York and London, 1992), 77.

[45] John Locke, *Two Treatises of Government*, ed. Peter Laslett (Cambridge: CUP, 1988 [1698]), 301.

[46] Jeremy Bentham, 'Security and Equality of Property,' in *Property: Mainstream and Critical Positions*, ed. Crawford Brough McPherson (Toronto: University of Toronto Press, 1978 [1843]), 52.

[47] McDonald, *Tribe* (2), 698.

displayed in the socio-political narrative of evictions, where the binary of being on the 'wrong side of the line' is imprinted through the rhetoric of illegality, and this is contrasted with the seeping violence of highly performative televised scene of evictions.[48] This display of the false dichotomy of the settler vs the sedentary as a battle performed live on air was transformed into a dramatic event in which the parameters of the dichotomy itself were never questioned, sequestered as they were against a background of disordered violence. Katherine Quarmby relates, as an example, a case of similar conflict over a site in Wales between 'a handful of families of Welsh, English and Scottish Romany Gypsy heritage ... [who had] moved on to a field in 2010 which they owned but for which they did not have planning permission, and ... the local settled community.'[49] Campaigners objecting to the sites—arguing they were protesting against inappropriate development—subjected them to harassment and surveillance in the form of constant pickets and a website which monitored the residents constantly. According to a local councilor, these protestors monitoring the site were both 'defend[ing] the green belt' and preventing 'further illegal acts from taking place.'[50] Although the planning committee voted eventually to evict those picketing, the discomforting thing here was that, as Quarmby observes:

> One set of residents—the 'legitimate'—were permitted, even encouraged, to police unwanted groups, just so long as they had permission to be on the plot from which they were doing their monitoring. It wasn't the surveillance that was a problem; it was the encampment on green-belt land.[51]

This demonstrates the way in which property and particular constructions of ownership, as the 'proper usage of land' are at the heart of the idea of belonging. It is firmly spatialized, but not in the way it is often portrayed. You could say, perhaps, that the dichotomy between the 'settler' and the 'travelling' community is not only a false one, but also a smoke screen for the dominant paradigm of spatial order, in which the only option left open to the Gypsies is, as Owen relates, to claim a role 'in the old amorphous brood—the doorstep third-world tribe. ... Playing a little part in the economics of a hostile society—yet

---

[48] Katherine Quarmby, 'Gypsies Belong Here Too. So Why Do We Always Expect Them to "Move On"? ' *The Observer*, 4 August 2013.
[49] Quarmby, 'Gypsies belong here too.'
[50] Quarmby, 'Gypsies belong here too.'
[51] Quarmby, 'Gypsies belong here too.'

keeping apart from it.'[52]

McDonald refutes such totality through the reconstruction of a more infinite space, however, his world of inhabitation is neither porous nor fluid; there are still defiantly rigid identities in the world in which Owen travels, marked by rituals and blood-lines and networks and a reaction to being marginalized by a 'gorgio' society. And yet, the space mapped out within the text is not a dead and easily segmented neutral space. Owen moves in and out of properties and campsites, but his response to the silent space of a post eviction site reflects a parallel with the closed space of the 'gorgia' kitchen flat he slinks back to. It is perhaps worth asking Massey's questions here, to register her potent analysis on the spatiality of power:

> The real socio-political question concerns less, perhaps, the degree (i) of openness/closure (and the consequent question of how on earth one might even begin to measure it), than the terms (i) on which that openness/closure is established. Against what are boundaries erected? What are the relations within which the attempt to deny (and admit) entry is carried out? What are the power-geometries here; and do they demand a political response?[53]

Massey's suggestion that the focus should shift from the boundary line to the way in which bound space is constituted reaffirms the attempt within this thesis to consider the actual condition of space. It posits that as boundaries are not constructed in a vacuum, it is important to read the topology in action. This lends itself to a more detailed study of the official narrative in which the boundary that is established is one between the sedentary and the nomadic, and that the only solution is to delineate a false equivalence between an ambiguous form of acknowledgement for what is termed 'the traditional and nomadic way of life of travellers while respecting the interests of the settled community.'[54] Indeed, the campaign group in Quarmby's case study established themselves as the settled community, *protecting* the land and promoting the legitimacy of ownership. Their leader, David McGrath, said 'We bear no malice to the travellers. They have a right to live *somewhere*' (just not 'here'!)[55] This 'somewhere' is identified by Owen's friend Litzy as 'near rubbish- tips or flyovers or sewage

---

[52] McDonald, *Tribe* (2), 1320.

[53] Doreen Massey, *For Space* (Sage: London, 2005), 179.

[54] Department for Communities and Local Government, *Planning Policy for Traveller Sites* (London: Department for Communities and Local Government, 2012), 1.

[55] Katherine Quarmby, *No Place to Call Home—Inside the Real Lives of Gypsies and Travellers* (London: Oneworld, 2013), 42. My emphasis.

plants or dangerous railways lines. Places that's useless to anyone else,'[56] spaces which are ordained as appropriate by 'some council clerk.'[57] Legislative policy appears to demonstrate the emphasis on a balance between two halves of society—in which the sedentary majority, in the place of elected councils and authorities, must provide sites, but in return for, as a 2006 circular reiterates, 'the responsibility of Gypsies and Travellers to *respect* the planning system.'[58] Similarly, the local conservative MP claimed that 'it is not about the Travellers, it is about planning laws being upheld.'[59] Thus, the positivist law affirmation of 'the boundaries of space [as] reinforced by the concepts of law' determines that the community is obliged to have respect for a system which purportedly marginalizes and excludes them.[60] It is not only an unbalanced scale, but a scale based on an extremely narrow definition of space. As Richardson and Ryder argue, all legislation constructed against this abyssal line is thus inherently flawed, as it reflects

> the contradictions in everyday discourse surrounding Gypsies and Travellers [through the suggestion] that this is a binary debate on the needs of the communities versus the needs of the wider 'settled' population. Approximately two-thirds of the Gypsy and Traveller population of England today live in bricks and mortar accommodation and are thus effectively hidden within the wider community.[61]

[56] McDonald, *Tribe* (2), 2606.

[57] McDonald, Tribe (2), 2606.

[58] 'UK Government circular 01/2006,' *Department for Communities and Local Government*, para. 18, my emphasis. This was withdrawn in 2014 and replaced with new planning practice guidance, namely, in August 2015, *Planning Policy for Traveller Sites*, Department for Communities and Local Government which still reiterates the spatial paradigm of a partitioned system, with an emphasis on an equitable 'balance' between 'two halves' of society: 'The Government's overarching aim is to ensure fair and equal treatment for travellers, in a way that facilitates the traditional and nomadic way of life of travellers while respecting the interests of the settled community' and pursue, to an even greater extent, the construction of a weighty threat on the 'settled society' and an ongoing narrative of containment: 'Local planning authorities should very strictly limit new traveller site development in open countryside that is away from existing settlements or outside areas allocated in the development plan. *Local planning authorities should ensure that sites in rural areas respect the scale of, and do not dominate, the nearest settled community*, and avoid placing an undue pressure on the local infrastructure.' My emphasis.

[59] Stephen Bates, 'Dale Farm Eviction: Essex Police's Use of Tasers at Close Range Criticized,' *The Guardian*, 19 October 2011.

[60] Jane Holder and Carolyn Harrison, 'Connecting Law and Geography,' in *Law and Geography*, eds. Jane Holder and Carolyn Harrison (Oxford: OUP, 2003), 6.

[61] Jo Richardson and Andrew Ryder, 'New Labour's Policies and Their Effectiveness for the Provision of Sites for Gypsies and Travellers in England,' in *Romani Politics in Contemporary Europe—Poverty, Ethnic Mobilization, and the Neoliberal Order*,

Thus the dynamic of proportionality, crucial to any decision on the rights and interests of Gypsies and Travellers (as a by no means homogenous) ethnic group weighed against public interest,[62] becomes part of a discourse on inside/outside spaces of legitimacy rather than a condition of the space itself, unevenly configured in terms of planning, accommodation and proper land use (because, one could argue the environmental defence is often conveniently forgotten when it comes to corporate exploitation or large scale industrial programs). It is this balancing act which O'Nions describes as the 'negative non-discrimination paradigm' which offers no challenge to the evictions which take place repeatedly within the Roma Diaspora.[63] Even those with objectives of protection thus situate this false dichotomy through a limited reading of identity and minority group membership, configured along extremely linear narratives of possession and belonging. As Thomas Hammerberg states, 'it is paramount that all efforts be deployed to identify sustainable solutions, which are acceptable to both local communities, Traveller and non-Traveller.'[64] Calls for increased protectionism, it is apparent, are simply not enough until the concept of space and its relationship to narratives of legitimate ownership is expansively deconstructed. Yet, minority rights protection validates the myth of a single space, barely able to contain two distinctly homogenous and directly antagonistic communities.[65] It is evident, therefore, that in a context of evictions, expulsions and ongoing discrimination a recognition of the paradox of planning, property and public order legislation is necessary, even if it risks inflating the instability in juridical discourse about cultural spaces.[66] A more robust critique of a sedentary spatial order would, for example, acknowledge that rather than seen as an aberrant anomaly to the progression of assimilation, the Criminal Justice and Public Order Act can thus be read as the truest manifestation of the focus of planning: as a singular definition of space, the 'correct' way to inhabit space,

---

eds. Nando Sigona and Nidhi Trehan (New York & Basingstoke: Palgrave Macmillan, 2009), 246–7.

[62] In Chapman v UK (2001) the court recognized that it could not decide for itself how the balance of interests between the community and the rest of the population should be ascertained so that it had a purely supervisory role.

[63] O'Nions, *Minority Rights Protection*, 47.

[64] Hammerberg, 'Letter to The Rt Hon Eric Pickles.'

[65] Judith Okely, 'Cultural Ingenuity and Travelling Autonomy: Not Copying, Just Choosing,' in Romani Culture and Gypsy Identity, eds. Thomas Acton and Garry Mundy (Hatfield: University of Hertfordshire Press, 1997), 191.

[66] See David Delaney, 'Tracing Displacements: Or Evictions in the Nomosphere,' *Environment and Planning D: Society and Space* 22/6 (2004), 847–60.

and the need to frame all alternatives to this as 'disorder.'[67] Whether or not adequate accommodation is found or planning permission is granted, there is always the legislative perspective of an 'inside' and an 'outside' space. McDonald's novel is a narrative of setting up this binary- he sets up the conceit of being in two different worlds, only to immediately prove its paradoxical instability. McDonald's novel draws attention to the uses of space as they are manufactured through spaces of legitimated access, which is more complex than a recognition of containment or exclusion. As Blomley writes:

> if space is a powerful medium through which property is enacted and by which its violences are legitimated, we must also acknowledge that the relation can become a little more ambivalent ... we are forced to recognize their contingency and ambivalences. Socialized space can prove contradictory ... The enactment of property is never completely contained by dominant regulatory norms.[68]

It is necessary to question this particular framing of space within a broader project of spatial justice. It is necessary to re-read space, to accept neither that territory must be carved up according to the extent of a subjective border,[69] nor that space is neutrally mandated through a Westphalian boundary paradigm. McDonald reflects a potentially radical framing of space in the text when he describes Owen's internal thoughts as he gazes down at a beach in Ireland:

> Here I stands then—on the edge of a continent. Surrounded by the barren acres of wild will-o'-the wisps and hearing in my head the lonely keen of a pagan piper from the side of some soulless hill. Looking up at the free sky and wishing again that I could fly. Not this time to love but to the face of the fucking sun. And from there laugh down at these poor cunts. Scuttling in their everlasting struggle to be free. Just like me.[70]

McDonald constructs a sense of space as emptiness—'barren acres' and 'free sky'—that is also simultaneously not an absence, as it is full of the potential of anonymous subjects also inhabiting the space. Owen is firmly located in a distinct position, but this location is also revealed as an 'edge' and marred by an ambivalent sense of above and below, in which Owen is also implicated. The potential to move freely

---

[67] Reflecting, as Blomley writes, that 'at its core, property entails the legitimate act of expulsion, devolved to the state.' (Blomley, 'Law, Property, and the Geography of Violence,' 130.)

[68] Blomley, 'Law, Property, and the Geography of Violence,' 135.

[69] Bryan Reynolds, *Transversal Subjects: From Montaigne to Delueuze after Derrida* (London and New York: Palgrave Macmillan, 2009), 136.

[70] McDonald, *Tribe* (2), 2921.

into the sky—'wish that I could fly'—is not the possibility of moving 'outside' the space, but rather a means of acknowledging both himself and others as complicit in the production of a space in which they are perpetually contained. Drawing on Michel Foucault's theory of space as a complex matrix of competing power relations, for example, territory is anything but static: it is not 'the dead, the fixed, the undialectical, the immobile,'[71] but is rather 'a socially produced space … saturated with power relations' which acts as both a transgressive and productive site of power. In this sense, legal space can be regarded as simultaneously constructing and constructed within a 'cadastral grid,' so that 'in enacting law, we enact space, and vice versa.'[72] Hence, 'belonging' is not a matter not the adequate provision of sites nor the allocation of planning, but is a question of the human right to inhabit space, of generating a framework of spatial justice which will insist upon unsettling the parameters implied by McDonald's assumption of neutral space in his description of the Gypsies as a 'mobile community surviving in a settled world.'[73] In reading these spaces of legality all modes of belonging should be spatialized, not through a binaric determination of marginality and exclusion but through a rendering of space as conditioned by violence: and therein, lies its potential for resistance against the ideology of disorder, as well as the source of its contamination. As Owen says, 'Somewhere I knows the sky is blue and the world is wide open':[74]

> 'You see,' property will say, "now I am not even my own idea. I'm just a bundle of other concepts, a mere chimera of an entity. I'm just a quivering, wavering, normative phantasm, without any home, without anything to call my own but an album full of fading and tattered images of vitality and consequence and meaning.[75]

It is crucial to consider this 'quivering, wavering, normative phantasm' in the context of diaspora, in order to consider its role in the constructions of narratives of ownership and paradigms of possession. To play on this idea of the concept of property as one that is effectively 'homeless' in terms of its implications, is important for a reading of the

---

[71] Michel Foucault, 'Questions in Geography,' in *Power/Knowledge: Selected Interviews and Other Writings*, 1972–1977, ed. Colin Gordon (New York: Pantheon, 1980), 70.

[72] Nicholas Blomley, 'Law, Property, and the Geography of Violence,' 31; see also David Delaney, 'Running with the Land: Legal-Historical Imagination and the Spaces of Modernity,' *Journal of Historical Geography* 27/4 (2001), 493–506.

[73] McDonald, *Tribe* (2), 572.

[74] McDonald, *Tribe* (1), 266. [sic].

[75] James E. Penner, *The Idea of Property in Law* (Oxford, Clarendon Press, 1997), 1.

'diasporic' as a potential refutation of sedentary orders of imperium. According to Margaret Davies, the idea of property 'has lost its solid reassuring, conceptual distinctiveness.'[76] This can be demonstrated through the way in which Gypsy and Traveller spaces of the camp are narrativized in the novel, for as Angus Bancroft writes, 'The forms of exclusion and ordering of marginal populations in modernity [can be understood] as an intimately spatial form of regulation.'[77] The concept of 'diaspora space'[78] may be a useful interpretive framework with which to examine the spatiality of 'dislocation' within this context as a means of deconstructing 'the intricate relationships between law, power and space' in 'unsettled' spaces, as a framework with which to analyze the operative 'legal codes of spatiality [which] have served to control and shape the lives of Gypsies and Travellers.'[79] The way in which diaspora space acts as a critique of settled society is particularly useful in explaining how 'the nomadism of Gypsies and Travellers contests the norms of sedentary living.'[80] The more radical implications of the concept of diaspora space which holds particular relevance for this analysis, are that it does not merely situate the diasporic subjects as those under the microscope, as it were, leaving the 'resident' or indigenous inhabitants unobserved as 'natural' or 'legitimate citizens,' but rather argues that diaspora space incorporates all subjects through its enactment as a process. This spatio-temporal dislocation is emphasized in *Tribe*, where

---

[76] Margaret Davies, *Property—Meanings, histories, theories* (Oxon and New York: Cavendish, 2007), 19.

[77] Angus Bancroft, *Roma And Gypsy—Travellers In Europe: Modernity, Race, Space And Exclusion* (Aldershot and Burlington: Ashgate, 2005), 17.

[78] Avtar Brah, *Cartographies* of Diaspora: Contesting Identities (New York and London: Routledge, 1996). The sociologist Avtar Brah introduced the concept of 'diaspora space' in her influential text *Cartographies of Diaspora*. This went on to become a particularly key concept within diaspora studies, signaling a move from a more root-based focus in diaspora studies to an analysis of the complex lives of the diasporic. What makes them diasporic, she posited, can be found in the layers of power relations at work in their contemporary spaces: it acted as a complication of the notion of location, suggesting instead that it had to be configured in a broader and simultaneously more nuanced sense than through the abstract label of 'hostland.' Hence, it can be argued that 'diaspora space' provides an antidote to the traditional or classical paradigm of diaspora, in which the critical focus was on the link to origin, or point of departure. Brah's concept is a distinct challenge to this, by instead suggesting we turn our attention to the lived spaces of diasporic communities as multi-layered, complex, dynamic and evolving.

[79] Margaret Greenfields and Robert Home, 'Women Travellers and the Paradox of the Settled Nomad,' in *Feminist Perspectives on Land Law*, eds. Hilary Lim and Anne Bottomley (New York and Abingdon: Routledge-Cavendish, 2007), 136, 138.

[80] Malcolm James, *Interculturalism—Theory and Policy* (London: The Baring Foundation, 2008),
368.

in attempting to forge a distinct path for himself between an itinerant nomadic identity and his sedentary 'gorgio' life with his girlfriend, he witnesses a new potentially of disorientating collision: 'sees the present and following in a dissolving mist—the future.'[81] For Brah, then, diaspora space is potentially all space. Her work is about not only complicating discourses of migrancy, then, but also discourses of 'Home,' offering an attempt to analyze 'discourses of fixed origins, while taking account of a homing desire.'[82] Brah explores:

> The nature of various structures of oppression [seeking] to theorize their (con)joint articulations in specific and contingent situations [culminating] in the conceptualization of difference as experience, as social relation, as subjectivity and as identity.[83]

Diaspora space, then, problematizes the construction of 'homeland' and 'hostland' as resolute and self-contained categories: to deconstruct what could be termed as the 'unspoken and rather cosy connotations of the concept "community".'[84] As Brah writes:

> Diaspora space as a conceptual category is "inhabited" not only by those who have migrated and their descendants but equally by those who are constructed and represented as indigenous. In other words, the concept of diaspora space (as opposed to that of diaspora) includes the entanglement of genealogies of dispersion with those of "staying put"[85]

This concept does not discount the idea of coming from one place and going to another, nor negate, for example, nomadic identity markers, but suggests it cannot be considered in isolation from narratives of settlement. In *Tribe*, this is manifested in Owen's attempts to flee that are similarly encounters with the impulse to return—'Falling in fright along the lanes of blackthorn and bramble until I'm completely lost and there's not a fucking sinner in sight to ask the way home. Collapsing onto the roadside.'[86] Thus, this notion of spacing implicates not only the diaspora, or those who are itinerant, but the subjects who are settled, and attempts to challenge the construction of space through discourses of power. Like Foucault, Brah doesn't suggest power is a simple phenomenon which is always oppressive, and exerted from the top down. Instead, she considers power as a dynamic and complex

---

[81] McDonald, *Tribe* (2), 2921.
[82] Brah, *Cartographies*, 196–7.
[83] Parita Mukta, 'Avtar Brah—Cartographies of Diaspora: Contesting Identities,' *Feminist Review* 63 (1999), 109.
[84] Sökefeld, 'Mobilizing in Transnational Space,' 280.
[85] Brah, Cartographies, 181.
[86] McDonald, *Tribe* (2), 2921.

process, which can be resistant as well as possessive, and is enacted, embodied and encountered in numerous instances and by all subjects and institutions. Brah describes her understanding of Diaspora as that which is 'embedded within a mutli-axial understanding of power; one that problematizes the notion of "minority/majority".'[87] For Brah, then, the concept of 'dislocation' is not distinctly one of itinerance, but rather a critique of how any localities develop.

Despite the presence of Gypsy and Traveller communities in the UK from the fifteenth century onwards, unremittting strategies of sedentarization have led to legislative measures which persistently enforce settlement. Identites have been spatialized through the trope of the nomad and 'caravan sites have become an integral part of the state's regulatory power over Gypsies.'[88] This is not merely a figurative construction, as the trope of nomadism is used metonymously to describe Romany ethnicity as a means of regulation.[89] McDonald subverts this synecdoche through an inversion of water imagery so frequently exploited to demonize the disordered flood of nomadic Roma:

> And the river water running away in the opposite direction as if it knows something I doesn't and chuckling as it flows with little cross-currents and bits of broken water and backwashes and whirlpools and the whole world wearing me down into the ground.[90]

In this instance, the water signifies both a current of preordained movement, and similarly a space in which multiplicities are colliding and interacting, disrupting the stronger path of the current with interruptions and breaks and new directions. McDonald's use of alliteration—'the whole world wearing me down'—introduces a sense of fluid continuity, gesturing towards an assemblage of unity; however, finally, this is subverted through the finality of a definite end point, a mortal limit to the space. This metaphor reflects the juridical technique of enclosure which McDonald explores within the text, reflecting the way in which the Gypsy community were often synecdochically associated with vagrancy, which carried harsh punishments.[91] Since 1835 various Highway Acts have prohibited movement to those who travel or attempts to camp on a highway. The use of nomadism as a metonymy for Gypsy ethnicity was established in Mills v Cooper, when the court declared that in fact 'gypsy means no more than a person

---

[87] Brah, *Cartographies*, 189.
[88] Greenfields and Home, 'Women Travellers,' 137.
[89] Greenfields and Home, 'Women Travellers,' 139.
[90] McDonald, *Tribe* (2), 392.
[91] Greenfields and Home, 'Women Travellers,' 136.

leading a nomadic way of life with no, or no fixed, employment and with no fixed abode.'[92] The same definition used to categorize them was simultaneously an aspect of criminal non-belonging, and established a rhetoric of spatiality which was both enclosing and ambivalent. The Caravan Sites Act held this judgement, so that Romany ethnicity was sublimated by a status based on nomadic behavior under planning, which meant that from now on, paradoxically, 'ethnic Gypsies could lose their legal status if they ceased to travel.'[93] This still presents a problematic form of labelling for the Romany in the UK, as the emphasis on nomadic behaviour as an identifying characteristic that is essential for the designation of minority status continues to dominate the official narrative. Judicial decisions have continuously emphasized this aspect of their identity, which creates a heavily specific form of spatiality by 'impos[ing] an increasingly restrictive reading of the definition [and thus] making it harder for Traveller families to set up legal sites.'[94]

It has been argued that in effect, contemporary Roma communities 'possess a continuity, rather than a community, of culture,' and are spatialized as persistently 'other.'[95] However, such an interpretation threatens to merely reiterate the temporal interruption imposed by the nomadic emphasis is not problematic as it points to a genealogical truth. On the contrary, McDonald identifies the mythology of this sense of continuity through his positioning of nostalgia as a dreamscape, in which as he is falling asleep, Owen imagines a former life lived by many:

> Thoughts running back a hundred years to the hopfields and hazel branches of the bender tents and 'tilters and the roadside verges and the broomdashing and colourful vardas drawn along at a leisurely pace by the little banners and the fift of the gum-sha-lack. Head dropping and eyes half-closed and don't even notice the soft little paws of sleep stealing.[96]

The evocative use of enjambment reflecting the movement of a unified—and yet disordered—cavalcade demonstrates the need for a spatio-temporal critique of the narrative of culture as a continuity, and particularly the way in which communities are supposedly 'shaped' by

[92] *Mills v Cooper* [1967] 2 All ER 100; cited in Greenfields and Home, 'Women Travellers,' 136.

[93] Greenfields and Home, 'Women Travellers,' 137.

[94] Greenfields and Home, 'Women Travellers,' 149.

[95] Derek Hawes and Barbara Perez, *The Gypsy and the State- The Ethnic Cleansing of British Society* (Bristol: SAUS Publications, 1995), 7.

[96] McDonald, *Tribe* (2), 587.

law.[97] This particular idea that the shaping of any space can effectively come 'from above' is problematized through the particularities of how this space is constructed, in other words, to focus on the legal spaces of the campsites or settlements themselves or to consider how this space is effectively 'mastered,' to use Derrida's terminology. Mark Wrigley writes that 'the traditional sense of space is only produced in the very gesture of its subordination'—yet it is impossible to reach the ultimate conclusion that from this we can only determine that there can only be legitimate inhabitation or marginal non-territoriality.[98] To contend with the inherent discrimination in the planning system, to aim for some form of spatial justice for the Gypsy and Traveller community, it seems to be evident that the debate itself must centre on new ways of 'investigating space.'[99] It is too simplistic to say that these sites must be then 'other spaces' (those places which are marginalized, uninhabitable, and liminal) as they are part of a systemized socio-legal construction in which nomadism has been both eradicated, and, simultaneously, exploited to determine the basis of a singular ethnic identity rendered as an illegitimate access to space.

---

[97]   Greenfields & Home, 'Women Travellers,' 145.

[98]   Mark Wigley, *The Architecture of Deconstruction—Derrida's Haunt* (Cambridge, MA & London: MIT Press, 1993), 71.

[99]   Jo Richardson and Maggie Smith-Bendell, 'Accomodation Needs and Planning Issues,' in *Gypsies and Travellers: Empowerment and Inclusion in British Society*, eds. Joanna Richardson and Andrew Richard Ryder (Bristol: Policy Press, 2012), 22.

INDEX